HAWTHORNE'S EARLY TALES, A CRITICAL STUDY

HAWTHORNE'S EARLY TALES, A
CRITICAL STUDY · BY NEAL FRANK
DOUBLEDAY · DUKE UNIVERSITY PRESS
DURHAM, NORTH CAROLINA · 1972

© 1972, Duke University Press
L.C.C. card no. 76–185462 · I.S.B.N. 0–8223–0267–5
Printed in the United States of America by Heritage Printers, Inc.

Second printing, 1974

To MARIE EDEL, gratefully

CONTENTS

Acknowledgments   ix

1. Beginning Writer   3

2. American Materials   13

   The Waverley Novels and Literary Theory   14
   Literary Theory and Hawthorne's Practice   18
   Literary Theory and Hawthorne's Purposes   26

3. The Development of Hawthorne's Literary Habit   32

   "All sorts of good and good-for-nothing books"   32
   The Hawthornesque before Hawthorne: Scott and William Austin   42
   "That tinge of the marvellous": Hawthorne's Gothic Habit   52
   Moral Purpose and Allegorical Method   62

4. The Selection for *Twice-Told Tales*   71

5. Literary Theory in Practice   85

   "The Gray Champion"   85
   "The Maypole of Merry Mount"   92
   "Endicott and the Red Cross"   101

6. The Gothic Naturalized: "The Prophetic Pictures"   109

7. The Air of Antiquity: "Legends of the Province House"   117

   "Howe's Masquerade"   122
   "Edward Randolph's Portrait"   123
   "Lady Eleanore's Mantle"   128
   "Old Esther Dudley"   130

8. Tales of a New England Traveller 138

 "The Shaker Bridal" 138
 "The Ambitious Guest" 141
 "The Great Carbuncle" 145

9. Two Speculative Tales 151

 "Wakefield" 151
 "Fancy's Show Box" 155

10. The Masterpieces in *Twice-Told Tales* 159

 "The Gentle Boy" 159
 "The Minister's Black Veil" 170
 "Dr. Heidegger's Experiment" 178

11. Early Tales in *Mosses from an Old Manse* 182

 "Drowne's Wooden Image" 186
 "Roger Malvin's Burial" 192
 "Young Goodman Brown" 200

12. Early Tales in *The Snow-Image* 213

 "The Wives of the Dead" 215
 "The Man of Adamant" 218
 "The Canterbury Pilgrims" 222
 "My Kinsman, Major Molineux" 227

13. Sympathy and Craftsmanship 238

 Bibliographical Note 253
 Index 255

ACKNOWLEDGMENTS

I am grateful to the editor of *American Literature* for permission to reuse material from three articles: "The Theme of Hawthorne's 'Fancy's Show Box'" (November 1938), "Hawthorne and Literary Nationalism" (January 1941), and "Hawthorne's Estimate of His Early Work" (January 1966). I am likewise grateful for the permission of the National Council of Teachers of English to reuse material from an article in *College English*: "Hawthorne's Use of Three Gothic Patterns" (February 1946). My textbook-anthology *Hawthorne: Tales of His Native Land* (Lexington, Mass.: D. C. Heath and Company, 1962) brought me back to my early interest in Hawthorne. Some matters of literary history briefly considered in that book are here discussed at length; my reading of "My Kinsman, Major Molineux" there suggested in outline is here developed within a discussion of the tale.

Millikin University granted me a leave for the year 1967–1968 to work on this book. I am glad to record my gratitude to Millikin here. And I am grateful to the entire staff of the Millikin library, especially to Mrs. Catherine S. Armitage, then librarian for interlibrary loans. Through her I am indebted to a number of great libraries.

My earliest debt in this book is to the late Harry Hayden Clark; I wish to record my respect for him, and my gratitude. My wife, Frances, has been unfailingly patient and helpful. My son, James F. Doubleday, read the manuscript; his suggestions have improved the book at many points. My sister-in-law, Miss Helen E. Honey, has generously used her librarian's skill in helping me to materials otherwise difficult for me to find. Dr. Marie L. Edel, to whom this book is dedicated, read the manuscript.

N. F. D.

HAWTHORNE'S EARLY TALES, A CRITICAL STUDY

1. BEGINNING WRITER

In the prefatory letter for *The Snow-Image and Other Twice-Told Tales*, his last collection of short pieces, Nathaniel Hawthorne remarks: "I am disposed to quarrel with the earlier sketches, both because a mature judgment discerns so many faults, and still more because they come so nearly up to the standard of the best that I can achieve now. The ripened autumnal fruit tastes but little better than the early windfalls." Hawthorne's judgment in 1851 is much like that of his readers and critics today. Our recent interest has turned to his early work, and we see that some of it is as mature and as subtle within its scope as *The Scarlet Letter* is in its. And although *The Scarlet Letter* remains Hawthorne's masterpiece, we realize that it was woven of strands that were spun in the tales.

In this book we will understand "tales" to mean pieces of some considerable narrative interest, pieces distinct from sketches like "Sights from a Steeple" or "The Toll-Gatherer's Day." Hawthorne's own terms are not particularly helpful in distinguishing his literary kinds; he may, as in the passage just quoted, use "sketches" as a covering term for short pieces, often with a disparaging intent. But he speaks, too, of "tales and essays," and implies a distinction between pieces with an interest of event, and pieces with little or none. We shall be concerned with tales, pieces that do have an interest of event.

The 1825–1838 time span is as clearly defined a "period" in Hawthorne's work as any we are ever likely to find in the study of any writer. Hawthorne was graduated from Bowdoin in 1825; in January of 1839 he was appointed measurer in the Boston Custom House. Thereafter he wrote very little fiction until the time of his residence at the Old Manse, after his marriage in 1842. By the end of 1838 he had written the thirty-nine tales and sketches collected in the two editions of *Twice-Told Tales* (1837 and 1842), and all but three had had a first printing in periodicals or the annual *Token*. He had also written at least fifteen[1] of the pieces later collected in *Mosses from an Old Manse* and in *The Snow-Image and Other Twice-Told Tales*. He had

1. Fifteen, counting two or three sketches collected under one covering title (as the three sketches in "Old News" in *The Snow-Image*) as one, and not counting "Drowne's Wooden Image," although it will be contended that it was probably written early.

recorded in his notebooks suggestions for a number of the pieces he wrote later, and he had written the remarkable North Adams journal that was to become the substantiation for the allegory in "Ethan Brand."

The title of this book may seem to make no special commitment and, indeed, I have no central interpretation, no key to Hawthorne, to express in title or subtitle. Yet I wish some commitment to be understood. We will be concerned with the tales themselves; and we will be concerned with the literary theory that influenced them, with the literary conventions within which Hawthorne worked, and with the materials he used. In order to know what is intrinsic in his work, we need to know something of its context. And when a writer is using historical materials—as Hawthorne does in his best work—we need to be able to distinguish his materials from his use of them. No writer's work can be understood without some attention to its place in its time and to the influences upon it—the most important of which are likely to be those of the time just preceding.

Admittedly a balance in such endeavors is difficult to maintain; sometimes in them it is the work itself that is neglected. We will try to avoid that neglect. We shall examine the tales separately without ignoring their context or their relationship one with another. So far as a balance is maintained, we shall be able to see in Hawthorne's tales something of the way in which both his materials and the conventions he uses become peculiarly his own. We shall consider the significance of Hawthorne's choices in making his collections and see how Hawthorne himself regarded some of the tales we consider. At any rate, these are things literary study *can* do to bring a writer and his readers together.

Hawthorne's literary habit was formed early in his career, and there is in his work curiously little development. The effective influences on his work were the literary theory and the literary conventions of a time before 1825. The interplay between those influences and his own temperament is fully apparent by 1837, the date of the first edition of *Twice-Told Tales*. These contentions need support; they will be our concerns in subsequent discussion.

Students in survey courses in American literature are likely to think of the writers they study coming one after another in the order that the writers are assigned. Their elders may think in a somewhat similar fashion. For example, an unfortunate result of F. O. Matthiessen's influential *American Renaissance* (1941) is that, in bracketing Hawthorne with Emerson, Thoreau, Melville, and Whitman, it has helped a generation of writers on Hawthorne to neglect some important relationships between his work and its time. What we need to remember, or to realize, is how completely Hawthorne's literary interests and literary habits were formed before any one of the other four was known as a writer at all—how early in our literary history Hawthorne developed. When in 1836—the year Emerson's *Nature* was published —Hawthorne selected the eighteen pieces for the first edition of *Twice-Told Tales*, he had more than forty pieces from which to choose, among them his finest tales.

We may need to remind ourselves, then, of what was happening in American letters during the time Hawthorne was developing into a writer. *Waverley* was published in 1814, and almost at once the great American vogue of Sir Walter Scott's fiction began. The *North American Review* was founded in 1815, and, largely through it, a new concept of fiction, with Scott's work at its center but with a clear American emphasis, developed and took a discernible shape by 1825. In 1819–1820, the years just before Hawthorne entered Bowdoin, Washington Irving's *Sketch Book* was serially published in the United States, and established an American standard for a highly finished sort of fiction. When Sidney Smith in 1820 asked his famous question in the *Edinburgh Review*—"In the four quarters of the globe, who reads an American book?"—a satisfactory answer was almost at hand. And in 1821, Hawthorne's first year at Bowdoin, James Fenimore Cooper's *The Spy* and William Cullen Bryant's *Poems* appeared. From our point of view today, a national literature, so long desired, was under way. But that is not to say there were literary conditions in which a young writer of fiction—however gifted—could reasonably expect recognition and support.

Yet in his college years Hawthorne determined to become a professional writer of fiction, and he devoted himself to fiction upon his graduation from college in 1825. By the end of 1826 he had begun a course of reading clearly intended to furnish him with literary capital. His first attempt at a romance, *Fanshawe*, was published at his own expense in 1828 (he soon thereafter suppressed it). By 1829 he had abandoned a projected "Seven Tales of My Native Land" and was corresponding with Samuel G. Goodrich, the publisher of the "Peter Parley" books and of *The Token,* about his projected volume of "Provincial Tales." Now Hawthorne had only what he calls "some slender means of supporting myself," yet he apparently intended to make a career of the writing of fiction without any other endeavor. Today we should consider a like determination on the part of a would-be writer almost desperate, even if he had foundation help. Hawthorne's determination seems to have ignored all reasonable estimates of possibility. But it is not surprising that as a college boy he did not understand the apparent impossibility of his intention. It is amazing that, when he learned the difficulties he faced, he persisted in it.

Hawthorne's disappointment with *Fanshawe* seems to have been largely a conviction that it was an artistic failure, although a little commercial success might have mitigated that. But he did soon learn what a young writer was up against. In "The Devil in Manuscript" (first printed in 1835), he has the despairing young writer, Oberon, repeat the statement of the one honest publisher among seventeen that "no American publisher will meddle with an American work,—seldom if by a known writer, and never if by a new one,—unless at the writer's risk." One suspects that Goodrich had been explaining the facts of literary life to Hawthorne. Goodrich says in his *Recollections of a Lifetime* that before 1820 "it was positively injurious to the commercial credit of a bookseller to undertake American works" (except schoolbooks and the like), and that in 1830 "the book production of the United States embraced forty per cent. of American works, and sixty per cent. of British works."[2]

American publishers, of course, preferred reprinting the work of well-known British writers to whom they paid no royalty (though sometimes they paid a set sum for advance sheets from England) to the risk of bringing out American works. The republishing of British work was very profitable and highly competitive: Scott's work, for instance, was sold in the United States for much less than it sold for in England.[3] Cooper, writing about 1828 in *Notions of the Americans* (Letter 23), considered the first great obstacle to the development of an American literature the lack of international copyright. "No man,"

2. New York, 1856, 2: 111 and 389.
3. See James D. Hart, *The Popular Book* (Berkeley, 1961), p. 75.

he says, "will pay a writer . . . when he can get a work of equal merit for nothing"; and he quotes "a capital American publisher" as assuring him that there were not a dozen American writers he would feel justified in publishing. Although Alexis de Tocqueville was quite aware in the 1830s that "almost all important English books are republished in the United States," he was unable to see that the United States had any literature of its own.[4]

Some American work, of course, was published. But in his first efforts at book publication Hawthorne had two handicaps. Without reputation, he had to seek publication in Boston. The Boston bookseller-publishers published for a local market, and work published in Boston usually did not become nationally known until, as William Charvat says, "Ticknor & Fields woke up in the late forties." After the second edition of *Twice-Told Tales* had gained Hawthorne a reputation, he took *Mosses from an Old Manse* to Wiley & Putnam in New York. The second handicap was his lack of means. Evidently after the failure of *Fanshawe* he was unable to pay for the publication of another work. But commercial success for a writer in the early nineteenth century ordinarily depended upon his having enough capital to finance the publication of his work. The initial commercial success of Irving and Cooper, for example, came from their financial ability to dictate the terms of the publication of their work.[5] Some writers on Hawthorne seem to suggest that Goodrich's unwillingness to bring out at his own risk a volume of Hawthorne's short pieces was somehow unjust or peculiarly ungenerous. But Goodrich probably made an ordinary business decision, just as Carey & Lea of Philadelphia

4. Statistics on early American publishing may be misleading. Some kinds of books—textbooks, for instance—stood a much better chance of finding an American publisher than did fiction. Eugene Exman defends Harper & Brothers from the charge that they neglected American writers, but his chapter "Launching American Authors 1834–1836" includes few fiction writers that Harper "launched" if that means published their first work. See *The Brothers Harper* (New York, 1965), pp. 60–86. W. S. Tryon, writing of the Boston bookseller-publishers who would have been available to Hawthorne, says that in 1832 they issued a total of 481 titles, of which 47 percent were of European origin, 53 percent American. But of the entire number of titles, only 10 percent was made up "of fiction, poetry, essays, and the *belles-lettres* in general." *Parnassus Corner: A Life of James T. Fields* (Boston, 1963), p. 51.

5. See William Charvat, *Literary Publishing in America, 1790–1850* (Philadelphia, 1959), pp. 27, 38–39, 44, and 51.

did when they refused Edgar Allan Poe's projected "Tales of the Folio Club."[6] At any rate, Hawthorne was forced to find his market in Goodrich's *The Token* and in magazines.

The Token was one of the best of the "annuals." The annuals were ornate, sometimes handsome and often expensive gift books designed for the Christmas trade and primarily for feminine tastes. They ordinarily appeared in the last months of the year and were dated the next. The text was secondary in importance to the plates in all annuals; "their existence had sprung, at least in part," Goodrich says, "from steel-engraving, which had been discovered and introduced by our countryman, Jacob Perkins" (about 1810). Often the text, particularly the poetry, was written to order to accompany the plates; and the publishers paid a great deal more for the engravings than they did for literary material—writers were ordinarily paid from a dollar to two dollars a page for prose, a little more for verse. But apparently almost all of the writers of the second quarter of the nineteenth century we now remember contributed to them, and even the *North American Review* reviewed them. There were a great many annuals, some persisting for years, some issued only for a year or in two or three more numbers.

The first American annual of importance was *The Atlantic Souvenir* for 1826, published by Carey & Lea (the *Souvenir* was taken over by *The Token* in 1832). Goodrich began *The Token* with the number for 1828. He prided himself upon using American engravers and artists (among them Thomas Cole). Two of his engravers, John Cheney and Asher B. Durand, were very skillful; Durand sometimes engraved his own subjects. Goodrich's list of contributors to *The Token* includes some distinguished names; among them there are Edward Everett, A. H. Everett, John Quincy Adams, Henry Wadsworth Longfellow, Willis Gaylord Clark, Oliver Wendell Holmes, Horace Greeley, and Catherine M. Sedgwick. The Hawthorne pieces printed in *The Token* appeared with the work of well-known writers.[7]

6. Carey & Lea wrote in refusing Poe that "small books of detached tales, however well written, seldom yield a sum sufficient to enable the bookseller to purchase a copyright." Quoted in Fred Lewis Pattee, *The Development of the American Short Story* (New York, 1923), p. 119.

7. For example, a single number, *The Token* for 1836, in which appeared "The Wedding Knell," "The Minister's Black Veil," and "The Maypole of

If *The Token* hardly seems to us now an appropriate place for such
work as "My Kinsman, Major Molineux," "The Canterbury Pilgrims,"
or "The Minister's Black Veil" to have first appeared, one does feel
in turning over its shaken volumes that "Sights from a Steeple,"
"David Swan," and "The Village Uncle" (called "The Mermaid" in
The Token) are quite at home in them.[8]

"The whole tendency of the age," Poe wrote in *Graham's Magazine*
in 1846, "is Magazine-ward," but Hawthorne could hardly have felt
so when he began as a writer. Frank Luther Mott estimates that there
were somewhat less than a hundred periodicals other than newspapers
in the United States in 1825, at the beginning of a period of expansion. When Hawthorne began as a writer, almost all magazines had
precarious existences. Most were ephemeral; many did not use fiction
at all; some, like N. P. Willis's *American Monthly Magazine* (1829–
1831), were written in large part by their editors; some depended
entirely upon extracts from other publications. The magazines that
used Hawthorne's pieces in the first part of his career were all started
after he had been writing for some time, but they were the best outlets
for fiction in the 1830s. The *New-England Magazine*, which Mott
considers the best general magazine in New England before the
Atlantic Monthly, had a short career, 1831–1835. The *Knickerbocker
Magazine*, founded just a little later, in 1833, had for its day a remarkable survival to 1865, and a distinguished list of contributors.
The *United States Magazine and Democratic Review* (founded in
1837) was Hawthorne's best market after the publication of the first
edition of *Twice-Told Tales*.

But to begin with, and indeed until the publication of the 1837
Twice-Told Tales, *The Token* was Hawthorne's most important out-
let. We do not know that any of his work was printed before 1834 in

---

Merry Mount," contained work by Catherine M. Sedgwick, J. G. Percival, Mrs.
Lydia Sigourney, J. K. Paulding, John Neal, and Grenville Mellon. Although
these writers are remembered for the most part only in literary history, they were
all popular writers of the day.

8. For a useful account of the annuals, see Ralph Thompson, *American
Literary Annuals & Gift Books, 1825–1865* (New York, 1936). Goodrich's account of *The Token* is in *Recollections*, 2: 259–64 and appendix, n. 1. A
recent study of *The Token* is Daniel Roselle, *Samuel Griswold Goodrich* (Al-
bany, 1968), pp. 99–114.

any publications other than *The Token* and the Salem *Gazette*, although some unacknowledged work may well have been.[9] But beginning with *The Token* for 1831, Goodrich used twenty-seven or more pieces by Hawthorne.[10] Since he used several pieces in single volumes of *The Token*—eight in the volume for 1837—he understandably did not wish to identify the pieces by their author's name; nor did the *New-England Magazine*, which took a great batch of Hawthorne's pieces in 1834 and printed them thereafter in rapid succession. Hawthorne's early anonymity was unfortunate for him, but it arose from the conditions under which he published and from a convention of his time: both Irving and Cooper kept their names off the title pages of their first work. Hawthorne was not known by his name to his readers until the time of *Twice-Told Tales*. We need not greatly blame Goodrich. He was not averse to literary excellence, and he seems to have recognized something of Hawthorne's merit; but he was publishing a gift book, a book for the parlor table. For him, Hawthorne was a source of supply of pieces of text as he needed them.

When Goodrich's smug and not entirely candid account of his relationships with the young Hawthorne appeared in his *Recollections* in 1856,[11] Hawthorne wrote to his sister-in-law Elizabeth Peabody: "It is funny enough to see him taking the airs of a patron; but I do not mind it in the least. . . . I have rather a kindly feeling towards him, and he himself is not an unkindly man, in spite of his propensity to feed and fatten himself on better brains than his own."[12] But relation-

---

9. It seems likely that there is a body of unacknowledged and unidentified work by Hawthorne, written before and perhaps after 1834. Moncure D. Conway prints a letter of January 27, 1832 from Hawthorne to Carey & Lea offering to contribute to the *Atlantic Souvenir* (*Life of Nathaniel Hawthorne* [London, 1895], p. 44). Since *The Token* took over the *Atlantic Souvenir* in 1832, this effort failed, but it is unlikely that Hawthorne made no others or that all failed. In the prefatory pieces to both the 1851 *Twice-Told Tales* and *The Snow-Image*, Hawthorne implies that there were printed pieces of his that he had never acknowledged. And in a letter to James T. Fields in 1851 he earnestly enjoins Fields not to seek out his unacknowledged work. Fields, *Yesterdays with Authors* (Boston, 1872), p. 48.

10. More, if some *Token* pieces (such as "The Haunted Quack," *Token* for 1831) are his. See Nelson F. Adkins, "Notes on the Hawthorne Canon," *Papers of the Bibliographical Society of America* 60 (1966): 364–67.

11. Goodrich, 2: 269–73.

12. Quoted in George E. Woodberry, *Nathaniel Hawthorne* (Boston, 1902), p. 70.

ships between writers and their publishers are commonly strained. Goodrich did interest himself in Hawthorne's well-being: he got him a job as editor of the *American Magazine of Useful and Entertaining Knowledge*—although it was a pretty poor job. And he had Hawthorne write one of the Peter Parley Books—*Peter Parley's Universal History on the Basis of Geography*. It was through Goodrich's offices that Hawthorne's work came to the *New-England Magazine. The Token* did bring Hawthorne's work if not his name before the public and, with the *New-England Magazine*, made possible his first collections.

The dozen years between his graduation from Bowdoin and the publication of the 1837 *Twice-Told Tales, Hawthorne* spent for the most part in Salem, writing with little reward either in money[13] or reputation, often discouraged but apparently unswerving in his intent. He may have romantically exaggerated his seclusion; and some writers on him have seemed almost to equate the Oberon of his sketches "The Devil in Manuscript" and "Fragments from the Journal of a Solitary Man" with Hawthorne himself.[14] We have no better interpretation of Hawthorne's early years than his own statement in a letter to Richard Henry Stoddard: "My long seclusion had not made me melancholy or misanthropic, nor wholly unfitted me for the bustle of life; and perhaps it was the kind of discipline which my idiosyncrasy demanded, and chance and my own instincts, operating together, had caused me to do what was fittest."[15]

13. See Seymour L. Gross, "Hawthorne's Income from *The Token*," *Studies in Bibliography: Papers of the Bibliographical Society of the University of Virginia* 8 (1956): 236–38; and Frank Luther Mott, A *History of American Magazines* 1741–1850 (New York, 1930), pp. 504–12. But we probably underestimate Hawthorne's income from his writing. The dollar of 1835 is roughly equivalent to $3.58 in 1969 purchasing power (*Monthly Labor Review* [April 1970], p. 113). And, compared to that of other writers in his time, Hawthorne's income from writing was perhaps better than we are likely to suppose. In 1836 Hawthorne wrote to Horatio Bridge that he could earn "but $300 per annum" by his writing (Bridge, *Personal Recollections of Nathaniel Hawthorne* [New York, 1893], p. 73). In 1840 Longfellow's income from writing was $219. See William Charvat, *The Profession of Authorship in America, 1800–1870* (Columbus, Ohio, 1968), p. 128.

14. This sentence was written before I had read Jean Normand's *Nathaniel Hawthorne*, trans. Derek Coltman (Cleveland, 1970), which in its own way continues the tendency.

15. The letter was written about 1853 when Hawthorne's friend Stoddard was preparing an article on Hawthorne. See Julian Hawthorne, *Nathaniel*

Certainly the conditions under which Hawthorne wrote his early tales account in part for their excellence. He was not meeting deadlines; he was not writing after a day's work. He could lavish upon his tales the care with detail, and give them the sort of finish, that made possible so subtle a texture as we find, say, in "Young Goodman Brown," or, to take rather a different example, in "Dr. Heidegger's Experiment." Such tales as these would be most unlikely in the work of a young man with editorial employment, or one who was dependent upon a rapid production for his daily bread. On Hawthorne's seclusion, so far as it was seclusion, depended something of the very qualities we most value in his work.

The seclusion was inevitable when Hawthorne, with only his "slender means," determined to devote himself to fiction under the literary conditions of the 1820s and 1830s. When he won a little recognition, he wrote in his notebook, "In this dismal chamber FAME was won." It was so slight a fame, in no proportion to his achievement, that the entry has a kind of pathos. But the achievement was real, although Hawthorne's estimate of it may have been rather different from our own.

Hawthorne, in an often-quoted letter to Longfellow in 1837, complains that, beside a lack of recognition,

> I have another great difficulty in the lack of materials; for I
> have seen so little of the world that I have nothing but thin
> air to concoct my stories of, and it is not easy to give a lifelike
> semblance to such shadowy stuff. Sometimes through a
> peep-hole I have caught a glimpse of the real world, and the
> two or three articles in which I have portrayed these glimpses
> please me better than the others.

Whatever two or three articles Hawthorne had in mind, they have not pleased his readers better than the work which he wrought out of the history of his Massachusetts. Hawthorne's feeling that his own experience and observation were insufficient literary capital urged him toward his greatest resource: there he found rich material, he was supported by a vigorous critical theory, and he responded to a need.

Hawthorne and His Wife (Boston, 1885), 1: 95–98. Subsequent references in the text to Hawthorne's letter to Stoddard are to this letter.

When early in his Salem years he wrote "Roger Malvin's Burial," "The Gentle Boy," and "My Kinsman, Major Molineux"—and probably other tales we consider important—he was not more than twenty-five.[16] Young writers ordinarily have no great wealth of experience by their middle twenties; those that have—Mark Twain and Herman Melville, for instance—often use it most effectively in retrospect. But in his tales with historical connections, Hawthorne was working in the record of a far wider and richer experience than any personal one.

2. AMERICAN MATERIALS

The long discussion of a national literature in the first part of the nineteenth century may seem to us now academic and beside any point. American writers did, after all, write vividly and interestingly about American scenes and events. But the writers themselves were quite aware of great difficulties; and what we may fail to remember is how much a matter of convention literature always is. American writers, nurtured on British literature, naturally enough felt that there was no convention for what should be their subject matter. Despite the often fervid insistence that there was about to be a full-blown American literature, unique not only in scene and subject, but in glory and power, the thoughtful theorists and the writers themselves fully realized what Robert Frost was to say so much later in "The Gift Outright": their land was "still unstoried, artless, unenhanced."

From the beginning of our national period, the necessity and the possibility of an American literature were vigorously affirmed. Royall Tyler in his prologue to *The Contrast* (produced in 1787) wrote: "On native themes his Muse displays her pow'rs; / If ours the faults, the virtues too are ours." And Charles Brockden Brown in his preface to *Edgar Huntly* (1799) insisted that "the sources of amusement to the fancy and instruction to the heart that are peculiar to ourselves

16. See Nelson F. Adkins, "The Early Projected Works of Nathaniel Hawthorne," *Papers of the Bibliographical Society of America* 39 (1945): 127–28.

are . . . numerous and inexhaustible." The eloquent peroration to
Emerson's "The American Scholar" only reaffirmed a resolve that
had been affirmed from the beginning. Yet the direction that American
literature, and particularly American fiction, was to take did not
come clear until after the publication of *Waverley*. The discussion of
Scott's novels directed the American literary mind to the discovery
of important American resources.[1]

Now Hawthorne was very much aware of the literary discussion in
his time. To neglect the connections between that discussion and
his tales is to obscure the motives of the best of the early tales and to
disregard the kind of appeal Hawthorne hoped they would have for
his first readers. This chapter reviews matters of literary history not
so much unknown as too often ignored; their connection with Hawthorne's practice will be evident in subsequent considerations of
the tales themselves.

THE WAVERLEY NOVELS AND LITERARY THEORY

In our time, when even to some persons concerned with literature
Scott means just *Ivanhoe*, we may fail to understand what a towering
figure Scott was in the first part of the nineteenth century. The
popularity of Scott's poems persisted even as his novels appeared—
Hawthorne at sixteen was reading both *The Lord of the Isles* (1815)
and some of the Waverley novels. But it was the novels that made
the great appeal to the American public, that made the reprinting of
Scott's work immensely profitable to American publishers,[2] and that

1. Robert E. Spiller's anthology *The American Literary Revolution, 1783–
1837* (Anchor Books, 1967) well represents the literary nationalism discussion
in its larger aspects, but it does not reprint the essay-like reviews in which
the American materials discussion went on. G. Harrison Orians, "The Romance
Ferment after *Waverley*" in *American Literature* 3 (1932): 408–31, is an
account of the impact of Scott on the theory and practice of early American
fiction.

2. James D. Hart's *The Popular Book* has an interesting account of Scott's
work in the United States (pp. 68–69, 73–79). The history of the American
publication of Scott is striking evidence of his popularity. For instance,
Matthew Carey, in some sense Scott's authorized American publisher, had in
1822 ten printing plants hurrying *The Fortunes of Nigel* into type in order to
get ahead of the pirates, and in 1823 produced *Quentin Durward* in twenty-

accounted for his American prestige. Cooper, however much he
may have disliked the appellation, was inevitably "the American
Scott." Irving's reverent—and charming—account of his stay with Scott
in *Abbotsford* (1835) seemed to Americans to bring their literature
into a tradition. John Gibson Lockhart's *Life of Scott* (1838) sold
more copies in America than it did in England.

There is no parallel in American literary history for the pervading
interest in the Waverley novels. A passage from a review of *York
Town: A Historical Romance* in the *American Quarterly Review* in
1827 helps us to recapture something of the American feeling about
Scott, the better because the writer—who is probably the editor,
Robert Walsh—does not wholly approve of Scott's influence.

> No author, probably, ancient or modern, was ever so well paid
> by the booksellers, or so universally read by all classes of
> people; nor can his acknowledged merits entirely and satis-
> factorily account for his overwhelming popularity. Good
> fortune, as well as uncommon felicity in the choice and manner
> of treating his subjects, undoubtedly co-operated in building
> up, almost in a single night, a reputation, which preceding
> writers, of at least equal merit, owed to time and posterity. . . .
> All those who read at all, from the highest to the lowest,
> devoured with unsated appetite, these fictions, as they appeared
> with unexampled rapidity; all admired with an intensity of
> fashionable enthusiasm, or at least those who did not admire,
> were ashamed to confess it; and even the critics, whose business
> it is to discriminate, did homage to the universal taste, by
> indiscriminate praise. It was not in the nature of man, that an
> author, so fashionable, so successful, and so munificently
> rewarded, should not have found imitators, even had he possessed
> only a tithe of the excellence of Sir Walter Scott. Accordingly,
> the old school novels underwent a complete French Revolution
> in England, and, by a natural consequence, in this
> country. [2: 33]

What is said here is everywhere confirmed. Hawthorne's publisher
Goodrich writes: "I suspect that never, in any age, have the produc-

---

eight hours after receiving copy for it. "Every hour counted with a public so
intense," and competition so cut-throat.

tions of any author created in the world so wide and deep an enthusiasm. . . . Everybody read these works; everybody—the refined and the simple."[3] The most serious and austere men of letters found in Scott a new concept of fiction and its possibilities. In a review of Catherine M. Sedgwick's *Redwood* in the *North American Review* in 1825, Bryant asks: "Twenty years ago, what possible conception could an English critic have had of the admirable productions of the author of Waverley, and of the wonderful improvement his example has effected in that kind of composition?" (20:248–49). Bryant's question is the more significant in that he is seeing Scott as a guide not only in the use of historical and legendary materials but in the use of contemporary materials too. In 1827 in the same journal William H. Prescott writes, "We of present generation can hardly estimate our own good fortune, in having lighted upon this prolific and entertaining epoch" in which Scott's example has worked a revolution in fiction (25:184).

Mark Twain in two chapters of *Life on the Mississippi* (40 and 46) blamed all the ills of the South on its fondness for the chivalric novels of Scott, and sober writers have taken his extravagance more seriously than perhaps he intended it.[4] But it was not the chivalric novels that influenced northern literary theorists. They recognized in Scott's ways of dealing with the recent past in his own country a pattern adaptable to their own needs and history. Francis R. Hart in a recent book defines Scott's "perennial concern" as "the problem of individual freedom and cultural continuity in historical change";[5] and that was also the concern of thoughtful men of letters in the new nation. They recognized, too, that Scott showed the way to supply that texture of association, that coming together of story and place, Americans lacked and needed. He seemed the best example of the Associationism of Archibald Alison. Scott supplied them not only with the example of his practice but with a basis for theory, for

3. Goodrich, 2: 107–8.
4. See for examples, W. J. Cash, *The Mind of the South* (New York, 1941), pp. ix, 62–65, and Edmund Wilson, *Patriotic Gore* (New York, 1962), pp. 440–50.
5. *Scott's Novels: The Plotting of Historic Survival* (The University Press of Virginia, 1966), p. 13. See also A. O. J. Cockshut, *The Achievement of Walter Scott* (New York, 1969).

they found implicit in the Waverley novels the principle made explicit in the introduction to his edition of *Sir Tristrem*:

> Tradition depends upon locality. The scene of a celebrated battle, the ruins of an ancient tower, the "historic stone" over the grave of a hero, the hill and valley inhabited of old by a particular tribe, remind posterity of events which are sometimes recorded in their very names. Even a race of strangers, when the lapse of years has induced them no longer to account themselves such, welcome any fiction by which they can associate their ancestors with the scenes in which they themselves live, as transplanted trees push forth every fiber that may connect them with the soil to which they are transferred.[6]

Urged by their own need and by Scott's example, our early writers, and in their behalf our early critics, searched for historical and quasi-historical incidents suitable for fictional use, so that American places might be storied and enhanced.

There is then in the literary theory of the period a strong sense of locality. Harry Levin remarks that Hawthorne "was never a nationalist; he was a regionalist";[7] but that is a twentieth-century distinction, one that the critical theorist of the early nineteenth century would hardly have understood. In 1827 a writer (who may be James Kirke Paulding) in the highly nationalistic *American Quarterly Review*, insists that "probably, no country in the world . . . affords more numerous and distinct characters than the United States. . . . And every state in the Union is a little world in itself, exhibiting almost the same degrees of difference that we observe in the English, the Scotch, and the Irish" (1: 341).[8]

By 1825, the year of Hawthorne's graduation from college, the influence of Scott had permeated American fiction. Jared Sparks, writing in the *North American Review*, and reviewing ten novels that had been published within a year, finds "it expedient first to settle . . .

---

6. *Sir Tristrem; A Metrical Romance of the Thirteenth Century*, ed., Walter Scott, Esq. (Edinburgh, 1804), p. xxvi.

7. *The Power of Blackness* (Vintage Books, n.d.), p. 47.

8. In the copy in the University of Illinois library this review of Dunlap's *The Father of an Only Child* and Barker's *Marmion* and *Superstition* is identified in faded ink as by "Paulding N.Y."—as indeed it seems to be.

the peculiarities" of the Waverley pattern, of which most of the ten novels are "acknowledged copies." Fiction in the Waverley pattern, he thinks, fits the needs of Americans: "The actors in these works have not only a human, but a national, and often a provincial character. . . . The subject of manners and customs is, moreover, one of general interest, and as an adherence to these serves to give individuality to the characters in these narratives, it is so far an improvement on the practice of the older novels, and advantageous to the writer" (21: 80–82). Hawthorne began as a writer just at the time of Scott's greatest American prestige.

LITERARY THEORY AND HAWTHORNE'S PRACTICE

The discussion of the question of American materials began when Hawthorne was a boy, and it flourished in his college years and for several years thereafter. Our early literary history is remarkable, indeed, for the development of a vigorous theory ahead of practice, a theory that influences subsequent practice in particular and discernible ways.[9]

American writers, to be sure, had attempted American themes from the beginning. In the epic Joel Barlow had at least displayed courage; in poetry Philip Freneau and in the drama Royall Tyler and William Dunlap had had some success. American fiction did not find itself quite so soon. In its best early examples, the response to the demand for a national literature was the transplanting of a European legend. In the third of his *Lectures on Poetry* (delivered in 1826), Bryant remarks, "It is especially the privilege of an age which has no engrossing superstitions of its own, to make use in its poetry of those of past ages." Irving's "Rip Van Winkle" and "The Legend of Sleepy Hollow" both have German legends at their cores, but the legends are naturalized in their new locale and become parts of American imaginative experience.[10] The naturalization of European legend is

9. So far as this literary theory was a nationalistic movement, it was reinforced —and perhaps in its influence on Hawthorne—by a parallel nationalism in historians. See Nelson F. Adkins, "Hawthorne's Democratic New England Puritans," *Emerson Society Quarterly*, no. 44 (1966), pp. 66–72.

10. See Henry A. Pochmann, "Irving's German Sources in *The Sketch Book*," *Studies in Philology* 27 (1930): 477–507.

more direct in Irving's "The Storm-Ship" and William Austin's "Peter Rugg, the Missing Man," both of which use the *Flying Dutchman* legend. Hawthorne was once led into the naturalization of a legend; in "Drowne's Wooden Image" he makes the Pygmalion story at home in eighteenth-century Boston.

Although the naturalization of foreign legends accounts for our earliest tales of distinction, it could not long fulfill the need Americans felt for a storied land and their own tradition. The discussion in which the quest for a tradition went on, however, had a strong negative side. To many Americans it was by no means clear that the new nation had the possibility of a literature. Bryant is one of the best proponents of an American national literature, but he sums up fairly and succinctly the negative argument.

> Our citizens are held to possess, in a remarkable degree, the heedful, calculating, prosaic spirit of the age, while our country is decried as peculiarly barren of the materials of poetry. The scenery of our land these reasoners admit to be beautiful, but they urge that it is the beauty of a face without expression; that it wants the associations of tradition which are the soul and interest of scenery; that it wants the national superstitions which linger yet in every district in Europe, and the legends of distant and dark ages and of wild and unsettled times of which the old world reminds you at every step. Nor can our country, they say, ever be more fruitful of these materials than at present.

As Bryant proceeds, he endeavors to answer these objections, but it cannot be denied that the difficulties were real.

Indeed, the very writers who first make a distinguished use of American materials seem as conscious of the deprivations of the fiction writer in America as Bryant's opponents are. In a well-known passage in Letter 23 of his *Notions of the Americans*, Cooper says that, after the lack of international copyright, "The second obstacle against which American literature has to contend is in the poverty of materials." There are in America, Cooper thinks, "no annals for the historian . . . no obscure fictions for the writer of romance," little or nothing of what the writer needs to work with. And in "The Author's Account of Himself," his prefatory piece for *The Sketch*

Book, Irving, although admitting the special beauty of American scenery, finds his county without "the charms of storied and poetical association," the richness of Europe's "accumulated treasures of age" and "shadowy grandeurs of the past." Belatedly and only after he had turned from the American past as his subject matter, even Hawthorne remarks, in his preface to *The Marble Faun*, "the difficulty of writing a romance about a country where there is no shadow, no antiquity, no mystery, no picturesque and gloomy wrong." The complaint continues to Henry James who, in his *Hawthorne* (1878), centers on the preface to *The Marble Faun* his famous discussion of the "blankness" of life in the United States, where history has left "so thin and impalpable a deposit," where experience has so little texture.[11]

But whatever of importance and influence the proponents in the American materials discussion had to say was said in an effort to obviate just the objections that Bryant sums up. And—whatever the writer's position on the question—it is clear that Scott's novels had become the standard for fiction, that fiction was defined in reference to them. As Bryant summarizes the case against the possibility of a great national literature, it is that the United States cannot offer the writer the sort of materials Scott used. Cooper's second obstacle against which American literature has to contend is the lack of such materials as Scott had to exploit. Yet at the same time the case for an American fiction rested upon Scott's example, on the contention that, in dealing with recent past in Scotland, Scott had shown American writers how to use their own history and experience.

Hawthorne had been in college but one year when William Howard Gardiner, in some prefatory paragraphs to a review of Cooper's *The Spy* in the *North American Review*, stated the three great historical resources of the American fiction writer: the Colonial period, the Indian wars, and the Revolution. "What would not the author of Waverley," Gardiner asks, "make of such materials?"

11. This attitude persisted beyond mid-century in James Russell Lowell as well as in James. In his essay on James Gates Percival (1867), Lowell writes: "It had been resolved unanimously that we must and would have a national literature. . . . We forgot that artistic literature, the only literature possible under our modern conditions, thrives best in an air laden with tradition, in a soil mellow with immemorial culture, in the temperature steady yet stimulating of historic and national associations. We had none of these." *Writings* (Riverside Edition, Boston, 1898), 2: 148.

(15: 255–57). Ten years later, when Hawthorne was beginning to publish, the young John Greenleaf Whittier was still calling for the use of the same materials.[12] Although Hawthorne was quite aware of these three matters of American romance, he makes extensive use of only one, the Puritan material. About sixty years ago W. C. Brownell said of Hawthorne's works, "Even the theme of many of them—the romance of Puritan New England—was Hawthorne's discovery."[13] No critic today would say that; but a good deal of discussion of Hawthorne has gone on as if it were true.

Parallels in literary theory to Hawthorne's literary thinking and his practice in the tales may be found as early as a Phi Beta Kappa address by William Tudor, the first editor of the *North American Review*. It was printed in 1815, the first year of the *North American Review* (2: 13–32), and it helps to mark the beginning of a New England literary consciousness. In it Tudor is thinking of poetry, and apparently of poetry in an epic vein, but what he urges has quite as much application to fiction, and was as much fulfilled in it. He is close enough to the beginning of the American materials discussion to think of the great resource of American literature as the epic treatment of Indian materials, an idea which, though never of great effect—for Tudor does not envisage Cooper's Indians—persisted long.[14] Hawthorne fully recognized it; he says in "Our Evening Party Among the Mountains": "No writer can be more secure of a permanent place in our literature than the biographer of the Indian chiefs. His subject, as referring to tribes which have mostly vanished from the earth, gives him a right to be placed on a classic shelf, apart from the merits which will sustain him there." For himself, however, he regrets

12. Whittier wrote: "New-England is full of Romance. . . . The great forest which our fathers penetrated—the red men—their struggles and their disappearance . . . the savage inroad and the English sally—the tale of super-stition, and the scenes of Witchcraft,—all these are rich materials of poetry." *The Literary Remains of John G. C. Brainard*, ed. J. G. Whittier (Hartford, 1832), p. 35.

13. *American Prose Masters*, Modern Students Library (New York, n.d.), p. 51.

14. Robert Walsh or a writer in his journal says ironically in 1827: "If . . . a writer of this country wishes to make its history, or its traditions the subject of romantic fiction, high wrought, obscure, and sometimes extravagant, agreeable to the taste of the times, he must go back to the aborigines." *American Quarterly Review* 2: 45.

that he is "shut out from the most peculiar field of American fiction." "I do abhor," he says, "an Indian story." Part of his distaste for Indian material seems to stem from his realization that the history of the relationships of white settlers and Indians was a horrifying one.[15]

The Revolution, Tudor thinks, is too recent to be proper literary material; "some centuries hence . . . when ages will have consecrated its principles," when its feuds and passions are forgotten, and only "a few memorable actions and immortal names shall remain"—then it may become usable (2: 14). Tudor is writing before Cooper showed the way in *The Spy*; nevertheless, Hawthorne seems to have felt this principle a right one, and to have kept away from the Revolution generally. The three of the four "Legends of the Province House" that concern the Revolution deal with it only peripherally; and Hawthorne is careful, as we shall see, to identify the time of the action of "My Kinsman, Major Molineux" in a confusing fashion.

Tudor's definition of the proper historical span for American imaginative writing is "from the close of the 16th to the middle of the 18th century"—not far from Hawthorne's chosen period. There, Tudor thinks, writers will find materials to their purpose (2: 14). Writing almost prophetically at the beginning of Scott's career as a novelist,[16] Tudor insists that there are resources in American history that will offer materials such as Scott uses: "Perilous and romantick adventures, figurative and eloquent harangues, strong contrasts and important interests, are as frequent in this portion of history, as the theatre on which these actions were performed in abundant in grand and beautiful scenery" (2: 28). The single sentence predicts something of Hawthorne's practice and suggests some of his likenesses to Scott: the perilous and romantic adventure of "The Gray Champion," the eloquent harangue of "Endicott and the Red Cross," the strong contrast of "The Maypole of Merry Mount," the important interest of "Edward Randolph's Portrait."

In a long footnote (attached to "Perilous and romantick adventures" in the sentence quoted above) Tudor makes some specific suggestions

15. See *Grandfather's Chair*, pp. 467–69. Unless otherwise indicated, references to Hawthorne's writings by title and page number are to the Riverside Edition of *Works* (Boston, 1883).

16. Tudor had reviewed *Guy Mannering* and *The Lord of the Isles* in the first volume of the *North American Review*.

of historical personages and incidents for the use of American writers—and even includes some bibliography. Two of the suggested subjects Hawthorne used some fifteen years later: the career of Ann Hutchinson in "Mrs. Hutchinson" and the striking "incident mentioned by President Stiles . . . of Dixwell, one of the regicides, suddenly emerging from his concealment, and by his presence animating an infant settlement"[17] in "The Gray Champion." The literary treatment of such subjects as he suggests will supply, Tudor thinks, a texture of association for American places: "If remarkable characters and actions are to be found in our history, the scenes where they lived or occurred, must be interesting from association of ideas."

The literary theorists were prone to suggest what writers should be writing about, both generally and specifically, and their suggestions were likely to be materials in some sort parallel to those Scott had used. John Gorham Palfrey, in reviewing a long poem called *Yamoyden*[18] in the *North American Review* in 1821, predicts that the first important writer of fiction will lay his scene in New England:

> We know not the country or age which has such capacities in this view as N. England in its early day; nor do we suppose it easy to imagine any element of the sublime, the wonderful, the picturesque and the pathetic, which is not to be found here by him who shall hold the witch-hazel wand that can trace it. We had the same puritan character of stern, romantic enthusiasm of which, in the Scottish novels, such effective use is made, but impressed here on the whole face of society, and sublimed to a degree which it never elsewhere reached. [12: 480]

Palfrey's long catalog of historical personages for the use of fiction writers suggests the bias of his own later historical work, but it includes a surprising number of figures that Hawthorne used in his tales:

> Here were consummate gentlemen and statesmen, like Winthrop . . . female heresiarchs of the stamp of Mrs. Hutchinson . . .

17. Tudor is in error; Ezra Stiles in his *A History of Three of the Judges of King Charles I* (1794) identifies the "Angel of Hadley" as William Goffe, just as Thomas Hutchinson does in the first printed account of the story.

18. *Yamoyden, a Tale of the Wars of King Philip*, in six cantos. By the late Rev. James Wallis Eastburn, A.M. and his friend (New York: James Eastburn, 1820). The friend is Robert Charles Sands.

soldiers . . . scrupulous as much as loyal, like Endicott, who dreaded not the king's enemies half as much as the scandal of the red cross on his colours . . . devotees to the established faith and hankerers after a new . . . exiles life Goff and Whaley . . . men like Morton, the author of New English Canaan, a cavaliar as true as ever felt his heart dance to the rattling of spurs and broadswords. [12: 481–83]

Likewise, John Neal, writing on American literature for *Blackwood's Edinburgh Magazine* about 1824, suggests the life of Mrs. Hutchinson and the accounts of the regicide judges as story material, as well as "the female Quakers . . . or the witches," the subjects of "The Gentle Boy" and "Young Goodman Brown." Neal complains, indeed, of the preemption of the story of the regicide at Hadley by Scott in *Peveril of the Peak* (1822).[19]

But there was yet a function of Scott-like American fiction to be defined: the way in which it might discover for Americans not only a colorful past but what has been lately called a usable past. A striking example of the definition of that function is an oration by Rufus Choate, called "The Importance of Illustrating New-England History by a Series of Romances Like the Waverley Novels."[20] The address was delivered at Salem in 1833 and is printed in Choate's *Addresses and Orations* (Boston, 1887). One would like to know whether or not Hawthorne heard it. It is most unlikely that Choate was at all aware that a citizen of Salem had begun his illustrations of New England history.

Choate contends that the writer of historical fiction vivifies and fills in for the imagination the story of the past, that every lover of literature and his country would like, not one, but a thousand Walter Scotts. He would wish the American writer to be "like Old Mortality

19. *American Writers: A Series of Papers Contributed to Blackwood's Magazine, 1824–1825*, ed. F. L. Pattee (Durham, N.C., 1937), pp. 191–92. Apparently every writer and critic thought of William Goffe's adventure at Hadley as an ideal subject: Paulding (?) in 1827 in commenting on Barker's *Superstition* (which uses the story) says that it "has often occurred to us as singularly striking and dramatic" (*American Quarterly Review* 1: 354).

20. Rufus Choate (1799–1859) was representative and later senator from Massachusetts, and a famous orator and courtroom lawyer. He has two other addresses in the vein of literary nationalism: "The Colonial Age of New England" and "The Age of the Pilgrims the Heroic Period in Our History."

among the graves of the unforgotten faithful, wiping the dust from the urns of our fathers,—gathering up whatever of illustrious achievement their history commemorates, and weaving it all into an immortal and noble national literature" (p. 2).[21] But Choate is asking for more than just preservation: "Something is wanting yet to give to [the Puritan] character and fortunes a warm, quick interest, a charm for the feelings and imagination, an abiding place in the heart and memory and affections.... It is time that literature and the arts should at least cooperate with history" (p. 23). For Choate, to cooperate with history is to make it intelligible and to universalize it: the fiction writer must accommodate "the show of things to the desires and needs of the immortal, moral nature" (p. 31).

That exalted aim includes for Choate not only selection but suppression too. The writer of historical fiction will neglect that large portion of history which "chills, shames, disgusts us," and specifically in New England history the evidences of Puritan intolerance.

> The persecutions of the Quakers, the controversies with Roger Williams and Mrs. Hutchinson, the perpetual synods and ecclesiastical surveillance of the old times; a great deal of this is too tedious to be read, or it offends and alienates you. It is truth, fact; but it is just what you do not want to know, and are none the wiser for knowing. Now, he who writes the romance of history takes his choice of all its ample but incongruous material.... He remembers that it is an heroic age to whose contemplation he would turn us back; and as no man is a hero to his servant, so no age is heroic of which the whole truth is recorded. He records the useful truth therefore, only.... [pp. 30–31]

This concept—so baldly stated—of a usable past gained largely by suppression may be a little embarrassing to read, although we are beginning to realize how often American writers have carried on a like suppression. But Choate's theory helps us to see what Hawthorne was doing.

21. Compare a stanza from Whittier's "The Garrison of Cape Ann":

So, with something of the feeling which the Covenanter knew,
When with pious chisel wandering Scotland's moorland graveyards
    through,
From the graves of old traditions I part the blackberry-vines,
Wipe the moss from off the headstones, and retouch the faded lines.

A few of Hawthorne's early tales seem to be directed by the sort of cooperation with history Choate recommends, but with ironic reservations. Yet—it is surprising when one thinks of it—Hawthorne was at the same time preserving in fiction "the persecutions of the Quakers, the controversies with . . . Mrs. Hutchinson," and witchcraft, a horror in New England history that Choate does not even mention. Hawthorne's concept of "useful truth" is far more complex than any Choate envisaged. Yet it stems from Choate's sort of literary theory.

Indeed, Hawthorne's debt to the literary theorists—obvious and specific as it often is—cannot be fully counted up in the recognition of their influence on his subject matter nor in the total of their particular suggestions he seems to have followed. They furnished him with a place of beginning, the place he might develop from, and with a kind of surrogate for an American literary tradition.[22]

LITERARY THEORY AND HAWTHORNE'S PURPOSES

The literary theory of the 1820s and 1830s, preoccupied as it was with Scott, centered on the novel. The conditions of Hawthorne's market, as we have seen, turned him toward the tale. He may have had no special propensity for it—when he had published one successful romance, he wrote no more short fiction except "Feathertop" and, of course, the stories for children. And it is clear that he did not in the beginning think of his tales as separate and unrelated works.

If Hawthorne had been able to find a publisher for either of the two

22. Hawthorne's own discussions of literary theory in reviews are all too late to indicate the effect of the American materials discussion on his thinking in the period of our concern. His review of *Evangeline* is pleasantly laudatory, repaying in kind Longfellow's review of *Twice-Told Tales*. His review of W. G. Simms's *Views and Reviews in American Literature, History and Fiction* (New York, 1845), which is a twenty-years–belated plea for a national literature, dismisses Simms's discussion as a critical anachronism. See Randall Stewart, ed., "Hawthorne's Contributions to the Salem *Advertiser*," *American Literature* 5 (1934): 327–41. Hawthorne's review of Whittier's *The Supernaturalism of New England* in *The Literary World* in 1847 has a little more interest, for in it he denies the complete availibility of all American materials for the fiction writer—which literary theorists had often assumed. See Randall Stewart, ed., "Two Uncollected Reviews by Hawthorne," *New England Quarterly* 9 (1936): 504–9.

collections of tales he projected early, his intention as a young writer—perhaps never quite fulfilled—might be clear to us.

From the beginning, he projected groups of tales in some connection. He had before him the example of Irving, who had experimented with various sorts of connections in three successive volumes, in *The Sketch Book*, in *Bracebridge Hall*, and in *Tales of a Traveller*. Since Hawthorne was using only American material, he almost surely envisaged a closer connection among the tales in his projected volumes than Irving achieved in any of the three.

According to the recollection of Elizabeth Hawthorne, her brother early projected a collection to be called "Seven Tales of My Native Land," tales which were written in college or soon thereafter, and among which was the first version of "Alice Doane's Appeal."[23] What we have from Hawthorne's own pen on the matter is a paragraph in the frame of "Alice Doane's Appeal" as it was printed in *The Token* for 1835—evidently reworked from the first version. (Hawthorne never collected or acknowledged the tale.) In this paragraph Hawthorne writes of "a series written long ago"; but he seems to write of more than seven tales. He says that "three or four of these tales had appeared in the 'Token' "; that "one great heap . . . had fed the flames"; and that "Alice Doane's Appeal" and one other tale "chanced to be in kinder custody at the time, and thus . . . escaped destruction."[24] But the paragraph was hardly intended as sober autobiography, and in particular the reference to the burning of a "great heap" of tales may be intended as an allusion to "The Devil in Manuscript," a tale which describes a holocaust a despairing young writer makes of "a pile of blotted manuscripts."

What emerges of importance for the study of Hawthorne as a writer is that, in college or very soon thereafter, he wrote a group of tales

23. Elizabeth Hawthorne on one occasion remembered the "Seven Tales of My Native Land" as having been written while Hawthorne was in college; on another she remembered them as having been written soon after his graduation. According to George P. Lathrop, Hawthorne had expected a Salem printer to bring out the collection, but took back his manuscript and burned it when the printer long delayed. If Lathrop's account is trustworthy and merely misdated, as Hubert H. Hoeltje believes, then the tales intended for the projected volume were written in college. See Hoeltje's *Inward Sky* (Durham, N.C., 1962), pp. 81–83. See also Adkins, "The Early Projected Works of Nathaniel Hawthorne," pp. 121–26.

24. *Tales, Sketches, and Other Papers*, p. 282.

projected as a series connected by a nationalistic subject matter. His second projected series he thought of as "Provincial Tales," and in 1830 he was hoping for its publication as a volume.

On December 20, 1829 Hawthorne wrote a covering letter for a group of tales in manuscript he sent to Goodrich. Among them, evidently, was the first version of "Alice Doane's Appeal." But some of these tales, at least, were tales he thought of as comprising the "Provincial Tales" volume. This projected volume he mentions by title in a letter of May 6, 1830, a covering letter for the transmission of two pieces for *The Token* of 1831. Hawthorne writes: "You can insert them (if you think them worthy a place in your publication) as by the author of 'Provincial Tales'—such being the title I propose to give to my volume. I can conceive no objection to your designating them in this manner, even if my tales should not be published as soon as the Token, or, indeed, if they never see the light at all." Nelson F. Adkins remarks that the four tales in *The Token* for 1832 "belonged, we may reasonably assume," to the volume Hawthorne had projected, and suggests other tales that might have been part of it. The four tales in *The Token* for 1832 were "The Wives of the Dead," "Roger Malvin's Burial," "My Kinsman, Major Molineux," and "The Gentle Boy." (Goodrich apparently rejected "Alice Doane's Appeal" in its first version.) Their appearance in *The Token* for 1832 seems to show that Hawthorne despaired, by 1831, of the separate publication of a "Provincial Tales" volume.[25]

The projected "Seven Tales of My Native Land" and "Provincial Tales" have more than a merely biographical interest. We know enough of them to realize that Hawthorne's first intention was to become known as a writer working in the materials of early American history, and to present his tales in historical connection. The connection among the tales in both projected volumes would have been a likeness of historical subject matter, perhaps some scheme of sequence, and possibly some sort of frame. What he did do

25. See "The Early Projected Works of Nathaniel Hawthorne," pp. 127–31. Richard P. Adams, "Hawthorne's *Provincial Tales*," *New England Quarterly* 30 (1957): 39–57 is an attempt to reconstruct Hawthorne's proposed volume. It seems likely to me that Hawthorne intended by his title to indicate that the tales dealt with the time Massachusetts was a province, not a colony. But he does use "provincial" in reference to colonial times, in "Mrs. Hutchinson," for instance.

in his first collection, the 1837 *Twice-Told Tales,* must be considered therefore in some sense a defeat. The young Hawthorne knew where his strength lay, and was prevented from exhibiting it fully. The nearest Hawthorne ever came to attaining his project of a series of connected tales published together is in the four "Legends of the Province House."

In both projected titles, Hawthorne uses the word "tales"; perhaps neither projected volume would have included a group of early biographical sketches of historical personages. These four pieces—"Sir William Phips," "Mrs. Hutchinson," "Dr. Bullivant," and "Sir William Pepperell"—were first printed from 1830 to 1832 and Hawthorne left them all uncollected. He did collect—belatedly in *The Snow-Image*—other historical sketches, "A Bell's Biography" and the three pieces in "Old News."[26] The later "Main Street" is in the vein of these early historical reconstructions.

In these early pieces Hawthorne was experimenting with historical materials and seems to be trying to give them what Choate calls "a warm, quick interest." Indeed, in the first paragraph of "Sir William Phips," Hawthorne states just such an intention:

Few of the personages of past times (except such as have gained renown in fireside legends as well as in written history) are anything more than mere names to their successors. They seldom stand up in our imaginations like men. The knowledge communicated by the historian and biographer is analogous to that which we acquire of a country by the map,—minute, perhaps, and accurate, and available for all necessary purposes, but cold and naked, and wholly destitute of the mimic charm produced by landscape-painting. These defects are partly remediable, and even without an absolute violation of literal truth, although by methods rightfully interdicted to professors of biographical exactness. A license must be assumed in brightening the materials which time has rusted, and in tracing out half-obliterated inscriptions on the columns of antiquity: Fancy must throw her reviving light on the faded incidents that indicate

26. "Old Ticonderoga," also collected in *The Snow-Image,* is of indeterminate genre; it seems to have come out of one of Hawthorne's summer excursions, but it is somewhat in the vein of the early historical reconstructions.

character, whence a ray will be reflected, more or less vividly,
on the person to be described.

Of the pieces Hawthorne wrote with this intent, "Mrs. Hutchinson"
seems especially worth remembering, both for its intrinsic interest
and for its connection with *The Scarlet Letter*. In the sketch
Hawthorne sees Ann Hutchinson as the prototype of the feminists
of his own day, and in chapter 13 of the romance remarks Hester's
likeness to her.

If Hawthorne seems not to have much valued—and if his readers
have usually ignored—"Mrs. Hutchinson" and the other three biographical sketches of historical personages, the sketches yet have their
importance in his development. He may have thought of them as
studies for more finished work. And it looks as if, after he had published
the children's historical stories now collected in *Grandfather's Chair*,
he felt that these early sketches were too much like material in it
to collect.[27] But they are clear evidence of the influence of the literary
theorists on his work—influence of the most direct sort. Indeed
he functions himself as one of them in the passage from "Sir William
Phips" that we have just considered.

Although Hawthorne's projected collections and his experiments
"in brightening the materials which time has rusted" in his own genre
of historical pieces are important as they show the influence of the
American materials discussion, of course our chief concern is the
tales. And we need to recognize at the outset both the significance and
the complexity of the relationships between them and literary theory.

Hawthorne cannot be considered one of the thousand Walter
Scotts for whom Choate wished, but such literary theory as that of
Tudor, Gardiner, Palfrey, and Choate brought him toward his best
work. If W. C. Brownell did not know the influence of literary theory
on Hawthorne's work, he was perceptive enough to recognize the
result of that influence. Hawthorne's success, Brownell says, "varies
directly as the density of his material. . . . Hawthorne succeeded in
the main when he dealt with the Puritans. . . . There, he had a background, material, and a subject of substance."[28] Brownell is but

27. There are treatments of Mrs. Hutchinson, Sir William Phips, and Sir
William Pepperell in *Grandfather's Chair*.
28. Brownell, pp. 71–72 and 96.

stating the judgment of common readers as it has been clear in their preferences for generations.

Puritan material, of course, was a subject of substance in a special way for Hawthorne. As he says in "The Custom House," the long history of his family in New England gave him "a sort of home-feeling with the past" and a certain "kindred" with the locality, "probably assignable to the deep and aged roots" of his family in Salem, "not love, but instinct." Since he was aware of himself, for good and ill, as an inheritor of the New England tradition, the demand for the use of American materials came to him with special force. As we shall see, five of the tales he wrote in answer concern events with which he had particular ancestral connections.

The American materials discussion, then, gave Hawthorne a convention suited to American needs and possibilities, and one that required the use of his ancestral tradition. Yet of course he worked in that convention in his own ways. We could understand his development better, perhaps, if we knew the sequence in which he wrote his early tales—a matter about which too much may be assumed. At any rate, we have in tales first printed within the years 1831–1835 remarkably different uses of American materials. There is, for example, "The Gray Champion"—one might suppose that in it Hawthorne was following critical prescription as closely as he could. There is "The Maypole of Merry Mount," which uses such materials as Palfrey and Choate urged, but uses them to substantiate an allegory of timeless purport. And there are "My Kinsman, Major Molineux" and "Young Goodman Brown," which make a use of American materials peculiarly Hawthorne's own.

When Hawthorne was graduated from Bowdoin, his classmate Henry Wadsworth Longfellow made his commencement oration on the topic "Our Native Writers." "Is then our land to be indeed the land of song?" the young Longfellow asked, "Will it one day be rich in romantic associations?" He answered himself: "Yes!—and palms are to be won by our native writers!—by those that have been nursed and brought up with us in the civil and religious freedom of our country. Already a voice has been lifted up in this land, already a spirit and a love of literature are springing up in the shadow of our free political institutions. . . . Every rock shall become a chronicle of storied allusions." Of course Longfellow was saying nothing new, but he was affirming his own resolve and, although he did not know it, the resolve of one of his auditors. Longfellow and Hawthorne, each in his own way, went about fulfilling the prophecy and, when their work was done, their land was "rich in romantic associations," and much that had been barren became "a chronicle of storied allusions."[29]

3. THE DEVELOPMENT OF HAWTHORNE'S LITERARY HABIT

Without attention to Hawthorne's reading and to the conventions in which he worked, the most subtle analysis of a tale is likely to misinterpret elements that belong as much to literary convention or example, or to the source of the tale, as they do to Hawthorne's temperament. His literary habit took shape by the interaction of his temperament and his reading, and if we know something of the resources on which he drew and of his attitude toward them, we are less likely to mistake his purposes in the use of them.

"ALL SORTS OF GOOD AND GOOD-FOR-NOTHING BOOKS"

One of Hawthorne's cherished possessions was the copy of Sir Philip Sidney's *Arcadia* his first American ancestor, William Hathorne, had brought with him from England. Hawthorne was born into a reading family, and his literary development began early. It will become clear for us that the reading most effective on his development as a writer was the reading of his boyhood and youth, as is so often true of writers.

For our knowledge of Hawthorne's earliest reading, we are depen-

---

29. "Our Native Writers" is reprinted in *The American Literary Revolution*, pp. 387–90.

dent upon Elizabeth Hawthorne's account, made at the behest of
James T. Fields.[1] She tells us that Nathaniel at six was reading
Bunyan's *Pilgrim's Progress*, that he bought Spenser's *Faerie Queene*
with his own money as a boy, and that Shakespeare, Milton, Pope,
and James Thomson, author of *The Seasons*, were early favorites. That
list gets some confirmation in Hawthorne's testimony in his letter
to Stoddard that as a boy in Maine he read "a good deal . . . on the
rainy days, especially in Shakespeare and *The Pilgrim's Progress*, and
any poetry or light books" within his reach. Elizabeth Hawthorne
also remembered young Nathaniel reading the *Newgate Calendar*,
particularly because it occasioned some family disapproval.

Yet we may easily overstress Elizabeth Hawthorne's recollection of
her brother so many years before. A passage in *Our Old Home* suggests
that Hawthorne did a good deal of the exploratory sort of reading
that a literate boy does on his own. He remembers that he read
Boswell's life of Dr. Johnson "at a very early period" of his life, and
comments,

> It is only a solitary child,—left much to such wild modes of
> culture as he chooses for himself while yet ignorant of what
> culture means, standing on tiptoe to pull down books from no
> very lofty shelf, and then shutting himself up, as it were, between
> the leaves, going astray through the volume at his own pleasure,
> and comprehending it rather by his sensibilities and affections
> than his intellect,—that child is the only student that ever gets
> the sort of intimacy which I am now thinking of, with a
> literary personage.

Such reading would yield a wider and less conventional list than
Elizabeth Hawthorne remembered. Hawthorne remarks that, with his
propensities "toward Fairy Land" and with the New England yeast
in his nature, an early acquaintance with Dr. Johnson was doubtless
wholesome.[2]

1. See Randall Stewart, ed., "Recollections of Hawthorne by His Sister
Elizabeth," *American Literature* 16 (1945): 316–31.
2. *Our Old Home*, pp. 149–50. Since Hawthorne in his mature years did
not care much for poetry, it is worth noting that he here speaks with admiration
of Dr. Johnson's "two stern and masculine poems, 'London,' and 'The Vanity
of Human Wishes.'"

Hawthorne surely also began getting his familiarity with the Bible early in life, for his knowledge of it is clearly the available kind that comes from long acquaintance. When his prose rises, one sometimes hears the cadences of the King James version in it. His Puritans and Quakers speak in biblical idiom convincingly—how convincingly one can judge by comparing their speeches with those of Cooper's Puritans in *The Wept of Wish-ton-Wish*. Old Testament allusions come to him easily and naturally; the cave of Richard Digby (in "The Man of Adamant") is like "Elijah's cave at Horeb" or like "Abraham's sepulchral cave at Machpelah." Sometimes he seems to pick up a biblical expression unconsciously: at the end of "Young Goodman Brown," "neighbors not a few" follow Brown's body to its grave, an echo of a mannerism of St. Luke in Acts.

But often biblical expressions are calculated: in "Main Street" the "dew of mercy" Hawthorne hopes will cleanse the guilt of the persecutors of the Quakers is a kind of allusion to a score of passages in both testaments. Sometimes he paraphrases a biblical passage to adapt it to his context, as in "The Old Manse" the expression "so long as an unlettered soul can attain to saving grace" paraphrases "the wayfaring men, though fools, shall not err therein" (Isa. 35:8). And what is more important than any other kind of allusion is the New Testament metaphor and imagery so pervasive in his work. No one familiar with the New Testament really needs to have explained to him what Hawthorne means by "heart." His imagery of light and darkness seems to come from St. John's Gospel and from the first Epistle of St. John.

We get a clear notion of Hawthorne's reading in the two years just before he entered college in two passages from letters to his sister Louisa:

> [1819] I have read "Waverley," "The Mysteries of Udolpho," "The Adventures of Ferdinand Count Fathom," "Roderick Random," and the first volume of "The Arabian Nights." [1820] I have bought the "Lord of the Isles," and intend either to send or to bring it to you. I like it as well as any of Scott's other poems. I have read Hogg's "Tales," "Caleb Williams," "St. Leon," and "Mandeville." I admire Godwin's novels, and intend to read them all. I shall read the "Abbot,' by the author of

"Waverley," as soon as I can hire it. I have read all Scott's novels except that. I wish I had not, that I might have the pleasure of reading them again. Next to these I like "Caleb Williams." I have almost given up writing poetry.[3]

Later, but apparently also in 1820, he made another list. He had read Charles Robert Maturin's *Melmoth the Wanderer* (1820 was the year of its first publication), Fielding's *Tom Jones* and *Amelia*, Rousseau's *Héloïse* (which he thought "admirable"), R. L. Edgeworth's *Memoirs*, Scott's *The Abbot*, and Matthew Gregory Lewis's *Romantic Tales*.[4]

The young Hawthorne confidently prefaced this last list by writing, "I have read all most all the Books which have been published for the last hundred years." He learned about a good many others later, and his lists are only what we should expect from a literate youth in 1819 and 1820. He was carried along on the new enthusiasm for Scott, but he was reading, too, the fiction that Scott was in the process of displacing in the affections of American readers. By 1827 it was old-fashioned; a writer in the *American Quarterly Review* says—doubtless with some exaggeration—"the Mysteries of Udolpho could no longer keep people awake at night; Tom Jones was ignominiously turned out of doors by the country squires, as he was by the good Squire Allworthy; . . . Miss Edgeworth was eclipsed" (2: 33). The number of Gothic works in Hawthorne's lists, although not at all surprising for the time, may indicate a propensity of his.

In college, Hawthorne studied the Greek and Latin classics, and there were "recitations in the Bible every Sunday evening." The curriculum prescribed no modern literature, although Hawthorne apparently studied French with a tutor during his senior year. We have no indication of his extracurricular reading in his college years save a remark in a letter from Jonathan Cilley about "the damned ranting stuff of John Neal, which you, while at Brunswick, relished so highly." Hawthorne later writes as if his reading of Charles

3. *Hawthorne and His Wife*, 1: 105; George P. Lathrop, *A Study of Hawthorne* (Boston, 1876), p. 108.
4. This third list is preserved on a scrap of paper in the Huntington Library. See Jane Lundblad, *Hawthorne and European Literary Tradition* (New York, 1965), p. 35.

Brockden Brown and of Horace Walpole's *Castle of Otranto* had been early.[5]

Useful as the information we have about his early reading is, the discussion of Hawthorne has probably depended too much upon what by its nature must be incomplete. For instance, in most books about Hawthorne there is very little mention of Irving, although Hawthorne worked in some of Irving's genres, and surely recognized a skill that was unrivaled in the United States before he rivaled it. But we do have evidence of Hawthorne's regard for Irving's work. In a graceful letter accompanying a copy of *The Blithedale Romance* and acknowledging "a friendly and approving" letter from Irving, Hawthorne writes:

> Ever since I began to write, I have kept it among my cherished hopes to obtain such a word; nor did I ever publish a book without debating within myself whether to offer it to your notice. Nevertheless, the idea of introducing myself to you as an author, while unrecognized by the public, was not quite agreeable, and I saw too many faults in each of my books to be altogether willing to obtrude it beneath your eye. At last, I sent you "The Wonder Book," because, being meant for children, it seemed to reach a higher point in its own way, than anything I had written for grown people.

Hawthorne is happy, he continues, in the "opportunity of expressing the affectionate admiration which I have felt so long; . . . and which, I think, you can hardly appreciate, because there is no writer with the qualities to awaken in yourself precisely the same intellectual and heart-felt recognition."[6] Hawthorne's admiration for Irving must have gone back to his college days.

By the time Hawthorne had begun to write his short pieces, he tells us in his letter to Stoddard, he had "read endlessly all sorts of good and good-for-nothing books." In the Salem years the scope of his reading became almost frightening. For fiction he depended upon a

5. Randall Stewart reproduces the Bowdoin curriculum in Hawthorne's time in *Nathaniel Hawthorne* (New Haven, 1948), pp. 16–17. For Hawthorne's references to Brown and Walpole, see *Mosses*, pp. 198 and 428; *English Note-Books*, 2: 528.

6. Quoted in Stanley T. Williams, *The Life of Washington Irving* (New York, 1935), 2: 205–6.

circulating library which, Elizabeth Hawthorne says, "supplied him with most of the novels then published." For other work, he depended upon the Salem Athenaeum. Marion L. Kesselring's transcription of the charge-book record of Hawthorne's use of the Salem Athenaeum and identification of the entries in it is indispensable in the study of Hawthorne,[7] and it will be frequently used as this book proceeds. But we need also to consider what the extensive reading it records meant in Hawthorne's development.

Other members of Hawthorne's family surely used his privileges at the Salem Athenaeum, and in particular his sister Elizabeth would have read a great many of the books charged out to him. But making every allowance, we must conclude that Hawthorne read or turned over an amazing number of books and magazines. Some of this reading, of course, has no discernible connection with his writing. He read rather systemically in French literature; the record shows, for instance, withdrawals of forty-nine volumes of a set of Voltaire over three years. Apparently he read all but the first volume of a set of Swift in 1830. Some of the reading in periodicals is the sort of keeping up with contemporary writing he could be expected to do and, as Marion Kesselring points out, many of the books Hawthorne read were recent books.

But much of Hawthorne's reading seems to be that of a young writer in search of materials. For instance, there are recorded well over a hundred withdrawals of volumes of the *Gentleman's Magazine*, an English publication that Hawthorne would have found a mine of various sorts of information. He withdrew separate volumes of William Hone's *Every-day Book and Table Book* (London, 1830) on six dates. And above all, he read or looked at a great number of volumes of New England history. Many of these books are secondary sources: "the grave pages of our New England annalists," he calls them. But he read a good deal of primary material too: local histories, sermons, pamphlets, tracts, and other original sources—the charge-

7. "Hawthorne's Reading, 1828–1850," *Bulletin of the New York Public Library* 53 (Feb., Mar., Apr. 1949): 55–71, 121–38, 173–94. Hawthorne's aunt, Mary Manning, took a "share" in the Salem Athenaeum in 1826, probably for Hawthorne's benefit, and in 1828 transferred it to him. Marion Kesselring's transcription includes the books and periodicals withdrawn under Mary Manning's name from 1826 to 1828, and those withdrawn under Hawthorne's name from 1828 to 1839 and again from 1848 to 1850.

books show forty-two withdrawals of volumes of the Massachusetts Historical Society Collections. Since he was searching for materials for use in his tales, he may have turned over more books than he read. When we find that he withdrew the second volume of Winthrop's *Journals* on April 16, 1828, and returned it on April 19, we have no evidence of his careful consideration of a major source in colonial history. Although we have a far more precise record of Hawthorne's reading as a young man than we have for most writers, not everything about it is clear.

For one thing, the record of a withdrawal does not always indicate when he used a book. For example, the only records of withdrawals of Caleb Hopkins Snow, *A History of Boston* (1825) are in 1827 and 1829. It is clear that Hawthorne made considerable use of this book when he was writing *The Scarlet Letter* in 1849 and 1850.[8] Certainly nothing we know of Hawthorne suggests that he would have taken elaborate notes in 1829 and used them in 1849. Furthermore, we should not assume that the charge-book record is a complete record of Hawthorne's reading in the Salem years. There is, for instance, no record of a withdrawal of James Sullivan's *History of the District of Maine* (1795), although Hawthorne cites it in his footnote to "The Great Carbuncle." Another instance is his use of Thomas Hutchinson, *The History of the Colony and Province of Massachusetts-Bay.* The charge-books show only withdrawals of volume one in 1826 and 1829. Now all of Hutchinson's history was important to Hawthorne: the first paragraph of "My Kinsman, Major Molineux" refers to passages in volume two, and "Edward Randolph's Portrait" depends upon a passage in the third volume, which was not published until 1828.[9] Such questions as these probably have simple answers if we could know them, but they suggest some caution in the use of the Salem Athenaeum record. Hawthorne doubtless bought some books,

8. See Charles Ryskamp, "The New England Sources of *The Scarlet Letter*," *American Literature* 31 (1959): 257–72.

9. Hawthorne closely follows a portion of Hutchinson's third volume in *Grandfather's Chair* and makes his narrator remark that Hutchinson "was more familiar with the history of New England than any other man alive," but that if he was favored with any inspiration, "he made but a poor use of it in his history; for a duller piece of composition never came from any man's pen. However, he was accurate" (pp. 561–62).

but apparently not very many. Although he began using Joseph B. Felt's *Annals of Salem* (1827) in 1833, he borrowed it from the Salem Athenaeum in 1849 for use with "Main Street."

But there is a really puzzling matter about Hawthorne's reading. As we know, Hawthorne felt his personal experience and observation most insufficient literary capital; his search among the annalists and documents of his region was a search for usable material. The wonder is, when we come to think of it, that he used so little of what he found. Anyone who follows Hawthorne in his reading even a little way will be struck, time and again, by the thought that here is material that should have interested Hawthorne and been useful to him. Yet the problem usually has been skirted. For example, this passage from James T. Fields has more than once been quoted as an indication of the connection between Hawthorne's reading and his fiction:

> Hearing him say once that the old English State Trials were enchanting reading, and knowing that he did not possess a copy of those heavy folios, I picked up a set one day in a bookshop and sent them to him. He often told me that he spent more hours over them and got more delectation out of them than tongue could tell, and he said, if five lives were vouchsafed to him, he could employ them all in writing stories out of those books. He had sketched, in his mind, several romances founded on the remarkable trials reported in the ancient volumes; and one day, I remember, he made my blood tingle by relating some of the situations he intended, if his life was spared, to weave into future romances.[10]

Now Hawthorne had withdrawn from the Salem Athenaeum five of the six volumes of *A Complete Collection of State-Trials*, edited by Sollom Emlyn (London, 1742) in 1832, long before he had any acquaintanceship with Fields, and he might have made a literary use of them anytime thereafter.[11] Alfred S. Reid may be right in his

---

10. Fields, *Yesterdays with Authors*, pp. 62–63.
11. Elizabeth Hawthorne remembered Hawthorne being fond of "6 vols. folio of [Thomas Bayly] Howell's State Trials." She may have confused Howell's better known and later work with the Emlyn work.

contention that accounts of the murder of Sir Thomas Overbury are sources for *The Scarlet Letter*,[12] but the connection is at best oblique, and beyond it there seems no influence upon his fiction from his reading of state trials. The passage from Fields, far from being an example of the connection between Hawthorne's reading and his work, points up one of the problems in understanding that connection.

Anyone familiar with Hawthorne's reading and work must sometimes have wondered how near he came to being a historian. He had some, but surely not all, of the instincts of a scholar; and he seems to have been attracted by the prospect of historical work even while he avoided it. In 1845 he replies to Evert A. Duyckinck's suggestion that he write a history of witchcraft:

> I had often thought of such a work, but I should not like to throw it off hastily, or to write it for the sole and specific purpose of getting $500. A mere narrative, to be sure, might be prepared easily enough; but such a work, if worthily written, would demand research and study, and as deep thought as any man could bring to it. The more I look at it, the more difficulties do I see—yet difficulties such as I should like to overcome. Perhaps it may be the work of an after time.[13]

But we cannot be quite sure that the difficulties Hawthorne saw are really of the sort he would have enjoyed. The most comprehensive use he ever made of his knowledge of Salem history is in the sketch "Main Street"—but that is designed to avoid the historian's difficulties. There is a tendency to overestimate the depth of Hawthorne's reading in history. Our consideration of individual tales will show a careful examination of particular sources and often a most adroit use of them; but for the most part the tales do not show, it seems to me, any great depth of knowledge of New England history or remarkable historical perceptiveness on Hawthorne's part. He learned much from Scott, but not until *The House of the Seven Gables* does he

12. See *The Yellow Ruff & The Scarlet Letter* (University of Florida Press, 1955). There are of course allusions to the Overbury affair in the romance: Chillingworth is said to have been an associate of Doctor Simon Forman (chap. 9). Mistress Hibbens, the narrator says, had been a friend of Ann Turner (chap. 20).

13. Quoted in Randall Stewart, ed., "Two Uncollected Reviews by Hawthorne," p. 505.

manifest much of the kind of insight into social change and the conflict of traditions that distinguishes Scott's best novels—perhaps "My Kinsman, Major Molineux" does have something of that quality.

Hawthorne's attitude toward his historical materials was, after all, very much the attitude of the literary theorists that so much influenced his early work; his difference from them was in his wider concept of the possibilities of fiction. But history was important to him only as it was, or might be, literary material. As late as *Our Old Home* we find him saying: "We neither remember nor care anything for the past, except as the poet has made it intelligibly noble and sublime to our comprehension. The shades of the mighty have no substance . . . save when the poet has thrown his own creative soul into them, and imparted a more vivid life than ever they were able to manifest while they dwelt in the body."[14]

Of course there is no intention here of saying that Hawthorne should have done other than he did; the intention is only to realize a condition of his literary habit. Hawthorne's reading seems never afterward to have been nearly so extensive as it was in the 1826–1838 period at Salem. And even in the 1826–1838 period his reading was not, on his own testimony, intensive: "I have indeed turned over a good many books," he wrote to Longfellow in 1837, "but in so desultory a way that it cannot be called study, nor has it left me the fruits of study."[15] There is no indication that in his later life Hawthorne was a great reader, and he seems never to have owned many books.[16]

For Hawthorne the reading and the turning over of many books and periodicals in the Salem years was perhaps a kind of indolence, but doubtless a kind necessary to the nurture of his talents. We can often see the relationships between one and another of his tales and work we know him to have read; and it is well to recognize them,

14. *Our Old Home*, p. 315.
15. Woodberry, p. 74.
16. In "The Old Manse" Hawthorne describes his books as "few, and by no means choice . . . chiefly such waifs as chance had thrown in my way." William Dean Howells, in an account of a call he made on Hawthorne at the Wayside, says: "After tea, he showed me a bookcase, where there were a few books toppling about on the half-filled shelves, and said coldly, 'This is my library.'" *Literary Friends and Acquaintances* (New York, 1911), p. 54. There is relatively little reference to his reading in Hawthorne's notebooks, but that is not particularly significant—he was not keeping the ordinary journal of his literary contemporaries.

for Hawthorne's great gift was for the transmutation of his materials. But the subtle influence of his twelve years of immersion in many books of no apparent connection with his work we shall not be able to trace.

THE HAWTHORNESQUE BEFORE HAWTHORNE: SCOTT AND WILLIAM AUSTIN

In 1856 Hawthorne visited Abbotsford and recorded his disappointment in his notebook. At the end of the account he confesses "a sentiment of remorse" for having visited the home of Scott "with so cold a heart and in so critical a mood,—*his* dwelling-place . . . whom I had so admired and loved, and who had done so much for my happiness when I was young." He still cherishes Scott "in a warm place," he says, and he looks forward to rereading all his novels.[17]

Hawthorne knew his debt for his own happiness in reading Scott; it is unlikely that he fully realized his debt as a writer. He must have known that in his first romance, *Fanshawe*, he had tried to reproduce the Waverley pattern—almost everyone who has commented on the story has recognized it. He had even tried to cast the story in the recent past as Scott often did—we are assured that this is a story of Harley College "about eighty years since."

Hawthorne's debt to Scott extends far beyond *Fanshawe*. We have seen that the quest for American materials became a quest for Scott-like materials in American history, and that Hawthorne pursued the quest. We shall remark specific relationships between Scott's work and particular tales. But beyond these matters, there are influences from Scott's work in fictional devices and in technique that help to account for important qualities in Hawthorne's tales.

About sixty-five years ago, George E. Woodberry wrote of Hawthorne: "Something of Scott is to be found permanently in his creative work,—in the figure-grouping, the high speeches, . . . and especially in the use of set scenes individually elaborated to give the high lights and to advance the story."[18] So long as Scott was generally read, Hawthorne's debt to him was probably sufficiently realized. Now that Hawthorne, in this country at least, has many more readers than has

17. *English Note-Books*, 2: 274.
18. Woodberry, p. 126.

Scott, some aspects of Hawthorne's work best accounted for by the preeminence of Scott in Hawthorne's time, and by particular influences of Scott's work on Hawthorne's, may seem to belong to Hawthorne more peculiarly than they do.

To begin with, there is the matter of pictorial quality. Scott, and Hawthorne after him, think of some episodes in their fiction as pictures; the pictorial quality in Hawthorne, of which—under various designations—so much has been written, has its antecedent in Scott. Now the pictorial quality in Hawthorne does not need critical analysis for its realization. Any reader who will try to recall one of Hawthorne's better tales that he has not read for some time will find that he recalls first a figure grouping in a set scene: perhaps the Gray Champion stopping the march of Andros and his company, or Endicott watching the Lord and Lady of the May as they take their way from Merry Mount, or Robin appalled at the spectacle of his kinsman carried on a cart "in tar-and-feather dignity," or Dr. Heidegger's guests in the illusion of rejuvenation acting out a youthful rivalry for the Widow Wycherly, with the doctor sitting silently by.

So also may a reader remember set scenes in a Waverley novel, and sometimes Scott remarks his own awareness of the likeness of a scene to a picture. When, for example, in *The Bride of Lammermoor* he is describing the interruption of the funeral of Allen Lord Ravenswood, he writes:

> The scene was worthy of an artist's pencil. Under the very arch of the house of death, the clergyman, affrighted at the scene, and trembling for his own safety, hastily and unwillingly rehearsed the solemn service of the church, and spoke dust to dust, and ashes to ashes, over ruined pride and decayed prosperity. Around stood the relations of the deceased, their countenances more in anger than in sorrow, and the drawn swords which they brandished forming a violent contrast with their deep mourning habits. In the countenance of the young man alone, resentment seemed for the moment overpowered by the deep agony with which he beheld his nearest, and almost his only friend, consigned to the tomb of his ancestry. [chap. 2]

In every expression here the reader is asked to imagine the scene as a painter's composition. Elsewhere Scott goes further and assigns particular scenes to artists appropriate for them. In *The Antiquary*, for instance, Scott says of the funeral of Steenie Mucklebackit (chap. 31): "In the inside of the cottage was a scene, which our [Sir David] Wilkie alone could have painted, with the exquisite feeling of nature that characterises his enchanting productions," and then proceeds to describe that scene as one might describe a genre painting by Wilkie. In the next chapter, when the Earl of Glenallan goes to the Mucklebackit cottage to see old Elspeth, the light from an opened window "illuminated, in the way that Rembrandt would have chosen, the features of the unfortunate nobleman, and those of the old sibyl."

In the tales (so far as I remember) Hawthorne does not make this sort of reference to particular artists. But he does point up the likeness of a scene in a tale to a picture. When the company that have gathered to seek the Great Carbuncle are described, we see them grouped about a fire, "each man looking like a caricature of himself, in the unsteady light that flickered over him." In "The Wedding Knell" the reference to a painting is explicit:

> The gorgeous dresses of the time, the crimson velvet coats, the gold-laced hats, the hoop petticoats, the silk, satin, brocade, and embroidery, the buckles, canes, and swords, all displayed to the best advantage on persons suited to such finery, made the group appear more like a bright-colored picture than anything real. But by what perversity of taste had the artist represented his principal figure as so wrinkled and decayed, while yet he had decked her out in the brightest splendor of attire, as if the loveliest maiden had suddenly withered into age, and become a moral to the beautiful around her!

When this sort of pictorial representation has an allegorical intent, Hawthorne may use *moral* as here, or more often *emblem* in connection with it. In "The Wedding Knell," the ancient widow between her young bridesmaids becomes an emblem. And when in "Lady Eleanore's Mantle," Jervase Helwyse, distraught by Lady Eleanore, prostrates himself beside her coach, the scene is thus represented:

> Then, though as lightly as a sunbeam on a cloud, she placed her foot upon the cowering form, and extended her hand to meet that of the Governor. There was a brief interval, during which

Lady Eleanore retained this attitude; and never, surely, was there an apter emblem of aristocracy and hereditary pride trampling on human sympathies and the kindred of nature, than these two figures presented at that moment.

Some recent criticism considers it well to substitute *emblem* for *allegory* in the discussion of Hawthorne's work generally. But his tendency is to use *emblem* when a scene of especial pictorial effect has also an allegorical intent, or when an object (a pine tree or a black veil) by its part in a tale has especially an allegorical significance. Yet he may never have reflected on the term; in much of his reading, *emblem* frequently recurred in senses very close to those we give to *metaphor* or to *symbol*.[19]

Although we do not have letters in which Hawthorne discusses what he is writing for the period of our concern, letters written later in his life show him very much aware of the pictorial quality of his work. The way in which his pictorial imagination turned toward emblematic effects is neatly shown in his suggestions to Sophia Peabody for some contemplated (but never used) illustrations for his children's history, *Grandfather's Chair*. In 1850 he wrote to Fields concerning *The Scarlet Letter*: "I found it impossible to relieve the shadows of the story with so much light as I would gladly have thrown in"; and later he says of *The House of the Seven Gables*: "Many of the passages of this book ought to be finished with the minuteness of a Dutch picture, in order to give them their proper effect." His suggestions in a letter to Fields about the illustrations for A *Wonder-Book* show that he thought of many portions of that volume pictorially.[20]

The influence of Hawthorne's pictorial habit of mind is pervasive in his work. Ever since Walter Blair's fine 1942 article, "Color, Light, and Shadow in Hawthorne's Fiction,"[21] Hawthorne's critics

19. For instance, Roger Williams writes: "The wolf is an emblem of a fierce, blood-sucking persecutor; the swine of a covetous, rooting worldling. Both make a prey of the Lord Jesus in his poor servants." Quoted in Moses Coit Tyler, A *History of American Literature 1607–1765* (Collier Books, 1962), p. 227. For an account of recent work on Hawthorne as an emblem writer, see Richard Harter Fogle in *American Literary Scholarship*, 1965 (Durham, N.C., 1967), pp. 15–16.

20. See *Passages from the American Note-Books*, pp. 238–40; Fields, pp. 51, 55, and 59. (Mrs. Hawthorne's edition of the American notebooks in the Riverside Edition of *Works* will hereafter be referred to as *Passages*.)

21. *New England Quarterly* 15 (1942): 74–94.

have been much concerned with such imagery as Professor Blair discusses, particularly as it suggests or enhances meaning or mood. Sometimes (as it seems to me) they are discussing only the details of what Hawthorne thought of as a composition; and generally his imagery of color, light, and shade is the concomitant of his pictorial approach to fiction. Of course we will agree that the analogy between literature and painting, if pushed very far, is not critically fruitful: neither poetry nor fiction is "a speaking picture." Yet the analogy, which Scott makes Dick Tinto and Peter Pattieson discuss in the first chapter of *The Bride of Lammermoor*, had a marked effect of Scott's practice, and after him on Hawthorne's.

We have been considering a quality of Hawthorne's imagination, but what the consideration seems to show is that the quality comes out in his work in fashion paralleled in Scott's. And if Hawthorne's pictorial habit has an antecedent in Scott, so also do some of Hawthorne's literary devices and one of his chief interests in human character have antecedents in Scott. It would be wearisome to parallel Scott and Hawthorne at anything near the length for which there is material; the likenesses in their literary habits may be conveniently illustrated by a consideration of Scott's *The Bride of Lammermoor*, 1819. Now admittedly this novel, which has a marked Gothic vein, suggests Hawthorne's work more often than would any other Scott novel; but that is only a matter of the concentration in it of elements that run throughout the Waverley novels. Although a passage in *The Bride of Lammermoor* is (unmistakably, it seems to me) a source of one of Hawthorne's least happy allegories, "Egotism; or, the Bosom Serpent,"[22] and another passage has a connection with "The

22. *The Bride of Lammermoor*, chap. 7, supplies a simple and obvious source for "The Bosom Serpent": Bucklaw has been saying that he has wasted himself with "wine, women, and dice, cocks, dogs, and horses." The conversation continues:

"Yes, Bucklaw," said the Master, "you have indeed nourished in your bosom the snakes that are now stinging you."
"That's home as well as true, Master," replied his companion; "but, by your leave, you have nursed in your bosom one great goodly snake that has swallowed all the rest, and is as sure to devour you as my half dozen are to make a meal on all that's left of Bucklaw . . . ."

In "The Bosom Serpent" the narrator remarks, "by Roderick's [the egotist's] theory, every mortal bosom harbored either a brood of small serpents or one

Prophetic Pictures" that we shall be considering in a discussion of that tale, these relationships are not so important as other parallels.

Throughout *The Bride of Lammermoor* there is suggestion—without affirmation—of preternatural influence upon the action, so that there is in the novel, as so often in Hawthorne's work, a residue of mystery.[23] Yet the action proceeds by human means and is accounted for by human motives. One especially effective suggestion is accomplished by the use of the Gothic device of the mysterious portrait, which as Woodberry long ago pointed out, is like Hawthorne's use of a mysterious portrait in "Edward Randolph's Portrait." When the marriage of Bucklaw and Lucy is about to be celebrated, the portrait of Sir Malise Ravenswood appears mysteriously in the great hall of what had been his house, where it seems "to frown wrath and vengeance upon the party assembled below" (chap. 34). The device of the mysterious portrait was well-worn; indeed it had been ridiculed in Jane Austen's *Northanger Abbey* which, although published the year before *The Bride of Lammermoor*, was written years before. But Scott uses the device only as a Gothic flavor, and suggests that the agency of its appearance had been ordinary physical means employed by old Ailsie Gourley (chap. 35).

Within this pattern of preternatural[24] suggestion in *The Bride of Lammermoor*, there is a narrative device that Hawthorne's critics think peculiarly characteristic of him. It is the trick of the narrator's recording a preternatural explanation, often as a tradition, without

---

overgrown monster that had devoured all the rest." For Hawthorne's notebook suggestions for the piece, see *Passages*, pp. 34 and 274.

23. Such suggestion is variously accomplished: Sir William Ashton looks up at the Ravenswood crest, a black bull's head, with its motto "I bide my time," and remembers its history (chap. 3). At the fountain which has an ominous legend, Lucy is frightened by a bull, swoons, and then has her first encounter with Ravenswood on his ancestral grounds (chap. 5). Old Alice, reputed witch, warns the Master away from Lucy (chap. 19). Ailsie Gourley, who may have had dealings with the devil, foresees the tragedy and that the Master will never have an ordinary burial (chap. 23).

24. I trust I may be allowed the pedantry of using the word *preternatural*— which is frequent in Hawthorne—where many writers would use *supernatural*. *Supernatural* should be kept, it seems to me, to designate what is above or better than nature, e.g., "the supernatural working of grace." The distinction is of some importance, because Hawthorne does not ordinarily deal with the supernatural.

specifically accepting it—sometimes ostensibly rejecting it. Here, for instance, is the passage that ends chapter 2 of Scott's novel: "The peasant, who shows the ruins of the tower, . . . even yet affirms, that on this fatal night the Master of Ravenswood, by the bitter exclamations of his despair, evoked some evil fiend, under whose malignant influence the future tissue of events was woven. Alas! what fiend can suggest more desperate counsels, than those adopted under the guidance of our own violent and unresisted passions?"[25]

Sir Leslie Stephen, in his essay on Hawthorne in *Hours in a Library*, affirms that "no modern writer has the same skill in so using the marvellous as to interest without unduly exciting our incredulity," and then, a page or so later, remarks that only Scott approaches Hawthorne in the quality of his use of the preternatural. What Hawthorne seems to have done was to understand and then to refine Scott's technique. Hawthorne, Sir Leslie says, "loves the marvellous . . . as a symbol of perplexity which encounters every thoughtful man in his journey through life." But he learned much from Scott about the use of it as a symbol.

Beyond these likenesses in the use of the preternatural, there is in *The Bride of Lammermoor* a character of a sort we have come to think of as peculiarly a Hawthorne character. Lady Ashton seems the ancestress of some of Hawthorne's figures, and the antecedent of one of his major preoccupations—although one that developed largely after the period of our special concern. Lady Ashton, with Dame Gourley as instrument, invades her daughter's mind and spirit, not only asserting her will but manipulating Lucy in her very person: "With this stern and fixed purpose, she sounded every deep and shallow of her daughter's soul, assumed alternately every disguise of manner which could serve her object, and prepared at leisure every species of dire machinery, by which the human mind can be wrenched from its settled determination" (chap. 30). Dame Gourley remarks to her attendants: "There's mair o' utter deevilry in that woman, as brave and fair-fashioned as she rides yonder, than in a' the Scotch witches that ever flew by moonlight ower North-Berwick

25. The reader may have noticed a likeness between the question that ends the passage and a narrator's remark in "Young Goodman Brown": "The fiend in his own shape is less hideous than when he rages in the breast of man" (*Mosses*, p. 100).

Law" (chap. 34). Lady Ashton's deviltry is allied to the pride of
the painter in "The Prophetic Pictures"; but it is more nearly like
the kind of wickedness in Ethan Brand, in Westervelt, and in
Chillingworth, "who violated, in cold blood, the sanctity of a human
heart."

Of course there are elements in Scott that have no parallel in
Hawthorne—he has, for instance, no Caleb Balderstone nor any character like him. But if we look back at *The Bride of Lammermoor*
through our familiarity with Hawthorne and find it often Hawthornesque, that may indicate how much Hawthorne was working
in the tradition of Scott. It may suggest, too, how careful one ought
to be before he insists upon an entirely temperamental or psychological
origin for Hawthorne's devices, his preoccupations, or even what may
seem the quality of his imagination.

Scott's influence on Hawthorne is as unmistakable as it was inevitable; William Austin's "Peter Rugg, the Missing Man" is curiously
like Scott on the one hand and Hawthorne on the other. The tale
was first printed anonymously in Joseph T. Buckingham's weekly
New-England Galaxy in 1824; its author was a successful Boston
lawyer and legislator who wrote only a few tales. Of them, only "Peter
Rugg" is much remembered. But it became famous at once; Hawthorne could not have helped knowing it soon after its first printing.[26]

Hawthorne uses the figure of Peter Rugg as the doorkeeper of the
museum in "A Virtuoso's Collection" (1842); the first readers of
the sketch would have at once recognized that doorkeeper as the title
character of Austin's naturalization of the legend of the *Flying
Dutchman*. As the skipper of that famous ship was fated forever to
seek and never to find the harbor of Cape Town, so Peter Rugg, as
a consequence of an oath like the skipper's, had been seeking Boston

26. Buckingham said of the tale: "This article was reprinted in other papers
and books and read more than any newspaper communication that has fallen
within my knowledge." The tale was familiarly alluded to within the year
of its first printing; it was reprinted in two gift books by 1827; and in the same
year a spurious sequel appeared. Austin, however, was not known as the
author for some time. See Walter Austin, *William Austin: The Creator of Peter
Rugg* (Boston, 1925), pp. v and 117–20. The tale is reprinted in Edmund C.
Stedman and Ellen M. Hutchinson, eds., *A Library of American Literature*
(New York, 1888–1890), 4: 372–80; in Walter Austin, pp. 207–19; and
in various collections.

since a time before the Revolution, traveling, accompanied by his daughter, in a "chair" pulled by a great black horse. Austin's narrator himself encounters Rugg, and records the accounts of several informants. The accounts take the reader back to the beginning of Rugg's wanderings, but leave the question of whether or not Rugg is a specter not quite determined. Hawthorne in "The Virtuoso's Collection" is continuing a legend: when his narrator leaves the Virtuoso's museum, the doorkeeper beseeches him, "For Heaven's sake, answer me a single question! Is this the town of Boston?"

Austin's tale is interesting, first of all, as a successful effort to supply a texture of legendary association for American places. As the narration moves about and in Boston, with a careful precision of reference, New England places become storied places. But the tale is interesting, too, for a skillful use of narrative point of view. It seems at first thought quite different from any Hawthorne uses, for the narrative is cast in what purports to be a letter to a named correspondent. But its effect is remarkably like the effect in some of Hawthorne's best tales. Thomas Wentworth Higginson, who considered himself the rediscoverer of Austin, thought of him, with some reason, as a precursor of Hawthorne.[27]

The striking characteristic of Austin's tale, and the one most Hawthornesque, is what Higginson calls *penumbra*, and what Hawthorne's critics call ambiguity, or more precisely in reference to the narrative technique Higginson is thinking of, the device of multiple choice or the formula of alternative possibilities. Austin, Higginson says, discredits his own witnesses as Hawthorne does—although in both the testimony of those witnesses remains effective on the reader. The technique runs through the tale; we shall have to be content with two instances.

The narrator records that when he had first seen Rugg on the road, the stage-driver warned him that the appearance of Rugg always heralded a storm, and called his attention to a remarkable configuration in a cloud:

He said every flash of lightning near its centre discovered to him distinctly the form of a man sitting in an open carriage

27. "A Precursor of Hawthorne," *Independent* 40 (March 29, 1888): 385–86; reprinted in Walter Austin, pp. 121–26.

drawn by a black horse. But in truth, I saw no such thing. The man's fancy was doubtless at fault. It is a very common thing for the imagination to paint for the senses, both in the visible and invisible world.

But the storm does come; and we remember that before the appearance of the cloud, the horses, who may be supposed to act from instinct and not superstition, had thrown "their ears on their necks, as flat as a hare's."

The narrator's final informant is a chance acquaintance who has heard his grandfather speak of Rugg "as though he seriously believed his own story." It is through this informant that the reader learns of Rugg's "fatal oath," and of the story of the toll-gatherer at Charlestown bridge who, one dark and stormy night, threw a three-legged stool at the appearance of a horse drawing a carriage.

> The toll-gatherer on the next day asserted that the stool went directly through the body of the horse, and he persisted in that belief ever after. Whether Rugg, or whoever the person was, ever passed the bridge again, the toll-gatherer would never tell; and when questioned seemed anxious to waive the subject. And thus Peter Rugg and his child, horse and carriage, remain a mystery to this day.

This testimony has the effective end position; yet the suggestion that Rugg is a specter comes to the narrator through his informant's memory of his grandfather's account of the toll-gatherer's experience.

But Austin's tale is no mere exercise in preternatural suggestion. Peter Rugg's fate represents a national experience: our break with the past and the restless movement that Frederick Jackson Turner found the dominant characteristic of American life. "If Peter Rugg," the narrator says, "has been travelling since the Boston massacre, there is no reason why he should not travel to the end of time. If the present generation know little of him, the next will know less, and Peter and his child will have no hold on this world." As Hawthorne does in "The Gray Champion," Austin is endeavoring to establish a continuing legend. And as in so much of Hawthorne's work, the preternatural is suggested but not affirmed.

Now, as we have seen, there is much the same sort of suggestion in Scott; and indeed there is something of the sort in Irving's "Legend of Sleepy Hollow" and a degree of ambiguity in his "The Stout Gentlemen" and "The Bold Dragoon," although humorously used. But neither in Scott nor in Irving is the ambiguity so much the texture of the work as it is in Austin's tale, nor so much the texture of the work as it is in some of the best of Hawthorne's tales, in "The Minister's Black Veil," or, to take an instance in a different temper, "Drowne's Wooden Image." If Hawthorne ever recognized the quality of ambiguity as a storyteller's resource before he discovered it in himself, it would have been in the work of Scott and in Austin's "Peter Rugg, the Missing Man."[28]

In Oliver Wendell Holmes's verses on Hawthorne in "At the Saturday Club," Hawthorne was the "Essex wizard"; in Longfellow's obituary poem Hawthorne's was "the wizard hand"; and Bronson Alcott, in his elegy for Hawthorne, wrote of "the wizard tale" that Hawthorne told. The word for them was inevitable; they knew the work of both Scott and Hawthorne, and they knew that they were celebrating the American heir of the magic of "the Wizard of the North."

"THAT TINGE OF THE MARVELLOUS": HAWTHORNE'S GOTHIC HABIT

From Hawthorne's youthful reading of Gothic romances to the abortive romances of his last years, he was preoccupied with Gothic patterns. His failure to complete the last romances was a failure to find a meaning for his Gothic symbols; the manuscripts of *Dr. Grimshawe's Secret* show his disgust and despair as he found himself unable to control materials he had been working with successfully throughout his career.[29] Indeed, the Gothic vein runs deeper in his

28. Curiously, Austin's artfully contrived tale has come to be regarded as if it were a piece of folklore; indeed, it is reprinted in folklore collections. Later writers have made it their own, much as Austin made the *Flying Dutchman* legend his own. There are verse treatments by Louise Imogen Guiney and by Amy Lowell, who says she knew an oral version long before she ever heard of Austin. *Legends* (Boston, 1921), p. xiii. Frank Luther Mott's story "Phantom Flivver" has Peter Rugg traveling on Kansas roads in a Model T Ford. *Saturday Evening Post Stories, 1950* (New York, 1950), pp. 155–65.

29. See *Dr. Grimshawe's Secret*, ed. Edward H. Davidson (Cambridge,

imagination than his collected fiction indicates. In the North Adams journal, for instance, he records this macabre idea for a story: a crow had followed his stagecoach, because, the driver thought, it scented some salmon in a basket under the seat. "This would be a terrific incident," Hawthorne writes, "if it were a dead body that the crow scented, instead of a basket of salmon. Suppose, for instance, a coach travelling along,—that one of the passengers suddenly died—and that one of the indications of his death was the deportment of the crow."[30] Now we will hardly agree that the incident would be terrific; yet scattered through Hawthorne's notebooks there are many unused suggestions for stories that seem as childish, and that at best could result in no more than a Gothic shiver.[31] Hawthorne was clearly planning within the Gothic convention, and he seems to have had an impulse to use it more than he actually did.

We think of the Gothic as an eighteenth-century convention, and of course it was Horace Walpole's *The Castle of Otranto, a Gothic Story* (1764) that gave currency to "Gothic" as a literary term. By the end of the century the Gothic romance had great American popularity: in the preface to his *The Algerine Captive* (1797), Royall Tyler wryly complained that "Dolly, the dairy maid, and Jonathan, the hired man . . . now amused themselves into so agreeable a terrour with the haunted houses and hobgobblins of Mrs. Ratcliffe that they were both afraid to sleep alone." The first American poet of distinction, Philip Freneau, and the first novelist of distinction, Charles Brockden Brown, both worked in the Gothic. English Gothic novels

Mass., 1954), pp. 147 and 183 for examples of marginal comments and pp. 163–69 for a reflection on the difficulties of the story.

30. *American Notebooks*, ed. Randall Stewart (New Haven, 1932), p. 36.

31. Here is a selection of examples of Gothic story suggestions: [1835] "In an old house, a mysterious knocking might be heard on the wall, where had formerly been a doorway, now bricked up." [1835] "An old volume in a large library,—every one to be afraid to unclasp and open it, because it was said to be a book of magic." [1837] "An ornament to be worn about the person of a lady,—as a jewelled heart. After many years, it happens to be broken or unscrewed, and a poisonous odor comes out." [1837] "A dreadful secret to be communicated to several people of various characters,—grave or gay, and they all to become insane, according to their characters, by the influence of the secret." [1839] "A stranger, dying, is buried; and after many years, two strangers come in search of his grave, and open it." *Passages*, pp. 24, 26, 107, 110, and 208.

were vastly popular; the American Isaac Mitchell's *The Asylum, or Alonzo and Melissa* (1804) had eleven editions; it is estimated that something like half the American plays written between 1794 and 1835 contain Gothic elements.[32]

But it would be a mistake not to see the Gothic as a continuing strain in our literature and literary taste. Sir Walter Scott, who in some sort displaced writers like Mrs. Radcliffe in the affections of the public, had yet a strain of the Gothic. Irving and Poe, for the most part in decidedly different ways, made tales of Gothic materials. And indeed the Gothic tradition has never died out; there are Gothic elements, or something very like them, in the work of William Faulkner, and one almost thinks he sees the influence of "Monk" Lewis in the work of some contemporary novelists who have probably never read him. Gothic story vigorously survives in various media and in various mutations, some of them repellent.

Hawthorne, as we have seen, had read the standard Gothic writers: Walpole, Mrs. Radcliffe, Godwin, Lewis, Charles Brockden Brown, and Maturin. But, even though some of the Gothic elements in his work can be paralleled in the work of these writers, we should probably be wrong in supposing them to be the chief Gothic influences upon him. In the circulating libraries he used, some large proportion of the novels would have had Gothic elements. He carefully examined *Blackwood's Magazine*, which we know Poe to have thought of as especially a repository of excellent examples of the tale of terror.[33] The American magazines of Hawthorne's time carried a good many Gothic tales; particularly those in the *Knickerbocker Magazine* are, it seems to me, often literate and entertaining, the work of skillful Gothic practitioners.[34] In Robert Charles Sands's "The Man Who

32. See Oral Coad, "The Gothic Element in American Literature before 1835," *Journal of English and Germanic Philology* 24 (1925): 72–93. The tradition of American Gothic fiction includes the perhaps unexpected figures of the Quaker Whittier and the dignified Bryant.

33. Poe, in his 1842 review of *Twice-Told Tales*, speaks of "those *tales of effect*, many fine examples of which were found in the earlier numbers of *Blackwood*." Hawthorne made twenty-six withdrawals of volumes of *Blackwood's* from the Salem Athenaeum, most of them of the "earlier numbers" and most of them in 1827.

34. Examples of good Gothic tales in *Knickerbocker* during its first years are these: "The Proselyte" and "The Whooping Hollow" in 1 (1833): 238–45 and 278–90; William L. Stone's "The Skeleton Hand" and "The Spectre

Burnt John Rogers" (1824) Hawthorne would have found a tale comparable to work he was to do.[35] And of course a great deal of work we do not even know by name was part of the convention as it presented itself to Hawthorne.

If we date the Gothic convention, rather arbitrarily, from Walpole's *Castle of Otranto*, it had persisted some sixty-five years by the time Hawthorne began to publish. It had developed a considerable paraphernalia of small properties recognized and even expected by readers. It had developed a type hero-villain, defined by William F. Axton as "a figure of great power, latent virtue, and personal magnetism tragically stained with criminality"[36]—or, if the central figure did not have all those traits, or did not have them quite fully, he was yet some recognizable modification of that hero-villain. The Gothic commonly made use of the preternatural, accepted as preternatural, or in the "explained supernatural" accounted for rationally at the end, or suggested but not affirmed—as often in Hawthorne. It had moved beyond the necessity of a medieval setting, or even of a ruined abbey or ancient castle, but it often kept some reminiscence of them. These elements were constantly, repetitively used; and that repetition was for readers a large part of the charm of the Gothic.

Indeed the effect of the Gothic convention depends upon a kind of extensive and insistent literary allusion. The interest or the thrill of terror belonging to any Gothic figure or property depends upon a complex set of associations. It is this element that Jane Austen ridicules in that best of satires of the Gothic convention, *Northanger Abbey*; it is nevertheless the capital and the chief appeal of the Gothic. Poe's "The Fall of the House of Usher" depends upon any number of literary experiences on the part of its readers, perhaps going back to the work of Horace Walpole—but of course the effect of allusion may work the other way round and Poe's work be a preparation for reading, say, Mrs. Radcliffe. Since the Gothic convention does de-

Fire-Ship" in 3 (1834): 57–63 and 361–70; John Water's "The Iron Foot-Step" in 15 (1840): 280–84.

35. Sands's tale was first printed in the *Atlantic Magazine*, but there called simply "A Story"; reprinted in Stedman and Hutchinson, eds., *A Library of American Literature*, 5: 482–92.

36. Introduction to *Melmoth the Wanderer* (University of Nebraska Press, 1961), p. x. Even Hawthorne's Fanshawe is an odd, pallid variety of the Gothic hero—set apart from his fellows, marked out for a special destiny.

pend so thoroughly upon this allusiveness, we should not insist that one or another Gothic element in Hawthorne's work depends entirely upon a particular source, even if that source offers a close parallel. A multiple allusiveness is just the quality that makes possible Hawthorne's most characteristic uses of the Gothic, uses which depend upon his readers' long familiarity with his materials, else he could not turn them to purposes beyond themselves.

In this regard the influence of Irving on Hawthorne's practice has probably been underestimated. In "The Legend of Sleepy Hollow" Irving discovers an American Gothic before Hawthorne. And in "The Stout Gentleman" and in the "Strange Stories by a Nervous Gentleman," the first section of *Tales of a Traveller*, Irving tries some half-playful uses of conventions that require experience in Gothic story on the part of readers for their success. Hawthorne could hardly have failed to see what Irving was doing, or to realize that it was adaptable to his purposes.

In the consideration of Gothic writers so late as Irving and Hawthorne, we must try not to ascribe to temperament what belongs to literary convention. Although we recognize that Hawthorne had some bent toward the Gothic, it is entirely natural, quite apart from temperament, that a young writer looking for material should work the Gothic vein—as natural, say, as Spenser's use of Ariosto. The pervasive appeal of the Gothic is strikingly illustrated by Poe's deliberate choice of the tale of terror as a genre calculated to win immediate acceptance.[37] Hawthorne, no less than Poe, wanted to write salable tales, and was as likely to consider what an established convention had to offer him. He does not, of course, proceed in Poe's fashion; rather he adapts the convention to his purposes, and combines it with American materials.

The problem of the adaptation of the Gothic convention to America and the American past Hawthorne shared with other writers. Perhaps the problem did not much concern Isaac Mitchell; Poe

37. In 1835 Poe wrote to T. W. White, owner of the *Southern Literary Messenger*, a defense of his "Berenice." In it he says, "The history of all magazines shows plainly that those which obtained celebrity were indebted for it to articles similar in nature to Berenice," and records his plan to fill a plainly evidenced demand. See Napier Wilt, "Poe's Attitude toward His Tales," *Modern Philology* 25 (1927): 101–5.

avoids it almost entirely, and the world of his tales is a Gothic world. But Irving (in his best tales) and Hawthorne naturalize their Gothic materials; and indeed Charles Brockden Brown before them had been concerned to do so, and in *Edgar Huntly* attempted to find an American Gothic in Indian material instead of, as he says in his preface, in "Gothic castles and chimeras." Hawthorne's ultimate triumph in localizing the Gothic is his substitution of the ancestral home of the Pyncheons in *The House of the Seven Gables* for the Gothic castle or ruined abbey of English romance. And even with the stock Gothic scientist he manages historical connections; his Gothic scientists have colonial antecedents, and he notes that an alchemist lived in his native Salem.[38]

In his later work, Hawthorne uses the figure of the Gothic scientist as an embodiment of the sin of pride. But the Gothic scientists of the early tales seem no very dangerous figures. Dr. Cacaphodel in "The Great Carbuncle" is intended to be comic; Dr. Heidegger hardly represents the sin of pride. The painter in "The Prophetic Pictures" is rather more sinister, and since his art is esoteric and nearly magical, he is allied to the Gothic devotee of mysterious arts. Later in Hawthorne's work, out of these figures and the Gothic convention develop Aylmer, Dr. Rappaccini, Ethan Brand, and Chillingworth.

But it was in the fictional treatment of witchcraft that Hawthorne found an American Gothic in some sense his own. Of course American fiction writers and playwrights had used witchcraft materials before him,[39] but save for a single passage in Irving's "Legend of Sleepy Hollow," no other writer, so far as I know, had used them with any real penetration. To be sure, Hawthorne's first efforts were not promising. Although the narrator of "Alice Doane's Appeal" says the tale has "good authority in our ancient superstitions," it has rather more relationship to the convention of Gothic story, in which the motif of potential incest is quite frequent enough[40]—the Gothic convention better accounts for the story, perhaps, than speculation about Hawthorne's psychological state. "The Hollow of the Three Hills,"

38. *Passages*, p. 206. See also *Snow-Image*, p. 456; *Tales, Sketches, and Other Papers*, p. 239.
39. See G. Harrison Orians, "New England Witchcraft in Fiction," *American Literature* 2 (1930): 54–71.
40. See Eino Railo, *The Haunted Castle* (London, 1927), pp. 269–72.

which Hawthorne liked well enough to include in the first edition of *Twice-Told Tales*, has a witch of sorts, but it makes no use of New England material and the setting is not localized. In his 1842 review of *Twice-Told Tales*, Poe, who speaks as an expert in the Gothic, finds the tale original in that it makes the ear instead of the eye the medium by which the witch's revelations are received, a substitution for the conventional pictures in a mirror or a cloud of smoke.

"Alice Doane's Appeal" and "The Hollow of the Three Hills" are at best apprentice work. In "Young Goodman Brown" Hawthorne found a way of using witchcraft material as imaginative substantiation for a complex and subtle parable. We shall be considering that tale by itself; what we may note now is that it has the closest connections with the witchcraft records—it shows far more detailed historical knowledge than any other Hawthorne tale—and that it uses the inherent symbolism in the material itself, even in its terror and wonder. Hawthorne also makes an effective secondary use of witchcraft in some tales laid in time after witchcraft days, but not so late that witchcraft beliefs might not linger in the minds of the elders. In "The Prophetic Pictures," in "Edward Randolph's Portrait," and in "Drowne's Wooden Image" such lingering remnants of witchcraft supply a counterpoint of preternatural suggestion. Finally, witchcraft elements persist into the romances: old Mistress Hibbens appears at crucial times in *The Scarlet Letter*, and in *The House of the Seven Gables* the memory of Wizard Maule's curse broods over the action.[41]

One motive for the use of the Gothic by Hawthorne and other early nineteenth-century American writers may easily escape the reader today. As we have seen, there was a conviction on the part of some literary theorists that American materials were all too new to be available for fiction, and even some of those who urged the use of American materials would limit writers to the colonial period. The use of the Gothic convention became a recognized method of making romance from American materials considered too new to be used quite by themselves. A passage in W. H. Gardiner's review of Cooper's *The Pioneers* and *The Last of the Mohicans* in the *North American Review* in 1826 makes the motive entirely explicit:

41. Two witches in his late work, Mother Rigby of "Feathertop" and Aunt Keziah in *Septimius Felton*, Hawthorne makes humorous, and hardly Gothic figures. Neither is much related to the New England witchcraft tradition.

The same sort of magical authority over the spirit of romance, which belongs in common to Scott, Radcliffe, Walpole, and our countryman Brown, is, for us at least, possessed by this writer in an eminent degree. Places, for example, familiar to us from our boyhood, and which are now daily before our eyes, thronged with the vulgar associations of real life, are boldly seized upon for scenes of the wildest romance; and yet our imaginations do not revolt at the incongruity. . . . A military conclave at the Province House possesses something of the same interest as if it were holden before the walls of Tillietudlem; and we attend a midnight marriage at the altar of King's Chapel, and feel our blood curdle at the overshadowing arm upon the wall, with the same superstitious terror as when the gigantic armor rattles in the purely imaginative Castle of Otranto. . . . It is the creation and adaptation of a kind of machinery, which may be original in its character, and yet within the narrowed limits of modern probability, that stretch to the utmost the inventive faculties of the novelist. [23: 152–53]

Hawthorne, we shall see, acknowledges this motive as his own in the frame of "Howe's Masquerade," and it is implicit everywhere in his use of the Gothic. Some effort of the historical imagination may be necessary to realize the strength of that motive in the new nation, but there is no doubt of its presence.

The air of antiquity, of course, depends upon the allusive quality of the Gothic. When Hawthorne used the mysterious portrait, he took what was perhaps the most frayed of Gothic properties, and found it useful just because his first readers had a prepared acceptance for it. The mysterious portrait goes back at least to *The Castle of Otranto*; it was used effectively more than fifty years later in *Melmoth the Wanderer* in the portrait that introduces the Wanderer to the reader, the portrait with "eyes . . . such as one feels they wish they had never seen." It was manipulated in any number of Gothic stories, including three of the tales in Irving's *Tales of a Traveller*. The allusion to the reader's experience with Gothic story evokes an awe that adds itself—or so Hawthorne intends—to the experience of "The Prophetic Pictures" and "Edward Randolph's Portrait." But the portraits in both tales are freighted with meaning; the Gothic device has become useful as a symbol. When Hawthorne returns to the mysterious portrait in

The House of the Seven Gables, he is refining his own earlier practice.

The magic mirror was perhaps more important to Hawthorne than the mysterious portrait. His preoccupation with mirrors and reflecting surfaces—which has been extensively discussed[42]—seems a function of the pictorial quality of his imagination expressing itself in a symbol. The magic mirror is of course older than what we call the Gothic convention. Cornelius Agrippa's magic mirror is among the wonders in "A Virtuoso's Collection." Hawthorne probably knew Cambuscan's mirror in Chaucer's "The Squire's Tale" and Prince Zeyn Alasnam's mirror in the *Arabian Nights.* He certainly knew Merlin's mirror in *The Faerie Queene* (bk. 3, canto 2) and Lao's mirror in Goldsmith's *The Citizen of the World* (letter 46). But the Gothic convention welcomed the device, and it persisted to Hawthorne's time. There is a magic mirror in Lewis's *The Monk* (1796); in 1828 Scott used a magic mirror in a fine Gothic tale, "My Aunt Margaret's Mirror," although he spoke apologetically of it in the introduction to the tale: his readers will remember "stories enow of much the same cast" if they have "dabbled in a species of lore" to which he had once given too much time.[43] We have seen that Poe thought the magic mirror a conventional device.

Allusions to magic mirrors are frequent in Hawthorne. In "Dr. Bullivant" the apothecary's powers of mimicry are exercised on his customers "as if a magic looking-glass had caught the reflection, and were making sport with it." Of the looking-glass in Dr. Heidegger's study "it was fabled that the spirits of all the doctor's deceased patients dwelt within its verge, and would stare him in the face whenever he looked thitherward." In "The Old Manse," Hawthorne says that, when he had found some old newspapers and almanacs, "It was

42. See F. O. Matthiessen, *American Renaissance* (New York, 1941), pp. 259–62; Malcolm Cowley, ed., *The Portable Hawthorne* (New York, 1948), pp. 8–9; Millicent Bell, *Hawthorne's View of the Artist* (New York, 1962), pp. 58–68; Marjorie J. Elder, *Nathaniel Hawthorne: Transcendental Symbolist* (Athens, Ohio, 1969), pp. 79–80 and passim; Hugo McPherson, *Hawthorne as Myth-Maker* (Toronto, 1969), index under "Images: mirror." This discussion seems to me to be somewhat confused by a failure to make a necessary distinction between the mirror used in the tales or romances as a metaphor for the writer's representation, on the one hand, and Hawthorne's remarks on reflecting surfaces in entirely different contexts, on the other.

43. *Short Stories of Sir Walter Scott,* ed. Lord David Cecil (Oxford World Classics), p. 262.

as if I had found bits of magic looking-glass among the books, with the images of a vanished century in them." And he puts down this story suggestion in his notebook in 1837: "An old looking-glass. Somebody finds out the secret of making all the images that have been reflected in it pass back again across its surface."[44] In "Old Esther Dudley," as we shall see in a subsequent consideration of the tale, the title character finds out the secret. But of course it is also the secret that Hawthorne worked hardest to discover, and in his best tales did discover.

Even the famous passage in "The Custom House" on Hawthorne's concept of romance represents it by a picture concentrated in its mirror image: "Glancing at the looking-glass, we behold—deep within its haunted verge—the smouldering glow of the half-extinguished anthracite, the white moonbeams on the floor, and a repetition of all the gleam and shadow of the picture, with one remove further from the actual, and nearer to the imaginative." The passage suggests that the use of the mirror image as the symbol of what the artist does with experience may well have come to Hawthorne from the Gothic convention.

The mirror image is framed; it has limits and focus; and of them, the suggestion is, art consists. At the end of a paragraph of description in "Lady Eleanore's Mantle," Hawthorne remarks, "What a pity that one of the stately mirrors has not preserved a picture of the scene, which, by the very traits that were so transitory, might have taught us much that would be worth knowing and remembering!" He is of course suggesting what he has endeavored to do in his function of historical painter. And in the next sentence he equates mirror and painter: "Would, at least, that either painter or mirror could convey to us some faint idea" of Lady Eleanore's mysterious mantle. Mirror and painter are also equated in "The Prophetic Pictures": "All men . . . shall find a mirror of themselves in this wonderful painter." But the magic mirror is focused by the artist who uses it and, as we shall see, sometimes focused obliquely according to his purposes.

Of all the tales, "Dr. Heidegger's Experiment" in its apparent simplicity will tell us most about Hawthorne's attitude toward his Gothic materials. In a single paragraph he catalogs enough Gothic paraphernalia for all the Gothic romances Jane Austen's Catherine

44. *Passages*, p. 109.

Morland ever read. Now no writer who wished from his reader the kind of response that Gothic story commonly aimed at would risk such a heaping together. Hawthorne has his ways—in this instance a whimsical way—of restraining one kind of interest so that another may emerge.

"There are some works in literature," Hawthorne wrote in his *Italian Notebooks*, "... where great power is lavished a little outside of nature, and therefore proves to be only a fashion, and not permanently adapted to the tastes of mankind."[45] The impulse of writers in the Gothic convention was often enough aberrant; it is one of Hawthorne's distinctions that in his best uses of Gothic materials (I do not say in all) he adapts them to a humane intent. His control is a double control—of his materials and of his readers' reactions—so that the response in his best tales is finally as much intellectual as emotional.

MORAL PURPOSE AND ALLEGORICAL METHOD

In his whimsical little preface to "Rappaccini's Daughter" (1844), Hawthorne accuses himself of "an inveterate love of allegory, which is apt ... to steal away the human warmth out of his conceptions." His critics, far from being content with his own deprecation of his allegory, have constantly repeated it. In the discussion of Hawthorne's allegory, therefore, one encounters at the outset the difficulty of a necessary consciousness of the weight of previous discussion.

Much of the older criticism, from Poe on, seems to be saying that Hawthorne's allegory was a wrong choice, and to consider it as if it were an easily avoidable mistake. More recent criticism has taken somewhat different tacks. One is to make a distinction between allegory and symbolism, and to say that so far as Hawthorne's method is allegorical, that is a misfortune. But then some critics talk of his symbolism, not really as a literary method, but as a collection of symptoms of his neuroses. And of course the terms of current criticism have come into the discussion: when the critic approves, Hawthorne's work is not so much allegorical as mythic, mythopoetic, or archetypal. Finally, as we have noticed, it has lately been felt that to speak of

45. *Italian Note-Books*, p. 143.

Hawthorne as an emblem writer somehow removes the curse of allegory.

Then there is another difficulty in discussing Hawthorne's allegory in special reference to his early work. What statements on his part about artistic purpose we have—beyond those incidental in the tales themselves—are all later in his career, after he had written some of his most interesting allegorical tales. What is said about art in the *Italian Notebooks*, for instance, may not have any close connection with Hawthorne's purpose when he wrote "My Kinsman, Major Molineux" or "Young Goodman Brown."

Under these conditions, one who wishes to discuss Hawthorne's practice without first writing a treatise on aesthetic theory can proceed (as it seems to me) only in this way: he can try to see how Hawthorne understood the term *allegory*, and what sort of allegory he wrote. But that of course involves to begin with some consideration of the bent of his mind, for he wrote what he calls allegory by a preference that has something of inevitability in it. However much he deprecated his allegory, he accepted it as a necessary condition of his work.

That bent of mind is not single, and not easy to fix. In a frequently quoted passage from a letter to Fields, Hawthorne remarks of Anthony Trollope's novels, "They precisely suit my taste; solid and substantial . . . and just as real as if some giant had hewn a great lump out of the earth and put it under a glass case."[46] No one who has considered the quality of the *American Notebooks* should be surprised at this admiration for Trollope, for many passages in them are solid and substantial—and often skillful—accounts of everyday experience and observation. They are just such passages as a writer practicing to be a realist of the Trollope sort might write. Indeed, Hawthorne seems to have regretted that he did not fully use his realistic power: in "The Custom House" he remarks, "A better book than I shall ever write was there." But Hawthorne's notebooks also show us that to see a symbolic quality in experience was part of his everyday habit of mind, even when there was no purpose of using the symbol in fiction,[47] for symbols were the natural coinage of his mind.

46. Fields, p. 63.
47. For striking examples of Hawthorne's tendency to find symbols in everyday experience and observation, see a passage on trees in autumn at the Old Manse (*Passages*, pp. 358–59), a passage on washing dishes (*Passages*, p. 364),

This tendency to see a second meaning in all experience is in Hawthorne a kind of residual Puritanism. His forebears saw in nature and experience revelations of God's will and purposes; some of their most impressive writings—Edward Johnson's *Wonder-Working Providence* or Increase Mather's *Illustrious Providences*—endeavor to discern the divine purposes as they run through experience. Where Emerson and Hawthorne are alike, they are so in a shared inheritance. In Emerson the conviction of a moral and spiritual meaning inherent in all nature and experience worked itself out, with some assistance from Swedenborg, in his Doctrine of Correspondences, which in its main assumptions was shared by the transcendentalists. Christopher Pearse Cranch wrote:

> All things in Nature are beautiful types to the soul that will
>   read them;
> Nothing exists upon earth, but for unspeakable ends.
> Every object that speaks to the senses was meant for the spirit.

We find sometimes in Hawthorne's later work statements very like Cranch's. "Everything, you know," Hawthorne makes Sybil Dacy say in *Septimius Felton*, "has its spiritual meaning, which to the literal meaning is what the soul is to the body." What may be said about a transcendental or a romantic literary theory in Hawthorne has this much basis.

Except for that likeness to transcendental thinking, Hawthorne's estimate of the nature of man—at least as it works itself out imaginatively in the early tales—is far closer to that of his Puritan forebears than is Emerson's. What Hawthorne sees in experience is often not what Emerson would expect the literary artist to find there; it is often what Emerson and the transcendentalists hoped was not there at all.

The feeling on Hawthorne's part that experience has a meaning beyond itself, and that the fiction writer should be busy about finding it, may manifest itself simply and ingenuously. He invites his reader to

---

a passage on the glow of sunset in Edinburgh (*English Note-Books*, 2: 500), and a passage on sunlight through a church window in Italy (*Italian Note-Books*, p. 187). A particularly interesting example is Hawthorne's reflection on the weeds in his garden, which may be symbols of sin, but may also be necessary to the well being of the world (*American Notebooks*, ed. Stewart, p. 186). This passage seems to contain the germ of a speculation in *The Marble Faun*, a speculation that the romance does not quite resolve.

go with him through Wakefield's vagary, "trusting that there will be
a pervading spirit and a moral, even should we fail to find them, done
up neatly, and condensed into the final sentence. Thought has always
its efficacy, and every striking incident its moral." It is true, as John
Caldwell Stubbs points out,[48] that in the romances Hawthorne deals
with his stated morals ironically in order to indicate that the romancer
has his own kind of moral purpose. But often enough in the early
tales he lets us know that he is in quest of a moral—and it may seem
to a reader that when the moral is unimpressive or its embodiment
unsuccessful, he calls it "a deep moral." Yet none but the most unperceptive reader ever found any great part of his reward in what
Hawthorne can state as a moral aphorism. But the statements are
there, and Hawthorne was impelled to make them.

Hawthorne was impelled to make them (as it seems to me) because
there was always in him some doubt—sometimes a consciously admitted doubt—of the validity of fiction itself. He says that, when he
began his residence at the Old Manse, he took shame to himself "for
having been so long a writer of idle stories," and that he hoped some
more important kind of writing would come out of his new life. And we
are forced to take with some seriousness the passage in "The Custom
House" in which he imagines his ancestors discussing their descendant:

> "What is he?" murmurs one gray shadow of my forefathers to
> the other. "A writer of story-books! What kind of a business
> in life,—what mode of glorifying God, or being serviceable to
> mankind in his day and generation,—may that be? Why, the
> degenerate fellow might as well have been a fiddler!" Such are
> the compliments bandied between my great-grandsires and
> myself, across the gulf of time! And yet, let them scorn me
> as they will, strong traits of their nature have intertwined
> themselves with mine.

The traits of his ancestors were strong enough in him so that he would
not wish to be a fiddler and feared that he might be. He well knew
how many literary men do not really matter to mankind; the type
figures of poets in "The Great Carbuncle" and "The Canterbury
Pilgrims" are made up of triviality, vanity, and pretense. Even the
dedicated artist Owen Warland, in "The Artist of the Beautiful,"

48. *The Pursuit of Form* (Urbana, Ill., 1970), pp. 16–19.

dedicates himself to an endeavor that not only separates him from his fellows but, after all, results only in the perfection of a toy.

Hawthorne demanded of himself and of any fiction writer some real purpose and importance to the lives of men. There is a characteristic reservation in his mature judgment of Scott. In his account in the *English Notebooks* of a visit to Abbotsford, he is led to reflect on the lack in Scott's character he thought Abbotsford represented:

> It is just like going to a museum, . . . and one learns from
> it, too, that Scott could not have been really a wise man, nor
> an earnest one, nor one that grasped the truth of life; he did but
> play, and the play grew very sad toward its close. In a certain
> way, however, I understand his romances the better for having
> seen his house; and his house the better for having read his
> romances. They throw light on one another.[49]

The passage seems surprisingly ungenerous and indeed unperceptive until one sees that what is said in it suggests a discomfort about the function and validity of fiction that extends to Hawthorne's own. Scott "did but play"; it behooves the fiction writer to be wise and earnest. Dare Hawthorne claim either wisdom or earnestness for himself?

Now given a man whose mind deals naturally in symbols, who sees experience freighted with a meaning beyond itself, and who is impelled in his fiction to seek some clear connection with the central interests of men, what should he do but write allegory? Hawthorne seems to have understood the term *allegory* in a standard fashion: a narrative in which persons, things, and actions have a second meaning, as the account of a journey in *Pilgrim's Progress* becomes the account of the difficulties and the encouragements of the Christian life. But in much of the work he called allegory, there is no figure that represents an abstract quality, no close parallel, for instance, for Bunyan's Giant Despair. Even Mary Goffe, in "The Man of Adamant," is not a personification of an abstraction.

Since we know Hawthorne to have been fond of reading Bunyan and

49. *English Note-Books*, 2: 273–74. Although Hawthorne writes in this passage as if the judgment had just occurred to him, the passage is an unconscious reminiscence of a passage in "P's Correspondence," written about 1845, long before he had seen Abbotsford. See *Mosses*, pp. 415–16.

Spenser as a boy (and indeed as a man), it has been rather too easy
to assume correspondences between his allegorical method and theirs.
But—except of course for the wonderful "Celestial Railroad"—there
is really not much of Bunyan's method in his work. There may be a
little more resemblance to Spenser in some of Hawthorne's best tales,
if only because Spenser is less consistently an allegorist than Bunyan.
This is not to say, of course, that Bunyan and Spenser do not influence
Hawthorne; doubtless they do,[50] and in more subtle ways than we
can trace. But we cannot clearly connect his allegorical method with
that of either.

A far more obvious influence on some of Hawthorne's allegories,
as he himself indicates in "The Threefold Destiny," is the eighteenth-
century "Eastern tale." He means, of course, such work as Addison's
"The Vision of Mirzah," Goldsmith's "Asem, an Eastern Tale" and
"A Dream" ("The Looking-glass of Lao"), and Dr. Johnson's oriental
tales in the *Rambler* and the *Idler*. "The Man of Adamant," "The
Lily's Quest," "David Swan," and "Fancy's Show Box" have analogues in the Eastern tale, as do several of the pieces in *Mosses from
an Old Manse*.

Hawthorne labels such pieces as these with the obvious intent of distinguishing their kind of interest; the label "An Apologue," for
instance, is used with both "The Man of Adamant" and "The Lily's
Quest." Whatever precise distinctions he may have intended when
he chose the several labels he uses, they indicate at the least that the
moral and not the narrative interest is to be the reader's chief reward.[51]
Certainly no one has an obligation to enjoy these "Eastern tale"
allegories; but they should not be lumped together with pieces of
another intent. And at any rate, no real problem of Hawthorne's
allegory arises with them; they belong to a recognizable genre, and
their weaknesses are the weaknesses of their models.

The problem arises in those tales that have a considerable narrative
interest and yet an allegorical intent. It is hardly to be solved by
applying to Hawthorne's work some distinction between allegory and

50. See David E. Smith, *John Bunyan in America* (Bloomington, Indiana,
1966), pp. 47–89.
51. The label "A Parable" with "The Minister's Black Veil" I take to have a
somewhat different intention from that of the other labels. *Parable* has
scriptural associations, and it may designate a piece of high narrative interest.

symbolism that does not inhere in it. Hawthorne uses—and very frequently—*symbol, type* (*type and symbol* in "The Minister's Black Veil"), and *emblem* without clear differentiation; the frequency of their occurrence is evidence of his propensity to point up his allegorical intent. Although he may speak of a symbol when his intent is not specifically allegorical, he speaks, too, of symbols as parts of an allegory. Had it ever occurred to him to make a distinction, he might have said that an allegory is a narrative pattern in which a number of symbols are organized; and that a symbol is an object, action, or typical person of such quality that it might be part of an allegory.

It would have been convenient for us had Hawthorne limited his use of the term *allegory* a little more strictly. Many characters and actions in fiction carry a meaning beyond their significance as individuals and separate sets of events; we say, perhaps, that they are representative, that the persons in these events stand for more than themselves, that in their predicaments, or their triumphs, something of the human condition is exemplified. But if the perception of that further meaning depends primarily upon our own reflection on the narrative, we do not call the work allegory. What distinguishes Hawthorne's work in his best allegorical tales is his insistence upon the recognition of a second meaning from time to time as the tale progresses.

Hawthorne's insistence on marking out this second meaning is so much an indication of his intent as a writer that it may be well to exemplify it here, even though we shall have to be concerned with it in subsequent discussions of the tales. In "The Maypole of Merry Mount," for instance, Hawthorne writes of the Lord and Lady of the May: "There they stood, in the first hour of wedlock, while the idle pleasures, of which their companions were the emblems, had given place to the sternest cares of life, personified by the dark Puritans." Or, in "Old Esther Dudley" the title character is left in the Province House, "dwelling there with memory; and if Hope ever seemed to flit around her, still it was Memory in disguise." When, in "Dr. Heidegger's Experiment," the old doctor protests the riot his friends are making, "it seemed as if gray Time were calling them back from their sunny youth, far down into the chill and darksome vale of years." It is such marking out as this that makes a tale otherwise only representative into an allegorical tale—perhaps we may not wish to say, quite, "into an

allegory." It is a special characteristic of Hawthorne as a fiction writer.
It is a strength or a weakness in his work, as it succeeds or as, in some
instances, it seems labored or even forced.

The second meaning is not always so explicitly confessed as it is in
the passages quoted above; particularly in some of Hawthorne's earliest
tales is the allegorical intent less obviously insisted upon; and one
wonders if, as he gained experience, he had less confidence in the
perceptiveness of his readers. But even in, say, "My Kinsman, Major
Molineux," the pointing up of a second meaning is there. Yet unless
Hawthorne is writing one of the pieces intended to be primarily an
allegory, he means to maintain an interest in his action for itself as
well as an interest in its moral significance.

Hawthorne was quite aware that fulfilling his intent required him to
keep a delicate balance between two kinds of interest, and apparently
he felt that he was most likely to fail to maintain a sufficient interest
in his persons and in the actions they carry out. He wrote in the 1851
preface to *Twice-Told Tales*: "Instead of passion there is sentiment;
and, even in what purport to be pictures of actual life, we have
allegory, not always so warmly dressed in its habiliments of flesh and
blood as to be taken into the reader's mind without a shiver." "Even
in what purport to be pictures of actual life"—Hawthorne is not here
writing about, say, "David Swan." He is writing about his problem
in the best of his tales.

In some tales Hawthorne's problem is to substantiate an allegorical
idea: to provide that idea with the action, figures, and setting that
will make it imaginatively acceptable, to write a tale as well as an
allegory. In other tales his problem is to find a moral or human significance in some concrete incident or event: to write what he considers
a meaningful tale. Now perhaps these two problems may be but two
sides of the same coin, yet they result in two procedures.

Sometimes a note to a tale lets us know how the tale got started;
sometimes a notebook entry does; less often we know from something
in the tale itself. In the first paragraph of "The Threefold Destiny,"
Hawthorne discusses his procedure in that tale:

I have sometimes produced a singular and not unpleasing effect,
so far as my own mind was concerned, by imagining a train of
incidents in which the spirit and mechanism of the fairy legend

should be combined with the characters and manners of familiar life. In the little tale which follows, a subdued tinge of the wild and wonderful is thrown over a sketch of New England personages and scenery, yet, it is hoped, without entirely obliterating the sober hues of nature. Rather than a story of events claiming to be real, it may be considered as an allegory, such as the writers of the last century would have expressed in the shape of an Eastern tale, but to which I have endeavored to give a more life-like warmth than could be infused into those fanciful productions.

"The Threefold Destiny" turns out to be feeble enough; the balance aimed at is not achieved; the "New England personages and scenery" are not well done and hardly infuse a "life-like warmth" to the "Eastern tale" allegory. But the aim is clear, and perhaps the tale is a little more interesting than, say, "The Lily's Quest," which is very much like what an eighteenth-century writer might have done as an Eastern tale.[52]

"The Threefold Destiny" illustrates that pattern in the development of a tale which starts with a moral idea for an allegory and works out its substantiation. That pattern is clearly illustrated, too, by tales later than the period of our concern, by "The Birthmark" and by "Ethan Brand."[53] But some of the best of Hawthorne's tales written before 1839 had their inception in historical matters or events which in the telling gather meaning beyond themselves. The imaginative movement from historical event to allegorical tale is clear in the pattern of a number of tales. Hawthorne explicitly describes it in his note to "The Maypole of Merry Mount," where he tells us that "the facts, recorded on the grave pages of our New England annalists, have wrought themselves, almost spontaneously, into a sort of allegory." But when we have no note to a tale, and no notebook entry for it—and the earliest notebook entries that have come down to us are dated 1835—the genesis of a tale must be a matter of inference.

Such inference is sometimes easy, but not always so. We have no extrinsic evidence about the inception of "Dr. Heidegger's Experi-

52. The allegorical scheme of "The Lily's Quest" is worked out with unusual fullness in a notebook entry, *Passages*, pp. 37–38.

53. See the notebook suggestions for these tales: *Passages*, pp. 106 and 210; *American Notebooks*, ed. Stewart, p. 106.

ment," for example, and we cannot confidently infer its genesis. We may suppose it had its inception with the imaginative turning-over of the elixir-of-life motif, familiar to Hawthorne at least since his reading of Godwin's *St. Leon* in 1820. We may equally well suppose that the tale had its inception as Hawthorne contemplated the idea that character is a kind of fate, and developed as he sought an embodiment for the idea.

But whatever the genesis of a particular tale (among those of any permanent importance) the degree of Hawthorne's success in it is the degree in which he maintains a balance of interest between the allegorical intent and the action.

4. THE SELECTION FOR
TWICE-TOLD TALES

About two years before the first edition of *Twice-Told Tales* was determined upon, Hawthorne planned his third projected volume, which was to have been a collection called "The Story-Teller," and which was to have had an elaborate frame. A number of pieces for it Hawthorne submitted to Goodrich, who, unwilling to undertake the publication of a volume, seems to have submitted the manuscripts to Joseph T. Buckingham, then editor of the *New-England Magazine*. Buckingham was apparently willing to publish the collection serially, and there appeared anonymously in the magazine for November and December 1834 the two installments of what was to have been the introductory piece, itself called "The Story-Teller" (collected in the second edition of *Mosses from an Old Manse* as "Passages from a Relinquished Work").[1] In the first installment the narrator tells us that the idea of becoming a wandering storyteller had been suggested, a year or two before, by an encounter with several merry vagabonds

1. "Passages from a Relinquished Work," however, does not include "Mr. Higginbotham's Catastrophe," which was a part of the second installment of "The Story-Teller" in the *New-England Magazine*, but which had been taken out of its context and printed as a separate tale in *Twice-Told Tales*.

in a showman's wagon—a reference to "The Seven Vagabonds"—
and announces the plan of the frame.

> The following pages will contain a picture of my vagrant life,
> intermixed with specimens, generally brief and slight, of that
> great mass of fiction to which I gave existence, and which has
> vanished like cloud shapes. . . . With each specimen will be
> given a sketch of the circumstances in which the story was told.
> Thus my airdrawn pictures will be set in frames perhaps more
> valuable than the pictures themselves, since they will be em-
> bossed with groups of characteristic figures, amid the lake
> and mountain scenery, the villages and fertile fields, of our
> native land.

But Buckingham relinquished the editorship of the *New-England
Magazine* at the end of 1834. The new editors apparently declined
to use Hawthorne's frame-work and printed his pieces as separate tales
and sketches. Park Benjamin became editor and proprietor in March
of 1835, and Hawthorne held him particularly responsible for the
breaking-up of the design of the collection. During 1835 the *New-
England Magazine* printed separate Hawthorne pieces month after
month, except for September and October.[2]

We cannot reconstruct the scheme of the "Story-Teller" volume
from the pieces in the *New-England Magazine*. They are so different
in genre that it does not seem possible that any frame, and certainly not
the one projected in the passage quoted above, could have held them
together. The pieces printed in 1835 include, for example, "Young
Goodman Brown," "Old News," and "A Rill from the Town Pump."
(It may be, of course, that the *New-England Magazine* had some
material not intended for "The Story-Teller.") But, although nothing
we know about "The Story-Teller" suggests that its plan could have
been successful, Hawthorne was disappointed and perhaps somewhat
bitter about the breaking-up of his design, and felt that the pieces
would have been better in their frame.[3] There was precedent for such

2. For an interesting discussion of the problem of "The Story-Teller," see
Adkins, "Early Projected Works of Hawthorne," pp. 131–46. It is worth
remark that Poe's projected "Tales of the Folio Club" apparently had a frame
comparable to that of "The Story-Teller."
3. See a statement by Elizabeth Peabody quoted in Conway, p. 32.

connection: he had surely considered the four sets of tales, each with its own frame, in Irving's *Tales of a Traveller* (1824). But he may have been thinking more particularly of Thomas Moore's *Lalla Rookh* (1817).[4] Yet when he came at last to designing the 1837 *Twice-Told Tales*, he gave up the frame principle entirely, and proceeded in a more commonplace fashion.

In 1836 Hawthorne's college friend, Horatio Bridge, without Hawthorne's knowledge, and working through Goodrich, secured the publication of *Twice-Told Tales* by guaranteeing the publisher, the American Stationers' Company, against loss. The story is familiar,[5] but Bridge deserves to be remembered in any study of Hawthorne. By a generous, sensible, and decisive action he brought Hawthorne's name into American letters. With the publication of the 1837 *Twice-Told Tales*, Hawthorne's long period of anonymity was over. The edition of 1000 copies was almost exhausted within its first year—something of a success for the day. But far more important to Hawthorne's career, he became a known writer. The book was reviewed by Longfellow in the *North American Review* in 1837, and in 1838 by Charles Fenno Hoffman in the *American Monthly Magazine* and Andrew Preston Peabody in the influential *Christian Examiner*. It was at last possible to determine what manner of writer Nathaniel Hawthorne was. We have now to consider what he did in presenting his work for the judgment of the public.

When Hawthorne went about assembling the eighteen pieces for his volume, he selected from forty or more pieces that had been printed in magazines, in the Salem *Gazette*, and in *The Token*. Certainly he made his selection carefully. We need to remember that, although nowadays even devoted students of Hawthorne do not often consider his collections as literary entities, their make-up and proportion were doubtless important to him. Moreover, he was putting his name to his work for the first time. He was not only presenting a

4. In "The Seven Vagabonds," which seems to record the idea for "The Story-Teller" in its germ, the narrator says: "My design, in short, was to imitate the story-tellers of whom Oriental travellers have told us, and become an itinerant novelist, reciting my own extemporaneous fictions to such audiences as I could collect."

5. The story may best be read in Bridge's *Personal Recollections of Nathaniel Hawthorne*, pp. 77–81 and Goodrich, 2: 272–73; Hawthorne's tribute to Bridge is in the prefatory letter to *The Snow-Image*.

selection of his work: he was presenting himself as a literary person. He was for the first time fully considering his relationship with the public he hoped would support his work. These matters are not extraneous to Hawthorne's function as a literary artist; they are conditions of that function, and they warrant some discussion.

At first consideration the pattern of Hawthorne's collection may be puzzling. The selection and arrangement of pieces seem to have no connection with his plans for any one of his three projected volumes so far as we know about them. The selection of pieces does not very well conform to our notions today about what his best work is. The principles that govern selection and arrangement are not immediately apparent.

Here is the table of contents of the 1837 *Twice-Told Tales* with a statement of when and where each piece had first been printed. (The dates for pieces in *The Token* and *Youth's Keepsake* are the dates of the actual publication of the volumes of the annuals; thus "Sunday at Home" here dated 1836 appeared in *The Token* for 1837.)

"The Gray Champion"	*New-England Magazine,* January 1835
"Sunday at Home"	*The Token,* 1836
"The Wedding Knell"	*The Token,* 1835
"The Minister's Black Veil"	*The Token,* 1835
"The Maypole of Merry Mount"	*The Token,* 1835
"The Gentle Boy"	*The Token,* 1831
"Mr. Higginbotham's Catastrophe"	*New-England Magazine,* December 1834
"Little Annie's Ramble"	*Youth's Keepsake,* 1834
"Wakefield"	*New-England Magazine,* May 1835
"A Rill from the Town Pump"	*New-England Magazine,* June 1835
"The Great Carbuncle"	*The Token,* 1836
"The Prophetic Pictures"	*The Token,* 1836
"David Swan"	*The Token,* 1836
"Sights from a Steeple"	*The Token,* 1830
"The Hollow of the Three Hills"	Salem *Gazette,* November 12, 1830

"The Vision of the Fountain"	*New-England Magazine,* August 1835
"Fancy's Show Box"	*The Token,* 1836
"Dr. Heidegger's Experiment"	*Knickerbocker Magazine,* January 1837

These eighteen tales and sketches had been printed during eight years; they had been written during ten or twelve; they are less than half of what Hawthorne had available.

Clearly Hawthorne had a problem in his selection. Elizabeth Peabody remembered him saying that his experience before the publication of *Twice-Told Tales* was like that of "a man talking to himself in a dark place."[6] A writer of any sort needs a response to what he has written; if he tries to assess his own work without it, he is beset by continual misgivings. Hawthorne may have had responses we do not know about, but they were few at best. Since he chose to identify some of his pieces as "by the author of 'Sights from a Steeple,' " others as "by the author of 'The Gentle Boy,' " and yet others as "by the author of 'The Gray Champion,' " we may suppose he thought well of those three pieces, probably on some indication beside his own taste. Henry F. Chorley, in a review of *The Token* for 1836 in the London *Athenaeum,* had praised "The Wedding Knell" and "The Minister's Black Veil," and reprinted "The Maypole of Merry Mount" in part. The editor of the *Knickerbocker Magazine* had written an enthusiastic letter about "Dr. Heidegger's Experiment." But beyond these indications, Hawthorne probably had little notion about how readers took his work.

The only public identification by name of Hawthorne as a writer before the publication of *Twice-Told Tales* came from Park Benjamin. In a notice of *The Token* for 1836 in the *New-England Magazine* of October 1835, Benjamin had spoken of "the author of 'The Gentle Boy' " as "the most pleasing writer of fanciful prose, except Irving, in the country." A year later, in the *American Monthly Magazine* of October 1836, he reviewed *The Token* for 1837 (which used eight pieces by Hawthorne). In this review he connected Hawthorne's name with his tales and sketches for the first time:

6. Conway, p. 32.

The author of "Sights from a Steeple," of "The Gentle Boy," and of "The Wedding Knell," we believe to be one and the same individual. The assertion may sound very bold, yet we hesitate not to call this author second to no man in this country, except Washington Irving. We refer simply to romance writing; and trust that no wise man of Gotham will talk of Dewey, and Channing, and Everett, and Verplanck. Yes, to us the style of NATHANIEL HAWTHORNE is more pleasing, more fascinating, than any one's, except their dear Geoffry [sic] Crayon! This mention of the real name of our author may be reprobated by him. His modesty is the best proof of his true excellence. How different does such a man appear to us from one who anxiously writes his name on every public post! We have read a sufficient number of his pieces to make the reputation of a dozen of our Yankee scribblers; and yet, how few have heard the name above written! He does not even cover himself with the same anonymous shield at all times; but liberally gives the praise which, con-centrated on one, would be great, to several unknowns. If Mr. Hawthorne would but collect his various tales and essays into one volume, we can assure him that their success would be brilliant—certainly in England, perhaps in this country. His works would, probably, make twice as many volumes as Mr. Willis's! How extended a notoriety has the latter acquired on productions, whose quantity and quality are both far inferior to those of this voluntarily undistinguished man of genius!

"The Token" would be richly worth its price for "Monsieur du Miroir," "Sunday at Home," "The Man of Adamant," and "The Great Carbuncle," if every other piece were as flat as the editor's verses. "David Swan" is, if we mistake not, from the same graphic hand; and so is "Fancy's Show Box;" we are sure of "The Prophetic Pictures." A little volume, containing these stories alone, would be a treasure. "The Great Carbuncle" is eminently good; and, like all the rest of our author's tales, both here and elsewhere, conveys an important moral.

"The Token" is further recommended by a tale from Miss Sedgwick, and one by Miss Leslie, about which we need not speak, as the authoresses' names are sufficient. We are happy to perceive that the Editor of "the Token" has this year followed

the sagacious advice with which we gratuitously favored him in
"New England Magazine," viz.—that he should rest the claims
of his work to public favor on the grounds of its intrinsic merits,
and not on the celebrity of contributors. We therefore stand
in the interesting light of a kind monitor, and not of a reproachful
critic. We are pleased; we therefore applaud. We commend
the Editor for his good taste in the selection of his prose papers,
and we can think of only one method by which he can do better
than he has done;—this is, next year to employ Hawthorne to
write the whole volume, and not to look at it himself till it be
for sale by all booksellers in town and country. [New series 2: 406]

Benjamin's notice was well-timed, and obviously it was not fortuitous,[7]
although some writers on Hawthorne seem to suppose so. It is a good
example of the standard practice the nineteenth century called
"puffing";[8] to use an expression of James T. Fields, Benjamin had been
persuaded to "do the amiable" for Hawthorne. If one remembers
Benjamin's connection with Hawthorne,[9] it is clear that his notice is
far from ingenuous, and that it is written to prepare the way for an
announcement of a Hawthorne collection.

    Benjamin's notice, keyed as it is to the taste and literary values of

7. This notice of Benjamin's may have stemmed from urging by Bridge.
Bridge had twice written to Hawthorne about his own intention of writing a
notice that should connect Hawthorne's name with his work (*Hawthorne and
His Wife*, 1: 139–41; Bridge, pp. 70–71). We do not have Hawthorne's
replies, but it looks as if it had been decided that Benjamin should break the
ice for the new collection.

8. See W. S. Tryon's account of the way in which James T. Fields arranged
puffs for the books he published (*Parnassus Corner*, pp. 183–204). Hawthorne
himself once wrote to Ticknor suggesting that Fields arrange a puff for the
poems of an English acquaintance, poems he confesses he has not read (*Letters
of Hawthorne to William D. Ticknor, 1851–1864* [Newark, N. J.: The
Carteret Book Club, 1910], 1: 102). See also Charvat, *The Profession of
Authorship in America*, pp. 46 and 171–81.

9. Benjamin owed Hawthorne a favor: when Benjamin left Boston for
New York and the *American Monthly Magazine*, Hawthorne gave him some
manuscripts to use in the new venture (Bridge, p. 69). Benjamin clearly does
his best in this rather too obviously adroit notice of *The Token*. There was
ill-will between Goodrich and Benjamin, and it is evident in what Benjamin
says of the plates and of some verses by Goodrich himself. Apparently the
negotiations with Goodrich and the American Stationers' Company were far
enough along so that any offense Goodrich might take was not feared.

the day, is helpful in our estimate of Hawthorne's intention. It is difficult to see what was to be gained by the exaggeration of the extent of Hawthorne's production, but for the rest Benjamin's motives in the notice are fairly obvious. The way in which the tales by Catherine M. Sedgwick and Eliza Leslie are dismissed may be invidious, but it shows Benjamin's recognition of what we so often forget, that it was these writers who had the public favor for which Hawthorne was aiming. The connection made with Irving must have gratified Hawthorne; but it also indicated a direction he would inevitably take, as inevitably as his friend Longfellow had taken it, about three years before, in his *Outre-Mer* (which is in some sort an imitation of the *Sketch Book*). Although of course Benjamin recognizes the pre-eminence of Irving, he makes an appeal to New England literary pride (the *American Monthly* was particularly intended to appeal to readers in both Boston and New York). Benjamin's prediction of an English popularity for Hawthorne is calculated and rather a good stroke, and his emphasis on the excellence of Hawthorne's style picks out a superiority that would hardly have been questioned.

Hawthorne's most obvious model in making a collection was the *Sketch Book*, and a glance at his table of contents suggests that he was trying for something of the sort of balance and variety that had worked so well for Irving.[10] If today we are far less interested in the sketches than we are in the tales, we might remember that it was in the sketch that Hawthorne was most like Irving:[11] in his 1842 review of *Twice-Told Tales* Poe wrote, "The Essays of Hawthorne have much the character of Irving, with more of originality, and less of finish." But Hawthorne surely did not consider the *Sketch Book* alone, for in the early 1830s there were, besides *Outre-Mer*, collections of tales and sketches by Theodore S. Fay, William Cox, Eliza Leslie, Lydia H.

10. Even the order of contents may owe something to the example of Irving, who put "Rip Van Winkle" early in the *Sketch Book* and "The Legend of Sleepy Hollow" at the end. Hawthorne considered the beginning and end positions the prominent ones: when the 1854 edition of *Mosses* was being planned, he instructed Ticknor to put "the patched-up article" ("Passages from a Relinquished Work") about the middle of the volume, "where it will not attract so much notice" (*Letters . . . to William D. Ticknor*, 1: 45).

11. See Fred Lewis Pattee, *Development of the American Short Story*, pp. 99–100; William L. Hedges, *Washington Irving: An American Study, 1802–1832* (Baltimore, 1965), pp. 147–53.

Sigourney, William Leete Stone, Sarah Josepha Hale, and Catherine
M. Sedgwick.[12] Even if we have forgotten them all, they represented for Hawthorne what was in his time getting acceptance, and
their acceptance must have helped him define his problems. Of course
he would have been aware, not only of the preponderance of women
writers, but also that his probable public would be largely feminine.
Doubtless he had to be reconciled to that, like Howells after him;
and doubtless he considered to whom he was making his bow, and how
the taste of his feminine readers had been formed. In that revealing
sketch "Main Street" (1849) the one sympathetic member of the
showman's audience is the young lady whose face reflects every
changing scene.

Since both Eliza Leslie and Catherine M. Sedgwick were writers of
reputation (and some merit) who were collecting pieces first
printed in the annuals, and since their work had appeared with his
in *The Token*, Hawthorne surely would have considered their volumes,
particularly Miss Sedgwick's, for her work was the closer to his. Her
Tales and Sketches (1835) was published by Carey, Lea, and
Blanchard of Philadelphia, the best American publishers of the day.
Ever since the appearance of her *Redwood* in 1824, she had had a
considerable reputation; her *Hope Leslie, or Early Times in Massachusetts* (1827) evinced historical interests somewhat like Hawthorne's
own. Although in *Tales and Sketches* she had fewer (eleven) and
longer pieces to work with, Hawthorne would have seen in her selection principles of balance and variety like those he followed in his own
selection for *Twice-Told Tales*. He must have been interested in her
"Mary Dyre," a redaction of William Sewel's account of the Quaker
martyr, the same material Hawthorne had used in "The Gentle
Boy."[13]

12. Theodore S. Fay's *Dreams and Reveries of a Quiet Man* appeared in
1832, and in 1833 Fay published William Cox's *Crayon Sketches by an Amateur*
—a title that seems designed to make a connection with Irving. In 1833 the
first series of Eliza Leslie's *Pencil Sketches; or, Outlines of Character* appeared;
in 1834 Lydia H. Sigourney's *Tales and Essays* and William Leete Stone's
Tales and Sketches; and in 1835 Sarah Josepha Hale's *Traits of American
Life*, Catherine M. Sedgwick's *Tales and Sketches*, the second series of Miss
Leslie's *Pencil Sketches*, and Stone's *The Mysterious Bridal and Other Tales*.

13. Besides "Mary Dyre," there are three other pieces that seem to have
some serious intent to use American materials. Two other tales have eighteenth-

We can see something of what Hawthorne was doing as he assembled his first volume for public approval. We cannot, of course, infer the reasons that Hawthorne chose one piece and rejected another very like it. But two principles of selection do seem to emerge. He intended to offer a variety of his pieces, in temper as well as in genre: if he chose "The Wedding Knell," for instance, he also chose "Little Annie's Ramble"; he included "Mr. Higginbotham's Catastrophe" as well as "The Minister's Black Veil." And he intended to offer fairly obvious, unsubtle pieces; he certainly did not foresee the kind of difficulty his critics have discovered in some of them.

Hawthorne's omissions from *Twice-Told Tales* make clear his intent to keep subtle pieces out of his first offering. He did omit just those tales in which recent criticism has been most interested: He omitted (1) "Roger Malvin's Burial," first printed in 1831 in *The Token* for 1832; (2) "My Kinsman, Major Molineux," 1831, in *The Token* for 1832; (3) "The Canterbury Pilgrims," 1832, in *The Token* for 1833; and (4) "Young Goodman Brown," *New-England Magazine*, April 1835. Ultimately, of course, all four were collected: "Roger Malvin's Burial" and "Young Goodman Brown" in *Mosses from an Old Manse* (1846); "My Kinsman, Major Molineux" and "The Canterbury Pilgrims" not until 1851 in *The Snow-Image*, about twenty years after their first appearance.[14]

---

century settings, but are highly "romantic." One tale, "St. Catherine's Eve," is laid in France in the thirteenth century. Three are tales of Miss Sedgwick's own time; of these, "Cacoethes Scribendi" is humorous; "The Elder Sister" highly sentimental; and "Old Maids" an embodiment of Miss Sedgwick's preoccupation with the lives of unmarried women, the concern of her last novel, *Married or Single?* (1857). The last piece in *Tales and Sketches* is a children's story, "The Canary Family" (a precedent for Hawthorne's inclusion of "Little Annie's Ramble"). All the pieces have some narrative interest; the term "sketches" in the title recognizes that the pieces have an informal, discursive technique. "Cacoethes Scribendi" includes an amusing ridicule of annuals, although the piece was first printed in the *Atlantic Souvenir* for 1830.

14. Of these four tales, "The Canterbury Pilgrims" was reprinted in Evert A. Duyckinck's *Arcturus* in 1842 (also three other tales as will be noted) and "Roger Malvin's Burial" was reprinted in John L. O'Sullivan's *Democratic Review* in 1843 (also "The Wives of the Dead," there called "The Two Widows"). Such reprinting was fairly common in the time, and what it may indicate about Hawthorne's attitude toward the tales is difficult to say. The Salem *Gazette* reprinted some thirteen Hawthorne pieces that had appeared in *The Token* and in magazines.

Hawthorne's preface to *Twice-Told Tales* was written for a reissue of the book and dated January 11, 1851, after *Mosses from an Old Manse* had been out for some time, and after the publication of *The Scarlet Letter*. Yet it tells us something of his intention in *Twice-Told Tales*, at least as he saw it in retrospect: "the sketches truly are . . . attempts, and very imperfectly successful ones, to open an intercourse with the world." When he made his decisions about what to include in *Twice-Told Tales*, he would surely have chosen those pieces he thought most likely to appeal to the readers he envisaged, and those that best represented his character as a writer as he wished it to be understood. Now what is most often noticed about this preface is Hawthorne's disparagement of his work: it is, he says, "pale," it has "an effect of tameness," and it is too persistently allegorical. That disparagement should not be dismissed as a pose Hawthorne liked to take in prefatory pieces: it accords well with remarks in his notebooks and letters.[15] But we ought to notice, too, what Hawthorne insists are the virtues of his "sketches": they are without "abstruseness of idea, or obscurity of expression. . . . Every sentence, so far as it embodies thought or sensibility, may be understood and felt by anybody who will give himself the trouble to read it, and will take up the book in a proper mood." It looks very much as if Hawthorne were saying that, in the first place, he had selected his work to interest as many readers as he could hope to, and that, in the second place, the concept of himself as a writer he had wished to project in *Twice-Told Tales* is one in which "Roger Malvin's Burial," "My Kinsman, Major Molineux," "The Canterbury Pilgrims," and "Young Goodman Brown" do not fit.

Nor is there any indication that Hawthorne's principles or procedures changed when he collected the 1842 *Twice-Told Tales*. Apparently nothing in the reception of the 1837 collection much altered his estimate of his readers and of what would be most acceptable to them.

Evert A. Duyckinck, who became a close friend of Hawthorne, endeavored to prepare the way for the 1842 *Twice-Told Tales* much as Benjamin had prepared the way for the 1837 edition. For the May 1841 issue of his magazine, *Arcturus* (1: 330–37), Duyckinck wrote an encomium of Hawthorne, taking a tack somewhat like that

15. See *American Notebooks*, ed. Stewart, p. 247; Fields, p. 75.

Benjamin had taken. Duyckinck presented Hawthorne as a neglected genius whose excellence was known to but few admirers, and suggested that he might have courted and preferred his obscurity. The essay includes oddly selected excerpts from "The Journal of a Solitary Man," "Edward Fane's Rosebud," and "The White Old Maid." Then, closer to the publication of the 1842 edition of *Twice-Told Tales,* in the issue of *Arcturus* for January 1842, there appeared a piece called "A Preamble to Nathaniel Hawthorne" (3: 152–55), ostensibly as a sort of introduction to the reprinting in *Arcturus* of Hawthorne pieces previously published elsewhere.[16] In this "preamble" is reprinted Longfellow's fulsome review of the 1837 *Twice-Told Tales*—"Words of our own may be laid aside," the writer (probably Duyckinck) says, "when we have by us so eloquent an introduction as Longfellow's review of his first book in the North American."

Twice-Told Tales, 1842, was reviewed in the April 1842 issue of *Arcturus* (3: 394). The reviewer, pointing out that with the 1842 edition there had been collected two series of Hawthorne pieces, remarks: "To these, the series we are at present publishing in Arcturus, will, we trust, be added and form a third. And thus collected, we know nothing to which to compare them, except, perhaps, the German tales of Tieck, as translated by Carlyle." Evidently, then, there was a projected volume of Hawthorne's work intended to include most or all of the pieces not collected in *Twice-Told Tales.* But the May 1842 issue of *Arcturus* was its last, and the design of reprinting a series of Hawthorne tales in the magazine came to little.[17] This project for a collection perhaps explains why the way for the 1842 *Twice-Told Tales* was prepared in the new and struggling *Arcturus* and not in the *Democratic Review,* where such promotion, one supposes, would have been more effective.

The second edition of *Twice-Told Tales* was published in two

16. *Arcturus* in 1842 reprinted "The White Old Maid" (there called "The Old Maid in the Winding Sheet"), first printed in the *New-England Magazine,* July 1835; "The Man of Adamant," first printed in *The Token* for 1837; and "The Canterbury Pilgrims" and "Sir William Pepperell," both first printed in *The Token* for 1833.

17. Duyckinck became the editor for Wiley & Putnam's Library of American Books. Horatio Bridge's *Journal of an African Cruiser,* edited by Hawthorne (1845) and *Mosses from an Old Manse* (1846) were both first published in this series.

volumes by James Munroe and Company of Boston. Although Haw-thorne's fiancée, Sophia Peabody, had misgivings about James Munroe,[18] he was probably a better publisher for Hawthorne than the American Stationers' Company had been. Munroe was Emer-son's publisher until about 1849 (although Emerson owned the plates of his books himself), and Munroe published some editions of the books of William Ellery Channing and of other distinguished writers. But like the other Boston bookseller-publishers, Munroe had inadequate means of marketing the books he published.

The first volume of the 1842 *Twice-Told Tales* has the same contents as the 1837 edition except for the addition of "The Toll-Gatherer's Day," first printed in the *Democratic Review*, October 1837. The second volume consists of twenty tales and sketches, and constitutes Hawthorne's second selection from his work. A number of the early pieces he was later to collect, including the four we have noticed as striking omissions from the 1837 volume, are here passed over for the second time. But, although this second volume is made up primarily of material that had been printed since the 1837 edition was made up (none later than 1839), Hawthorne did use five pieces that had appeared before 1836: "The Haunted Mind," "The Village Uncle," "The Seven Vagabonds," "The White Old Maid," and "The Ambitious Guest." The first four of these are not now considered of great importance, although one or another may be interesting as it is connected with some pattern in his work. "The Ambitious Guest" has interested generations of readers, yet Hawthorne a little be-latedly admitted it into his canon. Perhaps he had thought its irony too obvious or too labored for a collection he hoped might be his introduction to the public.

In general, just as in his first collection, Hawthorne seems to have intended to exclude the subtle and to offer a representative collec-tion. As in the 1837 collection it is the tales in Hawthorne's historical vein that most interest us, so in this new 1842 collection the four "Legends of the Province House" and "Endicott and the Red Cross" seem to have the most permanent interest. Some of Hawthorne's inclusions may puzzle us a bit, for we will feel that he had better

18. See Hawthorne's letter of September 10, 1841, in *Love Letters of Nathaniel Hawthorne* (Chicago: The Society of Dofobs, 1907), 2: 41. See also Charvat, *Literary Publishing in America*, p. 86, n. 25.

tales uncollected. There is "The Sister Years," for instance. It was first printed on January 2, 1839 in the Salem *Gazette* as a New Year's piece.[19] It is well enough done, but it is by its nature limited in interest to one time and place. Hawthorne must have included it for variety, or perhaps as evidence of his range. Or, to take another instance, "The Seven Vagabonds" seems somehow part of the scheme of "The Story-Teller," perhaps in its earliest form; the tale, in the shape we have it, is brought suddenly and unsatisfactorily to a close—it is difficult to see why Hawthorne collected this abortive tale. And that he gave the important end position to "The Threefold Destiny" certainly indicates an estimate of the tale quite different from what is likely to be ours.

At any rate, Hawthorne seems to have estimated accurately the taste of his own time in making up *Twice-Told Tales*. After the publication of the 1842 edition he was an established writer; his retrospective account of his lack of popularity in the 1851 preface hardly applies to any time after 1842. He wrote to Bridge in 1843 that "nobody's scribblings seem to be more acceptable to the public than mine," and in 1844 that he continued "to scribble tales with good success so far as regards empty praise, some notes of which, pleasant to my ears, have come from across the Atlantic"—although "the pamphlet and piratical system" forced him to work hard for small gains.[20] The reviews of the 1842 *Twice-Told Tales* were approving;[21] and in 1843 James Russell Lowell in the *Pioneer,* his new magazine, confidently described Hawthorne as "one whose pen always commands the loving admiration of his countrymen."[22]

19. Hawthorne had written a piece of this sort for the *Gazette* the preceding year: "Time's Portraiture" (in *Tales, Sketches, and Other Papers*). The pieces are in the tradition of Lamb's "All Fool's Day," and perhaps look forward to pieces like "A Select Party" and "The Hall of Fantasy" in *Mosses*.

20. Bridge, pp. 94 and 98.

21. There were notable reviews in 1842 by the two most independent-minded critics of the day: Orestes Brownson (in the *Boston Quarterly Review*) and Poe (in *Graham's Magazine*). Longfellow reviewed the second edition, as he had the first, in the *North American Review*. The reviews of both the 1837 and the 1842 *Twice-Told Tales* are surveyed in Bertha Faust, *Hawthorne's Contemporaneous Reputation* (Philadelphia, 1939), pp. 26–48.

22. *Pioneer* 1 (1843): 43. In 1845 Duyckinck felt able to say in the *Democratic Review* (16: 337) that Hawthorne's position was a "thing established."

5. LITERARY THEORY
IN PRACTICE

Which of Hawthorne's tales deserve separate discussion is not very difficult to determine. To begin with, there is the guidance of a consensus established over a century and a quarter. Then certain tales will be quite clearly convenient illustrations of Hawthorne's major preoccupations or skills, or both; and other tales will be of special interest because they fail relatively in the use of such materials or in the representation of such moral concerns as he elsewhere succeeds with.

We consider first three tales that have especially close relationships with the prescriptions of literary theorists. They may not be among the earliest-written of the tales, but one might expect the influence of literary theory to have been most effective as Hawthorne began. The three—"The Gray Champion," "The Maypole of Merry Mount," and "Endicott and the Red Cross"—are all done with remarkable economy and finish; they display a skill with the use of historical materials that Hawthorne's contemporaries who were working with them never attain. "There is a little infusion of color, a little vagueness about certain details," Henry James remarks in his *Hawthorne*, "but it is very gracefully and discreetly done, and realities are kept in view sufficiently to make us feel that if we are reading romance, it is romance that rather supplements than contradicts history." James seems to be saying that Hawthorne has found what Choate calls "the useful truth."

"THE GRAY CHAMPION"

"The later minstrels," Sir Walter Scott says, "prolonged and varied the description of events, which were no longer new in themselves."[1] In "The Gray Champion" Hawthorne is prolonging and varying a legend well known when he used it, and indeed giving it a new time and place. As we have seen, "The Gray Champion" has a particularly close relationship to the demand in early American literary theory

1. *Sir Tristrem*, p. lxxxv.

for the use of American materials; literary theorists had agreed in singling out the "Angel of Hadley" legend as eminently suitable for fictional use. Hawthorne's new setting for it in the Boston revolt against the government of Sir Edmund Andros has some connection with the history of his family. Major John Hathorne, Joseph B. Felt tells us in his *Annals of Salem,* was a member of the council of safety that took over the government after the revolt,[2] and one suspects that he had something to do with the revolt itself. The tale was first printed in the *New-England Magazine* in January 1835. Since Hawthorne used it to lead off the first edition of *Twice-Told Tales,* he must have thought highly of it.

The Angel of Hadley legend is, as the reader will remember, an episode in the romantic history of three of the judges who had condemned King Charles I to death, and who at the Restoration fled to New England and lived there, at first openly, but later, when it appeared that Massachusetts authorities would be ordered to apprehend them, in hiding. They were Edward Whalley, his son-in-law William Goffe, and John Dixwell, although Dixwell arrived in New England some time after Whalley and Goffe. All of these personages were at Hadley, Massachusetts, for a time; and according to tradition Goffe, on the occasion of an Indian attack in 1675, suddenly came out of hiding, directed the townspeople in their resistance to the attack, and then disappeared.

Hawthorne came to the legend somewhat tardily, for Sir Walter Scott and three American writers, one of whom was Cooper, had used it before him.[3] Cooper's use in *The Wept of Wish-ton-Wish* (1829) was the most recent, and Cooper had made the mysterious regicide judge a major figure in the novel. But it was Scott's use of the story that offered Hawthorne a problem in literary tact.

Scott's use of the Angel of Hadley legend comes in chapter 14 of *Peveril of the Peak* (1822) as a story the Presbyterian Major Bridge-

2. *Annals of Salem, from Its First Settlement* (Salem: W. & S. B. Ives, 1827), p. 291.

3. The Angel of Hadley legend was used, in pretty free adaptations, in James McHenry's novel *The Spectre of the Forest* (1823) and in James Nelson Barker's blank verse tragedy *Superstition* (1826, produced in 1824). McHenry and Barker both place the mysterious regicide judge in witchcraft times; Cooper involves him in King Philip's War. See G. Harrison Orians, "The Angel of Hadley in Fiction," *American Literature* 4 (1932): 257–69.

north tells to young Julian Peveril, who is from a Cavalier family. Bridgenorth tells the story from his severe point of view, and the story he tells is essentially the Angel of Hadley legend (although the identity of the regicide is confused).[4] Scott's version of the legend seems to have suggested Hawthorne's title for his tale: Scott's mysterious stranger had "locks of grey hair, which mingled with a long beard of the same colour"; "his grey eye retained all its luster; and . . . the grizzled beard covered the lower part of his face." Some persons, Bridgenorth says, "believed him an inspired champion." But, what is more important, Scott's version suggested the kind of extension of the legend Hawthorne carried out. In the course of his narration, Bridgenorth remarks: "Thou seest, young man, that men of valour and of discretion are called forth to command in circumstances of national exigence, though their very existence is unknown in the land which they are predestined to deliver." And he closes his narrative with this sentence: "Perhaps his voice may be heard in the field once more, should England need one of her noblest hearts."

Certainly if Hawthorne was to use the story he had to extend it; he could not simply tell over again the story of the saving of Hadley by the mysterious stranger's intervention. But even though Hawthorne does extend it, Scott's version is a difficulty as well as a source. Bridgenorth's narrative is a bright spot in *Peveril of the Peak*, and although we may think the novel a dull one, it is the work of Scott, who was still widely known and loved in 1835. Hawthorne invited comparison with Scott, a comparison many of his readers could be expected to make. He found a way to write a tale that could stand comparison.

Probably Hawthorne's first acquaintance with the Angel of Hadley story was by way of Scott. He may have known Ezra Stiles, *A History of Three of the Judges of King Charles I* (1794), but there is no record that he did; we do know that he was familiar with Thomas Hutchinson's history of Massachusetts. Hutchinson's telling of the legend within a long footnote on the regicide judges seems to be its first appearance in print:

4. Scott calls the mysterious stranger who comes out of hiding Richard Whalley. It was Edward Whalley, son of Richard Whalley, who was the companion of Goffe and Dixwell in New England. But both Hutchinson and Stiles, who are cited below, identify the Angel of Hadley as Goffe.

I am loath to omit an anecdote handed down through governor Leveret's family. I find Goffe takes notice in his journal of Leveret's being at Hadley. The town of Hadley was alarmed by the Indians in 1675, in the time of publick worship, and the people were in the utmost confusion. Suddenly, a grave elderly person appeared in the midst of them. In his mien and dress he differed from the rest of the people. He not only encouraged them to defend themselves; but he put himself at their head, rallied, instructed and led them on to encounter the enemy, who by this means were repulsed. As suddenly, the deliverer of Hadley disappeared. The people were left in consternation, utterly unable to account for this strange phœnomenon. It is not probable, that they were ever able to explain it. If Goffe had been then discovered, it must have come to the knowledge of those persons, who declare by their letters that they never knew what became of him.[5]

It is no wonder that this good and economical account of a distinct and striking incident persisted in New England tradition. One can see something of the influence of Hutchinson's pattern of narration coming down even through the retellings by Scott and by Hawthorne.

"The Gray Champion" tells of another near-miraculous appearance of the mysterious regicide judge, this time during the Boston revolt against the government of Sir Edmund Andros in 1689. The details of his sudden appearance and disappearance are closely parallel to those in the Angel of Hadley legend; the time of his appearance is fourteen years later, when, had he been alive, Goffe would have been about eighty-four (his dates are c. 1605–c. 1679). Even Hawthorne's decision to combine the history of the Boston revolt with the Angel of Hadley legend conforms to the thinking of the literary theorists. In 1834 Rufus Choate, in an address called "The Colonial Age of New England," made the resistance to Andros the prime example of the colonial spirit of liberty, an example to be remembered and taught to succeeding generations.[6]

5. *The History of the Colony and Province of Massachusetts-Bay*, ed. Lawrence Shaw Mayo (Cambridge, Mass., 1936), 1: 187. Hutchinson's friend, Ezra Stiles, follows Hutchinson's account closely. Compare Stiles's *A History of Three of the Judges of King Charles I* (Hartford, 1794), pp. 109–10.
6. *Addresses and Orations* (Boston, 1887), pp. 55–58.

The overthrow of the government of Sir Edmund Andros is a dramatic set of events, and might have made a good tale quite by itself. When William of Orange had landed in England late in 1688, he issued a declaration that magistrates unjustly turned out of office should resume their functions. The news reached Boston in April of 1689. The bearer of the news, John Winslow, was at once arrested, but not before the news was out. New Englanders were glad to assume that William's declaration applied to New England as well as old England, and a revolt at once ensued. Although it was successful and seems to have been without bloodshed, it was a courageous or, in Hutchinson's words, "a rash precipitate proceeding," for the Boston citizens were gambling on the success of what we now call the "Glorious Revolution." Hutchinson writes:

> The old magistrates and heads of the people silently wished,
> and secretly prayed, for success to the glorious undertaking,
> and determined quietly to wait the event. The body of the people
> were more impatient. The flame, which had been long smothered
> in their breasts, burst forth with violence, Thursday the 18th
> of April, when the governor and such of the council as had been
> most active, and other obnoxious persons, about fifty in the
> whole, were seized and confined, and the old magistrates were
> reinstated.[7]

The old magistrates made themselves into a council of safety, which became a provisional government headed by former Governor Bradstreet. In his tale Hawthorne follows the historical action with some accuracy,[8] although of course he simplifies it for dramatic effect. The first two paragraphs of the tale review the background of the action.

The tone of "The Gray Champion" may be a bit embarrassing to modern readers, but it is much like that of the nationalism of the time.

7. Hutchinson, 1: 317.
8. There is even something of a historical parallel to the role of the Gray Champion in the role Cotton Mather played in the revolt. It was Mather who wrote *The Declaration of the Gentlemen, Merchants, and Inhabitants of Boston*, a manifesto publically read at the time of the revolt. But of course Mather, associated in the minds of many readers with the idea of Puritan intolerance and superstition, could not have been used by any writer of fiction as a symbol of the American spirit of liberty.

Although the second sentence in the tale may remind one particularly of Macaulay, the tone of the tale in general is like that of the account of the revolt against Andros by George Bancroft, who was writing his account about the same time Hawthorne was writing his tale. Like Hawthorne, Bancroft suggests that this Boston rebellion was a miniature prototype of the Revolution: "Boston was the centre of the revolution which now spread to the Chesapeake; in less than a century, it would commence a revolution for humanity, and rouse a spirit of power to emancipate the world."[9]

But if the nationalism is not Hawthorne's in particular, and if Hawthorne is working with a legend well known to his readers, the narrative pattern is very much his own. Although the tale develops a single incident, it is developed in a pattern carefully calculated to an increasing tension and impressive release. The tale exhibits the adroit shifts of narrative technique that seem to belong especially to Hawthorne's early work. It exhibits, too, the kind of skillful imaginative reconstruction of Puritan society for which chapters 2 and 21–22 of *The Scarlet Letter* are distinguished.

At the end of the first two paragraphs of summary historical account, a time pattern is established with the roll of a drum at sunset. Throughout the first part of the tale, the approaching drum marks the advance of Andros and his company, which includes the well-hated Edward Randolph, the jesting Dr. Bullivant, Joseph Dudley, and, most objectionable of all to the Boston citizens, the Episcopalian clergyman of King's Chapel. The third paragraph is an account of the citizens assembled along King Street. At the beginning of the next paragraph the narrative becomes more immediate, as if by an eye-witness who can describe the order of Andros's company and report what old Governor Bradstreet says and what is said by voices out of the crowd.

But the immediacy of the narration does not preclude interpretation: the action is seen in a sharp, allegorical contrast, as sharp as that in

9. *History of the United States* (Boston, 1873), 2: 449. The tone of Bancroft's account may perhaps be suggested: he twice refers to Andros's party as "his creatures"; Bradford is "glorious with the dignity of four-score years and ten" (2: 445–47). The volumes of Bancroft's *History* began appearing in 1834.

"The Maypole of Merry Mount," and the contrast is unabashedly marked out:

> The whole scene was a picture of the condition of New England, and its moral, the deformity of any government that does not grow out of the nature of things and the character of the people. On one side the religious multitude, with their sad visages and dark attire, and on the other, the group of despotic rulers, with the high churchman in the midst, and here and there a crucifix at their bosoms, all magnificently clad, flushed with wine, proud of unjust authority, and scoffing at the universal groan.

Against that scene, so made emblematic, the mysterious stranger makes his sudden appearance, and with the single word "Stand!" and uplifted arm silences the drum and halts the march of Andros and his company.

Hawthorne's first readers, at least, would have had little doubt of the stranger's identity as soon as he addresses Andros: "I have stayed the march of a King himself, ere now. I am here, Sir Governor, because the cry of an oppressed people hath disturbed me in my secret place; and beseeching this favor earnestly of the Lord, it was vouchsafed me to appear once again on earth, in the good old cause of his saints." This, the reader is to recognize, is another appearance of him who had once appeared at Hadley, and thereafter in the work of historians and romance writers. An established legend is being extended to another time and place.

In the last paragraphs of the tale, the narrative takes a somewhat different tack. The question with which the next-to-last paragraph begins—"But where was the Gray Champion?"—is answered as if by traditional record: "Some reported . . . . Others soberly affirmed . . . . But all agreed that the hoary shape was gone." The shape may be specter or flesh—an ambiguity remains. The last paragraph begins with another question: "And who was the Gray Champion?" The answer, in highly cadenced prose, suggests that the extended legend is a continuing one, that the regicide judge has appeared in Revolutionary times, and may again appear at need, "for he is the type of New England's hereditary spirit; and his shadowy march . . . the pledge, that New England's sons will vindicate their ancestry."

There are some ironic touches—Hawthorne almost never wrote of the Puritan past without some ironic reservation. Among the assembled citizens are "the veterans of King Philip's war, who had burned villages and slaughtered young and old, with pious fierceness, while the godly souls throughout the land were helping them with prayer." The people in general expect, or fancy they expect, another St. Bartholomew's Day, or a Smithfield fire and a John Rogers "to take the place of that worthy in the Primer." The people of each parish gather round their minister, who looks upward in "apostolic dignity" as befits "a candidate for the highest honor of his profession, the crown of martyrdom." Edward Randolph would have appreciated this picture of Boston clergy smug in the role of prospective martyrs; after the revolt he wrote from jail: "All things are carried on by a furious rabble, animated by the crafty ministers."[10] Like the subtle narrative pattern, the irony in the tale is Hawthorne's own.

But to attempt to see much more of Hawthorne's own mind or psychological make-up in this tale is to ignore the tradition in which Hawthorne is working and the body of nationalistic and literary theory that urged him to work in it. If legends were in short supply in America, as writers frequently complained, here was one that Hawthorne made the most of. Were the mysterious regicide in the tale not pretty much of a stock figure, he could hardly have fulfilled his function. No other of Hawthorne's tales, not even "Endicott and the Red Cross," is written in such complete accord with the prescriptions of literary theory. The degree of Hawthorne's success with "The Gray Champion" cannot be judged entirely by our own enjoyment of the tale; we need to consider, too, how well the tale supplies those "associations of tradition" for which the young nation felt so real a need.

"THE MAYPOLE OF MERRY MOUNT"

Most literate Americans today know John Endicott chiefly as a personage made famous through "The Maypole of Merry Mount" and "Endicott and the Red Cross." But in Hawthorne's Massachusetts, Endicott was a revered figure, quite without Hawthorne's help. In

10. Quoted in Felt, *Annals of Salem*, 2nd ed. (Salem, 1845), 2: 543.

1825 (a little early) and in 1828 Salem celebrated the two hundredth anniversary of Endicott's landing: in 1825 Leverett Saltonstall was the speaker, in 1828, Joseph Story; and both of their performances, Felt tells us, "were in keeping with the eminent literature and talents of the authors."[11] George Bancroft, writing about 1834 of the founding of the Massachusetts Bay Colony, sees Endicott in this fashion:

> Endicott—who, "ever since the Lord in mercy had revealed himself unto him," had maintained the straitest judgment against the outward form of God's worship, as prescribed by English statutes; a man of dauntless courage, and that cheerfulness which accompanies courage; benevolent, though austere; firm, though choleric; of a rugged nature, which his stern principles of non-comformity had not served to mellow—was selected as a "fit instrument to begin this wilderness work."[12]

Bancroft characterizes Endicott very much as he loomed in the imaginations of the Massachusetts-born.

Hawthorne had an ancestral connection with Endicott. William Hathorne served under Endicott for thirteen years as one of the assistant magistrates for Essex County, and later during the persecution of the Quakers was in constant cooperation with Endicott's efforts to suppress the sect. In the tales here considered, Hawthorne exalts Endicott (but with ironic reservation), and in "Main Street" he paraphrases Edward Johnson's *Wonder-Working Providence* in this fashion: "The old settlers . . . like his bearded face . . . a visage resolute, grave and thoughtful, yet apt to kindle with that glow of a cheerful spirit by which men of strong character are enabled to go joyfully on their proper tasks."[13] But this passage hardly represents Hawthorne's whole judgment of the man. In "Mrs. Hutchinson" he remarks of Endicott that he "would stand with his drawn sword at the gate of heaven, and resist to the death all pilgrims thither, except they

11. Felt, 2nd ed., 2: 57.
12. Bancroft, 1: 340–41.
13. Johnson wrote that "Strong valiant John" was "a fit instrument to begin this Wildernesse-worke, of courage bold undanted, yet sociable, and of a chearfull spirit, loving and austere, applying himself to either as occasion served." Quoted in Morison, *Builders of the Bay Colony* (Boston, 1930), p. 36. Bancroft in the passage quoted above is, of course, also drawing on this passage.

travelled his own path"; and in "The Gentle Boy" he holds Endicott chiefly responsible for the extreme measures taken with Quakers. Indeed when, in "The Maypole of Merry Mount," Hawthorne calls Endicott "the Puritan of Puritans," the expression seems an evidence of a somewhat jaundiced attitude toward Puritanism itself. A writer who wished to represent early American Puritanism by an admirable example would probably pick John Winthrop as his Puritan of Puritans, as does Samuel Eliot Morison in his *Builders of the Bay Colony*.[14] Although in "Dr. Bullivant" and about twenty years later in "Main Street" Hawthorne recognizes the integrity of the spirit of the first Puritan emigrants—when "the zeal of a recovered faith burned like a lamp within their hearts"—no fiction of his, not even these two tales of the first years of the Bay Colony, represents that initial Puritan zeal.

The subject matters of both "The Maypole of Merry Mount" and "Endicott and the Red Cross" were suggested, we remember, by John Gorham Palfrey as particularly appropriate to American fiction. Both tales are closely related to the American materials discussion, although they develop from it in markedly different ways.

"The Maypole of Merry Mount," Professor Adkins thinks, "may possibly" have been one of the "Provincial Tales";[15] and if it was, it was written around the time of the anniversary year. We do know that Hawthorne withdrew one of the sources for the tale, Strutt's *Sports and Pastimes*, from the Salem Athenaeum in 1827, and another, Nathaniel Morton's *New England's Memorial*, in 1828. But he withdrew the Strutt volume again in January of 1835, perhaps when he was writing the tale, or perhaps when he was revising it.[16] The tale was first printed in 1835 in *The Token* for 1836.

The little colony at Merry Mount stands out vividly in the history

14. In "Mrs. Hutchinson" Hawthorne characterizes Winthrop as "a man by whom the innocent and guilty might alike desire to be judged; the first confiding in his integrity and wisdom, the latter hoping in his mildness."
15. "Early Projected Works of Hawthorne," pp. 130–31.
16. I cannot follow Daniel G. Hoffman's argument in *Form and Fable in American Fiction* (New York, 1961), pp. 134 ff. that "The Maypole of Merry Mount" depends on William Hone's *Every-day Book*. The argument seems to turn upon a mistaken notion that "The Maypole of Merry Mount" first appeared in *Twice-Told Tales*. It is of course true that Hawthorne was later familiar with Hone's work, but he made his first withdrawal of a volume of it in September of 1835, too late for use with "The Maypole of Merry Mount."

of early New England. First called Mount Wollaston, it was founded in 1623 by a Captain Wollaston at what is now Quincy, Massachusetts. A little later Thomas Morton, an adventurer whose life might make a picaresque novel, joined Wollaston's company. After Wollaston went to Virginia, Morton seems to have had some charge of the colony. It was he who renamed it Merry Mount, and he intended, he tells us in his *New English Canaan* (1637), to maintain there "Revels and merriment after the old English custome."[17] But he was soon in trouble with his neighbors. In 1627 a party from Plymouth cut down his maypole. In 1628 Captain Miles Standish took him into custody and he was sent back to England. The incident that Hawthorne uses in the tale took place in 1628 during Morton's absence. Endicott, who was serving as governor of the Bay Colony (then established at Salem) until Winthrop's arrival, went to Merry Mount and cut down another maypole.

Merry Mount was uncomfortably close to both the Plymouth Colony and Endicott's new Bay Colony. It is clear from William Bradford's *Of Plymouth Plantation* that, although both the Separatists and the Puritans were doubtless worried by neighbors who were Episcopalians and given to such practices as maypole rites, they had another concern. Bradford says that, in order to support the colony's "riotous prodigallitie and profuse excess," Morton, "thinking him selfe lawless," began furnishing the Indians with guns and employing them to hunt. And Felt tells us that in 1630 the Court of Assistants "passed a law for this and other plantations which forbid any to teach the Indians the use of firearms. This order appears to have had its rise principally from the conduct of Thomas Morton."[18]

Hawthorne's headnote to "The Maypole of Merry Mount" indicates something both of his sources and of the imaginative process of the tale:

There is an admirable foundation for a philosophical romance in the curious history of the early settlement of Mount Wollaston, or Merry Mount. In the slight sketch here attempted, the facts, recorded on the grave pages of our New England annalists,

17. *New English Canaan,* ed. Charles Francis Adams, Jr., for the Prince Society (Boston, 1883), p. 276.
18. *Bradford's History of Plymouth Plantation,* ed. William Thomas Davis (New York, 1908), pp. 238–39; Felt, 1st ed., p. 47.

have wrought themselves, almost spontaneously, into a sort of
allegory. The masques, mummeries, and festive customs, described
in the text, are in accordance with the manners of the age.
Authority on these points may be found in Strutt's Book of
English Sports and Pastimes.

Until a 1938 article by G. Harrison Orians, it was assumed in college
textbooks and like places that Hawthorne was drawing his material
from Bradford's *History of Plymouth Plantation* and Thomas Morton's
New English Canaan—and the assumption was indeed a natural one,
for the tale does seem to be related to both. But Morton's book was
virtually unknown in America until the edition of 1838; and Bradford's record of the Plymouth Colony remained in manuscript until
1856. Hawthorne had less to work with than we used to suppose, and
his tale is therefore the more remarkable feat of imaginative
reconstruction.

The New England annalist we are sure Hawthorne used, Nathaniel
Morton, Bradford's nephew, drew upon his uncle's manuscript.
Hawthorne found in *New England's Memorial*, first published in 1669,
a redaction of Bradford that outlines the central incident of his tale.

> That worthy gentleman, Mr. John Endicott, who brought over
> a patent under the broad seal of England, for the government
> of the Massachusetts, visiting these parts, caused the maypole
> to be cut down, and rebuked them for their profaneness,
> and admonished them that they walk better; so the name was
> again changed, and called Mount Dagon.

Another work by one of the annalists, Thomas Prince's *A Chronological History of New-England in the Form of Annals* (1736), also has
a redaction of Bradford, and it might have furnished Hawthorne with
some account of the maypole festivities (although there is no record
that he read it). Prince says that Morton and his company "set up a
May-Pole, got the Indian women to drink and dance about it, with
worse practices; as in the feasts of Flora, or the like mad Bachanalians;
and changed the name to Merry Mount, as if this jollity were to last
forever." Other annalists Hawthorne might have used furnish only like
materials.[19] But he used the material he did have with some care. He

19. See Orians, "Hawthorne and 'The Maypole of Merry-Mount,' " *Modern
Language Notes*, 53 (1938): 159–67.

does not have Thomas Morton present at the time Endicott cut down
the maypole, even though some of the annalists were not clear on
the matter. He does have Endicott arrest the revelers, but that is a
deviation from historical fact necessary to his allegorical purpose.
Needing a clergyman for his action, he introduces a historical personage, the Reverend William Blackstone, of whom he had read in Caleb
Snow's *History of Boston,* and whom William Howard Gardiner had
recommended to fiction writers as a striking figure.[20] Blackstone had
no connection with Merry Mount, and Hawthorne makes a kind of
apology in a footnote for his unhistorical use of him.

Hawthorne's headnote to the tale points to the way in which he
fleshed out the brief accounts of the annalists through Joseph Strutt's
The Sports and Pastimes of the People of England, first published in
1801. Strutt's work fits in with Hawthorne's sources in the annalists,
for Strutt's sources were often Puritan works, like Philip Stubbes's
The Anatomie of Abuses, 1583. Hawthorne's description of the maypole itself is drawn from Strutt's quotation from Stubbes:

> "Against Maie-Day, Whitsunday, or some other time of the
> year, every parish, towne, or village, assemble themselves, both
> men, women, and children; and either all together, or dividing
> themselves into companies, they goe some to the woods and
> groves, some to the hills and mountains, some to one place, some
> to another, where they spend all the night in pleasant pastimes,
> and in the morning they return, bringing with them birche
> boughes and branches of trees to deck their assemblies withal.
> But their chiefest jewel they bring from thence is the Maie-pole,
> which they bring home with great veneration, as thus—they

20. Hawthorne refers to Blackstone in *The Scarlet Letter* (chap. 7) as
"the Reverend Mr. Blackstone, the first settler of the peninsula; that half-
mythological personage, who rides through our early annals, seated on the back
of a bull." Caleb Snow says he was "a very eccentrick character" and cites
Cotton Mather, who "allows him to have been a godly episcopalian, though
he was of a particular humour, and would never join himself to any of our
churches, giving this reason for it: *I came from England, because I did not
like the* LORD-BISHOPS; *but I cannot join with you, because I would not be
under the* LORD-BRETHERN." See Caleb Snow, *A History of Boston,* 2nd ed.
(Boston: Abel Bowen, 1828), pp. 50–53. It is hard to understand why
Hawthorne, who knew about Blackstone from at least four sources, never used
him for a tale or sketch. Gardiner's account of Blackstone (or Blaxton) is in
his review of *The Spy, North American Review* 15 (1822): 257.

have twentie or fourtie yoake of oxen, every oxe having a sweete
nosegaie of flowers tied to the tip of his hornes, and these oxen
drawe home the May-poale, their stinking idol rather, which they
covered all over with flowers and hearbes, bound round with
strings from the top to the bottome, and sometimes it was
painted with variable colours, having two or three hundred men,
women, and children following it with great devotion. And thus
equipped it was reared with handkerchiefes and flagges stream-
ing on the top, they strawe the ground round about it, they bind
green boughs about it, they set up summer halles, bowers, and ar-
bours hard by it, and then fall they to banquetting and feasting,
to leaping and dauncing about it, as the heathen people did
at the dedication of their idolls. I have heard it crediblie reported, by men of great gravity, credite, and reputation, that of
fourtie, threescore, or an hundred maides going to the wood,
there have scarcely the third part of them returned home againe
as they went."[21]

But it is not only this passage that Hawthorne depends on. To watch
him weave material from Strutt into his American materials throughout the tale shows us something of his way of working. He pays careful
attention to the illustrations as well as the text. In the third paragraph of the tale he describes three of the several figures in two plates
representing fourteenth-century mummers. The "likeness of a bear
erect" and the dancing bear come from four amusing plates of dancing
bears, and "the Salvage Man" comes from another plate.[22] Hawthorne's description of the attire of the Lord of the May comes from
Strutt's account of a scene in a play by Beaumont and Fletcher, *The
Knight of the Burning Pestle*, and particularly from a bit of it Strutt
quotes: "With gilded staff and crossed scarf the May / Lord here I
stand." Strutt's quotation from the antiquarian Henry Bourne informs
Hawthorne that maypoles in England sometimes stood for the whole
year, as the maypole in Merry Mount was intended to stand.

Hawthorne has some responsibility for our image of Puritans as
"grave, bearded, sable-cloaked and steeple-crowned" personages, whose

21. Joseph Strutt, *The Sports and Pastimes of the People of England*, ed.
William Hone (London: T. T. and J. Tegg, 1833), pp. 352–53.
22. The plates are these (in the order Hawthorne describes them): 47 and
48, p. 160; 71–74, pp. 239–40; and 115, p. 373.

austerity was "sinister to the intellect, and sinister to the heart."[23] But
in "The Maypole of Merry Mount," at least, the sharp contrast between Endicott and his party on the one hand and the Cavaliers of
Merry Mount—far out Cavaliers we might call them—on the other is
inherent in the sources. The account of maypole festivities he found
in Strutt intensified the contrast. And if Hawthorne could have read
the parallel accounts in Bradford's *Of Plymouth Plantation* and
Thomas Morton's *New English Canaan*, he would have found the
contrast sharper still. Indeed, Puritan attitudes toward maypoles should
be understood not only in regard to Hawthorne's sources, but in a
larger historical context. As is clear in Bradford, maypoles were understood as holdovers from pagan fertility rites. Moreover, maypoles were
associated with a number of traditional activities the Anglican church
fostered but the Puritans abominated. Archbishop Laud's insistence
that every English clergyman read from his pulpit the declaration
in favor of traditional Sunday pastimes was an important reason for
the emigration from England of some New England clergy. The
wonder may be that Hawthorne finds idyllic qualities in the Merry
Mount festivities, and that he makes Endicott regard them, with dislike
certainly, but with a grim humor too.

In their opposition, the Puritans and the company at Merry Mount
assume symbolic qualities, but the "sort of allegory" into which the
facts in the record by the New England annalists "have wrought themselves almost spontaneously" is not a nationalistic sort. Yet, although
an imaginative procedure from "the facts" to a meaning beyond them
was natural enough to Hawthorne, it was certainly given direction
by the literary theorists who had so constantly pointed out the concrete
resources of American experience, and who were so insistent that the
fiction writer in America had his materials ready to hand.

One can see in the tale itself something of the process by which the
allegory emerged "almost spontaneously." The Lord and Lady of the
May are part of the maypole tradition, but not part of Hawthorne's
American sources in the annalists. Hawthorne's scene is "at sunset on
midsummer eve," and a marriage at Merry Mount a natural occasion
for a Lord and Lady of the May as it were out of season—although we
remember that Theseus in *A Midsummer-Night's Dream* thinks the

23. The quoted expressions are from "The Custom House" and "Main
Street."

lovers may have risen early to observe "the rite of May" (4. 1. 135). If the impetus of the tale is in the strong contrast Hawthorne finds between Puritans and the untypical Episcopalians of Merry Mount, the Lord and Lady of the May, as representatives of youth about to take on the responsibilities of maturity, preempt the final interest. The maypole itself, therefore, comes to stand not only for what Puritans must dislike in Merry Mount, but for all refusal to see human life for what it is.

In its closing paragraphs, "The Maypole of Merry Mount" becomes, in Harry Levin's fortunate phrase, "a *Paradise Lost* in provincial miniature." The last paragraphs of the tale have a pattern of imbedded allusion. In *Paradise Lost*, Michael is told how to dismiss Adam and Eve from Eden:

> Yet lest they faint
> At the sad Sentence rigorously urg'd,
> For I behold them soft'nd and with tears
> Bewailing thir excess, all terror hide.
> If patiently thy bidding they obey,
> Dismiss them not disconsolate; . . .
> [11. 108–13]

Endicott, bearing the keen sword with which he had cut down the maypole, is no bad representative of the cherubim and the flaming sword in Gen. 3:24 or of Milton's Michael. Michael is instructed, "So send them forth, though sorrowing, yet in peace" (11. 117), and so Endicott sends forth the Lord and Lady of the May. The last sentence of the tale is: "They went heavenward, supporting each other along the difficult path which it was their lot to tread, and never wasted one regretful thought on the vanities of Merry Mount." We are reminded of the closing lines of *Paradise Lost*. As Adam and Eve went forth from Eden, so the Lord and Lady of the May go into adulthood and responsibility, leaving an Eden which had never been innocent, except indeed for them.

In the course of the tale, Endicott makes a grim joke: "I thought not to repent me of cutting down a Maypole, yet now I could find in my heart to plant it again, and give each of these bestial pagans one other dance round their idol. It would have served rarely for a whipping-post!" Now the whipping post was very much a Bay Colony institution; Caleb Snow gives instances of its use in 1630.[24] But neither a whipping post nor a maypole can stand for the best in life; and we may hope that the "difficult path" the young lovers take may be something of a middle way between them. At any rate, Edgar and Edith have the pathos that belongs to youth in any time, at any place. Endicott himself smiles "at the fair spectacle of early love" and almost sighs "for the inevitable blight of early hopes."

"ENDICOTT AND THE RED CROSS"

Hawthorne's second tale with Endicott as the central figure, "Endicott and the Red Cross," was first printed in 1837 in *The Token* for 1838, too late for inclusion in the first edition of *Twice-Told Tales*. It seems likely that it was written not long before its first printing, for in it Hawthorne speaks of the 1634 incident of which he writes as "more than two centuries ago."

"Endicott and the Red Cross" deals with a single incident in the career of John Endicott. On a muster day for colonial militia in Salem in the late autumn of 1634, Endicott, then an "assistant" in the colony's government, actuated by a religious motive or scruple, rent the red cross from the English colors under which the company of militia were drilling. His act is partially understandable in the context of Puritan attitudes. For New England Puritans the use of any sacred symbol was idolatry, and they had come to think of the cross, not as a symbol of the Christian faith, but as a symbol of what they called popery. In his *New English Canaan*, Thomas Morton tells of "a silenced Minister" who, when he came to New England, brought "a great Bundell of Horne books with him and careful hee was (good man) to blott out all the crosses of them for feare least the people of the land should become Idolaters." And no edition of the *New England Primer* had the cross at the beginning of the alphabet, as English primers commonly had.[25] Governor Winthrop insisted that the name of a town, Hue's Cross, be changed to Hue's Folly.[26] But such things

24. The instances are of a man being whipped for stealing a loaf of bread, and of another for shooting a fowl on Sunday (Snow, p. 41).

25. See Paul Leicester Ford, ed., *The New-England Primer* (New York, 1899), pp. 51–52.

26. Felt, 2nd ed., 2: 493.

had no political implications; and if they were signs of a kind of bigotry, they were contained in a region provided for it. Endicott's act, however, was likely to make trouble in England.

Hawthorne might have found the story in a number of places. He is not following its ultimate source, Winthrop's *Journal*, nor does he seem to be influenced by Hutchinson's history. Since the specimens of seventeenth-century punishments in the tale undoubtedly come from Felt's *Annals of Salem*, it seems likely that Hawthorne is using Felt for the story of Endicott's act—Felt tells it sufficiently.[27] His own ancestral connection with the incident of the tale he could have gathered from Felt and Winthrop. Elizabeth Hathorne, William Hathorne's sister, had married Richard Davenport, who was ensign bearer for the Salem company of militia. It was he who was initially called before the court of assistants to answer for the defacing of the flag, although Endicott seems to have at once taken the responsibility for his act.[28]

Although Hawthorne frequently uses his historical materials with some freedom, in this tale he unabashedly twists them to his narrative purpose. The connection in the tale between Endicott's act of rending the cross from the colors and the threat of a governor general sent from England seems to have been suggested by an account in Felt of a meeting of the court about two months after the defacing of the colors, a meeting in which both matters were discussed.[29] Winthrop does record, however, in a journal entry for September 18, 1634, that he had been sent "a copy of the commission granted to the two archbishops and ten others of the council, to regulate all plantations," and advised that its intention was to force the colony "to receive a new governor, and the discipline of the church of England."[30] But the contrast—so important for the tale—between Endicott and a mild, "elderly," and sadly ironical Roger Williams has no historical justification. The historical Endicott was inspired to his act by the

27. Felt, 1st ed., pp. 72, 75, and 77–78.
28. Vernon Loggins, *The Hawthornes* (New York, 1951), p. 18; Felt, 1st ed., p. 72; *Winthrop's Journal "History of New England,"* 1630–1649, ed. James Kendall Hosmer (New York, 1908), 1: 137.
29. Felt, 1st ed., p. 73. See the entry for January 19, 1635 in Winthrop's *Journal*, 1: 145.
30. *Journal*, 1: 134–35. See Edward J. Gallagher, "History in 'Endicott and the Red Cross,'" *Emerson Society Quarterly*, no. 50 sup. (1968), pp. 62–65.

religious teaching of the historical Williams (then about thirty years old), teaching which was an important cause of Williams's banishment the next year.[31] And Hawthorne's account of various malefactors and of public punishments is, historically regarded, very curious. It comes from accounts of punishments and instruments of punishment scattered through Felt, but the instances are later—some much later—than the date of the action of the tale.[32] It must occur to even a casual reader of the tale that the little town of Salem—about six years old in 1634—had a remarkably high proportion of malefactors in its population.

Hawthorne ignores in the tale the aftermath of Endicott's act, as indeed he must if Endicott is to emerge a heroic figure. The record in Winthrop's *Journal* may seem comic to a reader today. Entries on the affair appear now and again from November 5, 1634 to May 31, 1636 and record the proceedings of the court of assistants. The matter was embarrassing to Winthrop: of course he must have respected a religious scruple, but clearly he wished that Endicott had not had this one, and there is no slightest sign that he shared it. He knew that if Endicott's act were to become known in England, it would add to his already sufficient troubles. There is every indication that the matter was considered delicate.

Finally, after a discussion from time to time during six months, a special committee, with members elected by the towns as well as members chosen by the magistrates, was formed to consider Endicott's case. Although Endicott was censured and debarred from holding public office for a year, Winthrop's summary account of the committee's resolution shows an oddly troubled and confused consensus:

31. Hutchinson, 1: 35.
32. Hawthorne used such passages as this one:

"Oct. 15th [1697]. It is enacted by the Legislature, that persons, guilty of blasphemy or denying the Canonical Books of the Bible, shall be imprisoned, not above 6 months, or be set in the pillory, be whipped, or have their tongues bored through with red hot iron, or sit on the gallows with a rope about their necks.—Not more than two of these sorts of punishments, were to be inflicted for one and the same offence."
[Felt, 1st ed., pp. 328–29]

See G. Harrison Orians, "Hawthorne and Puritan Punishments," *College English*, 13 (1952): 424–32.

> They found his offence to be great, viz., rash and without dis-
> cretion, taking upon him more authority than he had, and not
> seeking advice of the court, etc.; uncharitable, in that he, judging
> the cross, etc., to be a sin, did content himself to have reformed
> it at Salem, not taking care that others might be brought out
> of it also; laying a blemish also upon the rest of the magistrates,
> as if they would suffer idolatry, etc., and giving occasion to the
> state of England to think ill of us;—for which they adjudged him
> worthy of admonition, and to be disabled for one year from
> bearing any public office; declining any heavier sentence, because
> they were persuaded he did it out of tenderness of conscience,
> and not of any evil intent.

The discussion of the cross in the colors continued, however, and
apparently the cross was removed in new flags for the militia com-
panies. Winthrop's entry for May 31, 1636 records a compromise made
when some English shipmasters protested that the royal colors were
not flying over the fort in the harbor: "We replied, that for our part we
were fully persuaded, that the cross in the ensign was idolatrous,
and therefore might not set it in our ensign; but, because the fort was
the king's, and maintained in his name, we thought that his own colors
might be spread there."[33]

Now Hawthorne may have known all about these historical matters;
indeed his account of Endicott and the red cross in his children's book
Grandfather's Chair is closer to the historical record than is the tale.
If he chooses to disregard some historical facts—or to treat others in
a backhanded fashion—it is for the purposes of his tale. Those purposes
are difficult to define, and one is tempted by the term *ambivalence*.
But the difficulty in the tale is not so much a matter of a split emotional attitude as it is a tension between a deference to nationalistic
critical prescription on the one hand and Hawthorne's sceptical irony
on the other. Something of this tension we found in "The Gray
Champion."

The tension is evident in the structure of the tale itself. Even as
he introduces Endicott, Hawthorne describes the scene in Salem as it is
reflected on Endicott's breastplate—an odd but effective variety of

33. *Journal*, 1: 149–50, 174, and 182.

magic mirror. The description occupies about a fifth of the space of the tale. The first image is the meeting-house, with a wolf's head nailed to the porch, "according to the regular mode of claiming the bounty." The detail is from Felt;[34] the succeeding sentence—"The blood was still plashing on the door step"—is not from Felt, but Hawthorne's own suggestive addition to the image (an image he liked so well that he used it again a dozen years later in "Main Street"). And then Hawthorne continues, "There happened to be visible, at the same noontide hour, so many other characteristics of the times and manners of the Puritans, that we must endeavor to represent them in a sketch, though far less vividly than they were reflected in the polished breastplate of John Endicott."

The "characteristics of the times and manners of the Puritans"—with the exception of three sentences concerning the trainband and the few Indian spectators—turn out to be instruments of punishment, persons being punished, and persons who bear the marks of former punishments. But, besides the apparently inordinate number of persons punished, the punishments themselves are probably no more typical of the Massachusetts Bay Colony or of Puritans than they are of the age. Branding, ear cropping, the stocks and the pillory were common enough in England. Nevertheless images of cruelties are reflected on Endicott's breastplate—they are the images we see when we regard him. And they are presented—with some historical keeping but not much historical proportion—as characteristic of the Puritans.

These images are striking illustrations of Hawthorne's facility in picking up historical detail and turning it to his purposes. For example, the pair on the meeting-house steps—the Wanton Gospeller and the woman with the cleft stick on her tongue—come from widely separated passages in Felt followed pretty closely.[35] The account of

34. "March 6th [1665]. It is voted, that whoever kill any wolves within the precincts of this town, shall have 40s. each wolf, *provided they bring the heads and nayll them on the meeting house*" (Felt, 1st ed., Appendix, p. 538).

35. Felt records an order of November 4, 1646 "that if any interrupt and oppose a preacher in season of worship, they shall be reproved by a Magistrate on lecture day; and for a repetition of their offence, shall pay £5, or stand two hours on a block four feet high, with the following inscription in capitals on his breast: 'A wanton Gospeller.' " And, depending on Winthrop, he tells of Mary Oliver, who had once been whipped for reproaching the magistrates, and who "for slandering the Elders, Aug. 1646 . . . *had a cleft stick put on her*

the young woman "whose doom it was to wear the letter A on the breast of her gown" depends upon another passage in Felt, a passage which describes a Province law of 1694:

> Among such laws, passed this session, were two against Adultery and Polygamy. Those guilty of the first crime, were to sit an hour on the gallows, with ropes about their necks,—be severely whipt not above 40 stripes; and forever after wear a capital A, two inches long, cut out of cloth coloured differently from their clothes, and sewed on the arms, or back parts of their garments so as always to be seen when they were about. The other crime, stated with suitable exceptions, was punishable by death.[36]

Hawthorne's use of this passage in "Endicott and the Red Cross" adds to the tale a bit of historical color striking in itself, quite apart from his return to it for *The Scarlet Letter*.

As the tale develops, three of the figures whose images we have seen reflected on Endicott's breastplate become in their own persons a sort of chorus, speaking out their comments on Endicott's harangue and on his act, and providing an ironic counterpoint for the central action of the tale. When Endicott comes to the end of his first period, he asks why the citizens of Salem have come to the new world—"Was it not for liberty to worship God according to our conscience?" The man who wears the label "A Wanton Gospeller" interrupts: "Call you this liberty of conscience?" Roger Williams smiles sadly. But Endicott shakes his sword at the Wanton Gospeller, "an ominous gesture from a man like him," and plunges on. And at the moment Endicott rends the cross from the flag, the high churchman in the pillory cries out, "Sacrilegious wretch! thou has rejected the symbol

---

tongue for a half hour." Governor Winthrop, Felt says, thought she excelled Ann Hutchinson in zeal and eloquence (Felt, 1st ed., pp. 118, 175–76). Hawthorne would have also read of Mrs. Oliver in Snow's *A History of Boston*, see p. 94.

36. Felt, 1st ed., p. 317. The wearing of colored letters, the initials of the offenses, was a common punishment; Snow records an instance of 1634: "A man that had often been punished for drunkenness, is now ordered to wear a red D about his neck for a year" (p. 64).) Felt describes offenders being branded with the initial letters of the words for their offenses; a cloth "A" seems to have been a mitigation of what might have been a brand.

of our holy religion!" and the royalist in the stocks roars, "Treason, Treason! He hath defaced the King's banner!"

The concluding paragraph of the tale is as blatantly nationalistic as the concluding paragraph of "The Gray Champion," and like it makes the action of the tale a foreshadowing of the Revolution:

> With a cry of triumph, the people gave their sanction to one of the boldest exploits which our history records. And forever honored be the name of Endicott! We look back through the mist of ages, and recognize in the rending of the Red Cross from New England's banner the first omen of that deliverance which our fathers consummated after the bones of the stern Puritan had lain more than a century in the dust.

But before that judgment is in, Endicott has been judged intolerant, sacrilegious, and traitorous by persons who have reason enough for their judgments. What Endicott finally stands for in the reader's mind will surely not depend upon the concluding paragraph alone. His reservations have been effectively suggested to him by images on Endicott's breastplate that Endicott cannot see, by cries of protest that he will not hear. The Endicott in this tale is not the rough humorist of "The Maypole of Merry Mount"; perhaps Hawthorne intended to use the two tales to make this "Puritan of Puritans" represent both what is admirable and what is repellent in the Puritan temper.

"Endicott and the Red Cross" has, of course, a special interest for its connection with The Scarlet Letter, and it is clear that when Hawthorne wrote the initial description of Hester in the romance he had his eye on the passage in the tale describing the young woman who wore a scarlet "A" on her breast. Yet it looks as if he returned to the image by an indirect route. In 1844 he wrote in his notebook an entry that suggests he had newly come upon some record of an "A" worn as punishment: "The life of a woman, who, by the old colony law, was condemned to wear the letter A, sewed on her garment, in token of her having committed adultery."[37] But in January of 1849

37. American Notebooks, ed. Stewart, p. 107. If Hawthorne is thinking of the passage about a letter "A" in Felt, it is a province and not a colony law

he used Felt's *Annals of Salem* for "Main Street," in which he returns to Puritan punishments, and his mind must have turned to the tale he had written out of Felt some twelve years before.

"Endicott and the Red Cross" contributes not only the central symbol to *The Scarlet Letter*, but the important symbol of the pillory as well. And certainly the tale is connected with the scene in chapter 7 in which Hester is reflected on Governor Bellingham's breastplate as it hangs on a wall, reflected so that her scarlet letter assumes gigantic proportions—an ambiguous suggestion that our knowledge of the tale may help us to deal with.[38]

In the conceptual process of the romance, two other tales and "Endicott and the Red Cross" seem to coalesce. When in that tale, after his account of the woman wearing the scarlet "A," Hawthorne is led to remark that "It was the policy of our ancestors to search out even the most secret sins, and expose them to shame, without fear or favor, in the broadest light of the noonday sun," he is thinking of the spiritual implications of an enforced and public confession. Some years before he had dealt with the spiritual implications of a concealed guilt, like Dimmesdale's, in Reuben Bourne in "Roger Malvin's Burial." And in "The Prophetic Pictures," the painter's fascination in his belief that he controls the destinies of Walter and Elinor foreshadows Chillingworth's delight in the power he exercises over Dimmesdale. The major concerns of *The Scarlet Letter* had long been in the well of Hawthorne's memory; perhaps they came together without his full awareness of the process, for he seems to have written the romance with a rapidity unusual for him.

---

that is recorded there. He may be thinking of an earlier law of the colony of New Plymouth, or of a record of a woman there forced to wear an "AD" in token of adultery. See Orians, "Hawthorne and Puritan Punishments," pp. 430–31.

38. Yvor Winters's interpretation—possibly ironic in intention—of this ambiguous symbol is an example of how not to read Hawthorne, for it makes a detailed and contrived allegory out of what is effective only in its disturbing multiple suggestion. See *Maule's Curse*, reprinted in *In Defense of Reason* (Denver, n.d.), pp. 165–66.

6. THE GOTHIC NATURALIZED: "THE PROPHETIC PICTURES"

Hawthorne identifies one source for "The Prophetic Pictures" in his note to the tale: "This story was suggested by an anecdote of Stuart, related in Dunlap's *History of the Arts of Design,*—a most entertaining book to the general reader, and a deeply interesting one, we should think, to the artist." Since the tale was first printed in 1836 in *The Token* for 1837, and since Hawthorne withdrew Dunlap's book from the Salem Athenaeum twice in the first part of 1836, his note suggests that the tale was written then.[1] Although "The Prophetic Pictures" intends to be more than a tale of terror, and although its Gothic elements are skillfully made to seem at home in colonial New England, the term "Gothic tale" might apply a little more fully to it than to any other piece by Hawthorne except "Alice Doane's Appeal." It is a troublesome tale to discuss, not only because the stated moral in the last paragraph does not seem to arise from the action, but also because there is some difficulty in being sure about Hawthorne's intention.

The scene of the tale is Boston. The time of the action is indicated. The painter has done a portrait of Governor Burnet, which looks

1. The charge book, however, shows both withdrawals as of volume two; the passage Hawthorne refers to is in volume one. Dunlap's account of John Smibert (1688–1751) may possibly have suggested to Hawthorne the painter in the tale. Smibert, who was born in Scotland and had studied in Italy, arrived in America with Bishop (then Dean) George Berkeley in 1729; Berkeley considered making him a professor in his projected university. By the end of 1729 Smibert was established in Boston. He had one of the first collections of paintings in America (the painter in the tale has some very old paintings in his apartment). Smibert may have had some influence on Turnbull and Allston. The mysterious and picturesque Robert Feke, who appeared in Newport, Rhode Island and later in Boston as a portrait painter, and who seems to have disappeared about 1750, seems more like the painter in "The Prophetic Pictures" than does Smibert, but Hawthorne could have learned nothing of Feke from Dunlap save that he painted a portrait of a Mrs. Welling in 1746. See *A History of the Rise and Progress of the Arts of Design in the United States,* ed. Frank W. Bayley and Charles E. Goodspeed (Boston: C. E. Goodspeed, 1918), 1: 17–28, 30, ed.'s note 30, and the self-portrait of Feke facing 28.

as if its subject had just received "an undutiful communication from the House of Representatives." William Burnet was governor of New York and New Jersey from 1720 to 1728; after trouble with the assembly during his first governorship, he was made governor of Massachusetts and New Hampshire in 1728, and he died in 1729. Since Walter and Elinor seem to think of his portrait as that of a living person, we may suppose the action to begin in 1728 and to span many months thereafter. There is some point to this fixing of the time of the action, for the tale requires a Boston society developed enough to make use of a gifted and skillful portrait painter, but a time far enough in the past to accommodate its Gothic vein, and close enough to witchcraft times for witchcraft to be entertained as a real possibility.

There is a good deal of the conventionally Gothic in the tale. The prophetic pictures are veiled in a Radcliffean fashion:

> In course of time, Elinor hung a gorgeous curtain of purple silk, wrought with flowers and fringed with heavy golden tassels, before the pictures, under pretence that the dust would tarnish their hues, or the light dim them. It was enough. Her visitors felt, that the massive folds of the silk must never be withdrawn, nor the portraits mentioned in her presence.

Since the denouement comes with the unveiling of the portraits, the purple curtain is more than mere Gothic flavor. And the portrait painter himself—although Hawthorne's treatment of him has been taken as a serious consideration of the nature and function of the artist[2]—is very much a stock Gothic figure, a man marked out and set apart by his peculiar gifts and destiny. He sometimes uses "mystical language"; even a servant is made to recognize "that picturesque effect of which the painter could never divest himself."

These conventional Gothic elements fuse with Hawthorne's own kind of American Gothic. The citizens of Boston who keep a lingering belief in witchcraft are "inclined to consider the painter as a magician, or perhaps the famous Black Man, of old witch times, plotting mischief in a new guise." Even for the educated, the character

2. See an interesting discussion of the tale in Mary E. Dichmann, "Hawthorne's Prophetic Pictures," *American Literature* 23 (1951): 188–202. See also Millicent Bell, *Hawthorne's View of the Artist*, pp. 114–27.

of the painter is "invested with a vague awe, partly rising like smoke wreaths from the popular superstitions." It is the central irony of the tale that the painter, despite his gifts and cultivation, falls into a comparable delusion.

Now this artist is a portrait painter; Hawthorne is careful to point out that all his interest is directed to the single kind of painting.[3] Yet the tale does not reflect anything we know Hawthorne to have felt about portraits and portrait painters. When he remarks about the old portraits belonging to the Essex Historical Society, he finds their symbolic value in their age, not in the insight of the artists. In later notebook passages he records so complete a cynicism about portraits—almost a disgust with them[4]—that it looks as if, at least by 1850, Hawthorne could have given no more than a willed imaginative assent to the action of his tale, or even taken seriously the anecdote on which he says it is based.

The anecdote from William Dunlap's *History of the Rise and Progress of the Arts of Design in the United States* (New York, 1834) to which Hawthorne refers in his note to the tale is this:

> Lord Mulgrave employed Stuart to paint the portrait of his brother, General Phipps, previous to his going abroad. On seeing the picture, which he did not until it was finished, Mulgrave exclaimed, "What is this?—this is very strange!" and stood gazing at the portrait. "I see insanity in that face," was the brother's remark. The General went to India, and the first account his brother had of him was that of suicide from insanity. He had

3. Although the painter travels widely and in the wilderness, it is "seldom his impulse to copy natural scenery, except as a framework for the delineations of the human form and face, instinct with thought, passion, or suffering."

4. Hawthorne's remarks on the portraits belonging to the Essex Historical Society are in *Passages*, pp. 87–89. In 1850, in reference to a portrait of himself, he writes: "In fact, there is no such thing as a true portrait; they are all delusions, and I never saw any two alike, nor hardly any two that I would recognize merely by the portraits themselves, as being of the same man" (*Passages*, pp. 372–73). In 1857 he writes: "I have a haunting doubt of the value of portrait-painting; that is to say, whether it gives you a genuine idea of the person purporting to be represented. . . . Considering how much of his own conceit the artist puts into a portrait, how much affectation the sitter puts on . . . I question whether there is much use in looking at them" (*English Note-Books*, 2: 528–30).

gone mad and cut his throat. It is thus that the real portrait-
painter dives into the recesses of his sitter's mind, and displays
strength or weakness upon the surface of his canvass. [1: 187]

Gilbert Stuart had been able to see a latent insanity in his sitter's face;
the painter in the tale sees in Walter Ludlow's face an insanity or
an inherent evil. But beyond that, anecdote and tale do not have
much in common. In the tale the artist's prophecy is not only in the
expressions on the faces of the portraits, but also in his crayon sketch,
which is a prophecy of an action, of an attempted murder. The
portrait painter in the tale foreknows or thinks he foreknows an action.
It is likely that the tale has another impetus in Hawthorne's
reminiscence—perhaps an unconscious reminiscence—of a passage
in Scott's *The Bride of Lammermoor*. It is a passage which seems a
good deal closer to the tale than Dunlap's anecdote.

   The Bride of Lammermoor is one of the "Tales of My Landlord": in
its whimsical first chapter Peter Pattieson tells of a sketch that Dick
Tinto has done of a crucial scene in the story the novel is to tell.
Pattieson complains to Tinto that the implications of the picture are
not clear without a knowledge of the story, and Tinto replies:

> "That is the very thing I complain of; you have accustomed
> yourself so much to these creeping twilight details of yours, that
> you are become incapable of receiving that instant and vivid
> flash of conviction, which darts on the mind from seeing the
> happy and expressive combinations of a single scene, and which
> gathers from the position, attitude, and countenance of the
> moment, not only the history of the past lives of the personages
> represented, and the nature of the business on which they are
> immediately engaged, but lifts even the veil of futurity, and
> affords a shrewd guess at their future fortunes."

Now of course the lifting of the veil of futurity that Tinto is talking
about is a prophecy after the fact: the story of Ravenswood and the
Ashtons has completed itself before he makes his sketch. What
Hawthorne does is to explore the idea of a picture that prophesies a
future development in the characters of the persons represented, as the
portraits do; and then to extend that idea to a picture that lifts the
veil of futurity concerning the fortunes of the persons represented,

as Dick Tinto's sketch seems to do, and as the portrait painter's crayon sketch seems to do. What sort of moral problem would arise were such foreknowledge possible?

Hawthorne is transferring to the portrait painter's self-consideration a problem that used to be discussed frequently enough in theology, where it took some such terms as these: If we attribute to the Deity omniscience, we attribute to him foreknowledge of all events; and if he has foreknowledge, then is the Deity also necessarily responsible for all that he foresees? The problem is older than Calvinism; when, in Canto 17 of the *Paradiso*, Dante's ancestor Cacciaguida prophesies Dante's future for him, Cacciaguida says that, although all is clear in the eternal vision, yet the future does not take from that vision necessity, "any more than does a ship which is going down a stream from the eye in which it is mirrored." But the painter in "The Prophetic Pictures" cannot escape the idea that foreknowledge—or, to make up a term, forerepresentation—is foreordination:

> He had pried into their souls with his keenest insight, and pictured the result upon their features with his utmost skill, so as barely to fall short of that standard which no genius ever reached, his own severe conception. He had caught from the duskiness of the future—at least, so he fancied—a fearful secret, and had obscurely revealed it on the portraits. So much of himself—of his imagination and all other powers—had been lavished on the study of Walter and Elinor, that he almost regarded them as creations of his own, like the thousands with which he had peopled the realms of Picture.

He has skill and insight; he believes he has hit upon a single rift in the veil of futurity; and he confuses himself with God. He is not (as I read the tale) a type of the artist, but he is surely a type of the sin of pride.

Although in his delight in the penetration of other minds, the painter may be thought of as a study for Ethan Brand and for Chillingworth in *The Scarlet Letter*, in his particular manifestation of the sin of pride he may seem something of a comic figure. His transfer of a theological speculation to himself *is* comic the moment the reader's intellect is involved in perceiving it. And a sort of secondary comic apprehension on the reader's part may not have been quite beside

Hawthorne's intention. Our dominant impression of Ethan Brand, for instance, may be of a tragic figure, yet Ethan himself is made to perceive some "remote analogy" between his quest and a cur that chases his own tail in circles. The sin of pride must have something comic in it when it is perceived in others—however impervious we are to its comic aspects in ourselves.

The portrait painter says in soliloquy: "O glorious Art! thou art the image of the Creator's own. The innumerable forms, that wander in nothingness, start into being at thy beck." That may remind us of Coleridge's analogy between the Creator and the artist.[5] But Coleridge's concept of the Imagination—he calls it the esemplastic power—is wholly inapplicable to the art of the portrait painter, for Coleridge is thinking of a new combination of materials that results in a *new* unity. The familiar analogy between the Creator and his creation, on the one hand, and the novelist who imaginatively constructs a little world and peoples it with persons of his own devising, on the other, is in one way closer to the analogy the portrait painter is making. The novelist's imaginative activity involves a futurity for his persons, and the painter supposes he has the power of knowing the future of his sitters. But in any case, the painter's analogy is his own, not one to which Hawthorne gives his assent, for the narrator comments: "Reading other bosoms with an acuteness almost preternatural, the painter failed to see the disorder of his own." He exalts his powers beyond their possibility, and fails to recognize, as in other endeavors Aylmer and Ethan Brand fail to recognize, the limits on man.

Hawthorne is careful to distinguish between the painter's notion of his powers and their real limits. His skill does enable him to show forth in his sitters' portraits their essential characters. But his inference about their future does not belong to him alone or to his art; it is an inference possible to a perceptive—or only a "fanciful"—person not an artist:

> A certain fanciful person announced, as the result of much scrutiny, that both these pictures were parts of one design, and that the melancholy strength of feeling, in Elinor's countenance, bore reference to the more vivid emotion, or, as he termed it,

5. Hawthorne withdrew the *Biographia Literaria* from the Salem Athenaeum on October 29, 1836. This reading was too late to have influenced "The Prophetic Pictures," although he may have read the book earlier.

the wild passion, in that of Walter. Though unskilled in the art,
he even began a sketch, in which the action of the two figures
was to correspond with their mutual expression.

The painter merely carries out the same sort of inference in his crayon
sketch, which, we learn at the end of the tale, shows Walter about
to thrust a knife into Elinor's bosom. The painter arranges that Elinor
see his sketch; and Elinor, we are told, is aware that Walter has been
close enough to the sketch so that he might have seen it, although
she is not sure that he has. Nor can the reader be sure. In the
denouement, as Walter is about to stab Elinor, he says, "Our fate is
upon us!" But we do not know that he speaks from anything other
than some premonition of his own. Yet this doubt opens an ambiguous
and unresolved line of speculation. If Walter has seen the sketch—
even if we suppose the painter has no real insight into futurity—the
painter may still have a responsibility for Walter's attempt on
Elinor's life, so far as his sketch influences an unstable person. But
this speculation is the reader's—not the painter's.

The painter mistakes his ability to make an inference for a god-like
power over human destiny, and the irony of his delusion is that it
leads him into the crudest of superstitions, into a belief in what Sir
James Frazer designates as "Homoeopathic Magic," in which "the
magician infers that he can produce any effect he desires merely by
imitating it."[6] Nor is the painter guiltless of desiring the effect he
imitates, since he glories in his supposed power: "O potent Art! as thou
bringest the faintly revealed Past to stand in that narrow strip of
sunlight, which we call Now, canst thou summon the shrouded Future
to meet her there? Have I not achieved it? Am I not thy Prophet?"
His belief—however exalted his language—is precisely the belief of
the old women of Boston as Walter describes it: "After he has once got
possession of a person's face and figure, he may paint him in any act
or situation whatever—and the picture will be prophetic."

It is true that the painter, returning from long journeys into
unsettled territories just at the penultimate moment before the murder
his sketch had prophesied, is able to prevent it. As he approaches
Walter and Elinor he thinks, "Was not his own the form in which
that destiny had embodied itself, and he a chief agent of the coming

6. *The Golden Bough*, Abridged, (New York, 1951), p. 12.

evil which he had foreshadowed?" And he interposes himself between Walter and Elinor, "with the same sense of power to regulate their destiny as to alter a scene upon the canvass." At last he stands "like a magician, controlling the phantoms which he had evoked." On that image we leave him: in this tale so far as we can tell, as in "The Birthmark" and in "Ethan Brand," the pride of the central figure remains unrepented, indeed, undiminished. Nor does the moral with which the tale concludes have any reference to him.

But the concluding moral is very curious. We may often feel that the stated moral in one of Hawthorne's tales is less than the significance of the action; here we can hardly help seeing that the stated moral has little to do with the action: "Is there not a deep moral in the tale? Could the result of one, or all our deeds, be shadowed forth and set before us, some would call it Fate, and hurry onward, others be swept along by their passionate desires, and none be turned aside by the PROPHETIC PICTURES." But from what deed or deeds does this action result—or from what decisions? The answer can hardly be the falling in love of Walter and Elinor, for that is neither a deed nor a decision, but a manifestation of their temperaments. If we answer that the deed is the marriage of Elinor to Walter after she has been warned by the crayon sketch, it is a poor answer, since the painter's inference is not an inference from the marriage or from any deed or decision, but from his insight into the characters of the pair, characters formed long before their marriage.

The moral idea that emerges from the action seems rather different, then, from the stated moral. It is that human propensities inevitably work themselves out, that character is fate—an idea that is not really invalidated by the interruption of the murder, since the tragic results of character remain, and since no happiness can be supposed for Walter and Elinor.

"The Prophetic Pictures" is not a simple tale; yet it may be that we are too prone to see it primarily as a piece of speculation on Hawthorne's part. There is a critical trap easy to fall into in the discussion of a Hawthorne tale (and of course in the discussion of other very well-known narratives too). Any critic who discusses a tale by Hawthorne does so after he has read the tale a number of times; unless he is a very young critic he cannot remember when he first read the tale or what he felt on first reading. A critic's discussion of the tale after long familiarity with it and repeated readings may find nuances that it is well to find; but he may also be unable to realize what Hawthorne was probably most concerned with: the response of the reader to his first reading.

It may be well, therefore, to try to think what the effect of the tale would be at first reading. Would the tale not be first of all a tale of terror? The portrait painter is a recognizable Gothic figure and the initial insistence upon his skill and power is designed to build up a foreboding in the reader. Then, as the tale proceeds, a realization of the nature of the painter's crayon sketch takes shape in the reader's mind in increasing fullness, so that the final scene comes as confirmation of a carefully built up expectation. The effect of the tale depends upon foreshadowing and then fulfillment. But that effect is a first effect; it can be strongly felt only on first reading; and it may be entirely lost in a number of readings. Now of course if that were all, if there were no other interests, the tale would not bear rereading. But one's very familiarity with the tale may obscure the primary interest, and obscure something of the terror that belongs to the painter, whose great powers are so corrupted in his pride.

7. THE AIR OF ANTIQUITY: "LEGENDS OF THE PROVINCE HOUSE"

In April of 1837 Hawthorne received a letter that must have gratified and surprised him. It was from John L. O'Sullivan, who wrote to solicit Hawthorne's contributions to the new magazine he was planning, *The United States Magazine and Democratic Review*. In his letter O'Sullivan says that "this magazine is designed to be of the highest rank of magazine literature," that it will pay three and even five dollars a page for contributions (princely sums for the time if ever actually paid), and that "it will afford to Mr. Hawthorne what he has not had before, a field for the exercise of his pen, and the acquisition of distinction worthy of the high promise which the editors

of the 'United States Magazine' see in what he has already written."
This grandiose letter is charmingly characteristic of the twenty-
three-year-old O'Sullivan, who later described himself and his partner,
S. D. Langtree, as "both very young, very sanguine, and very democratic" at the time of the founding of their magazine. The letter was
the beginning of a long connection between Hawthorne and
O'Sullivan and his magazine. It printed altogether twenty-five
Hawthorne pieces, and Hawthorne and O'Sullivan became close
friends. O'Sullivan was "Uncle John" to Hawthorne's children, and
he interested himself in political appointments for Hawthorne. During
his Liverpool consulate, Hawthorne seems to have lent O'Sullivan a
large sum of money.

The *Democratic Review* was rather a distinguished publication.
Bryant, Paulding, Whittier, Longfellow, Lowell, Miss Sedgwick, the
young "Walter" Whitman, and others whose names we still
remember wrote for it. But since O'Sullivan was his own chief
political writer as well as an editor, it was colored by his own views.
He intended the magazine, he said, "to strike the hitherto silent
string of the democratic genius of the age and country." He was a
militant nationalist; indeed he was twice indicted for violations of neu-
trality laws in his support of filibustering expeditions against Cuba.
James W. Patton says his magazine "became the mouthpiece for the
exuberant nationalism of the period, glorifying all things American
and predicting the expansion of the United States till its boundaries
should embrace the North American continent and Cuba as well."
It is believed that O'Sullivan was the first to use the expression
"manifest destiny."[1]

Now Hawthorne's four "Legends of the Province House" take some
color from their environment in the *Democratic Review*; indeed
they are so clearly calculated to be pleasing to O'Sullivan that one
wonders if he had not asked for such a series. At any rate, Hawthorne
had surely read O'Sullivan's pretentious introduction to his magazine
in its preliminary issue, October 1837, which concludes with these
paragraphs:

1. The account of O'Sullivan and the *Democratic Review* is drawn from
Julian Hawthorne, *Hawthorne and His Wife*, 1: 159–60; Mott, *A History
of American Magazines*, 1741–1850, pp. 677–781; and James W. Patton's
article on O'Sullivan in the *Dictionary of American Biography*.

The anti-democratic character of our literature, then, is a main cause of the evil of which we complain; and this is both a mutual cause and effect, constantly acting and re-acting. Our 'better educated classes' drink in an anti-democratic habit of feeling and thinking from the copious, and it must be confessed delicious, fountain of the literature of England; they give the same spirit to our own, in which we have little or nothing that is truly democratic and American. Hence this tone of sentiment of our literary institutions and of our learned professions, poisoning at the spring the young mind of our people.

If the "United States Magazine and Democratic Review" shall be able, by the influence of example and *the most liberal* encouragement, to contribute in any degree towards the remedy of this evil, (as of the other evils in our institutions which may need reform,) by vindicating the true glory and greatness of the democratic principle, by infusing it into our literature, and by rallying the mind of the nation from the state of torpor and even of demoralization in which so large a proportion of it is sunk, one of the main objects of its establishment will have been achieved. [1: 15]

Hawthorne's four "Legends," which appeared so early in the magazine's history—three of them within its first year—seem Hawthorne's effort to help fulfill O'Sullivan's aim, although the effort is of course made in Hawthorne's own way.[2]

2. Hawthorne would have been willing to assent so far as he could to O'Sullivan's wishes. The *Democratic Review* seemed to offer him the best opportunities for periodical publication he had ever had. He was ambitious for political appointment, and indeed the publication of his sketch of Jonathan Cilley in the *Democratic Review*, September 1838, recommended him to Democratic politicians. He could hope that O'Sullivan would further his career as a political appointee, and O'Sullivan later made every effort to do so. In 1845, for example, O'Sullivan wrote to Hawthorne: "For the purpose of presenting you more advantageously I have got [Evert A.] Duyckinck to write an article about you in the April Democratic. . . . By manufacturing you thus into a Personage, I want to raise your mark higher in Polk's appreciation." Quoted in John Stafford, *The Literary Criticism of "Young America"* (New York, 1967), p. 10. Duyckinck's article appears in 16: 376–84. Longfellow, in a letter to George W. Greene in 1839, when the *Democratic Review* was not yet two years old, complains: "The *Loco-focos* are organizing a new politico-literary system. They shout Hosannas to every *loco-foco* authorling,

The "Legends" are related to the literary nationalism prescriptions that had been before effective on Hawthorne's work, but they have a decided cast of doctrinaire nationalism of O'Sullivan's sort. When, in his playful preface to "Rappaccini's Daughter," Hawthorne pretends that he is a French writer, he makes the *Democratic Review* into *La Revue Anti-Aristocratique*, and the jest has its point. The reader who finds the nationalistic conclusions to "The Gray Champion" and "Endicott and the Red Cross" a little shrill will find passages in the "Legends" strident. Hawthorne was himself a Democrat, of course, and owed his three political appointments to the party; in "The Custom House" he refers to himself as "the Locofoco Surveyor." Yet at bottom his democratic thinking was doubtless different from O'Sullivan's; for Hawthorne the basis of human equality is mankind's heritage of mortality and sin. Something of his own attitude may emerge in a doctrinaire fashion in "Lady Eleanore's Mantle."

"Howe's Masquerade," the first of the "Legends," appeared in the *Democratic Review* for May 1838; "Edward Randolph's Portrait" and "Lady Eleanore's Mantle" appeared in the same year; the last legend, "Old Esther Dudley," in January 1839. The "Legends" are frame stories, and in each the person to whom the tale is ascribed is established. These storytellers are Mr. Bella Tiffany for the first three and another called "the old loyalist" for "Old Esther Dudley." They tell their stories in the bar-room of the Province House, for the former residence of the royal governors of Massachusetts has become an inn. They are not, however, narrators of the tales in the technical sense; Hawthorne, having characterized them, does not use them as narrators. It is made clear in the frame of each tale that it is to be taken as Hawthorne's redaction of a tale he has heard, that we are to think of the author as narrator. In the frame of "Old Esther Dudley," for instance, Hawthorne remarks that "the sentiment and tone of the affair may have undergone some slight, or perhaps more than slight, metamorphosis, in its transmission to the reader through the medium of a thorough-going democrat."

"Howe's Masquerade" and "Old Esther Dudley" have their actions

---

and speak coolly of, if they do not abuse, every other. They puff *Bryant* loud and long; likewise my good friend Hawthorne of 'Twice-told Tales'; also a Mr. O'Sullivan . . . ." Quoted in *American Notebooks*, ed. Stewart, p. 288.

during the Revolution; "Edward Randolph's Portrait" in 1770, and "Lady Eleanore's Mantle" in 1721. Hawthorne is somewhat ill at ease in historical narrative as late as Revolutionary times. He remarks his discomfort in the frame of "Howe's Masquerade": "In truth," he says, "it is desperately hard work, when we attempt to throw the spell of hoar antiquity over localities with which the living world, and the day that is passing over us, have ought to do."

The spell of hoar antiquity was not only part of Hawthorne's literary habit; it was, as we have seen, part of the concept of fiction in the period in which that habit was formed. But some of the historical personages in three of the legends had been living within the memory of Hawthorne's older contemporaries; the Province House still stood, and some of his readers might have remembered it before the row of shops that screened it from the street was built. And if 1770, say, seems antiquity to us, it did not to Hawthorne's first readers.

Sir Walter Scott remarks in *The Bride of Lammermoor* (chap. 4) that tradition is "always busy, at least in Scotland, to grace with a legendary tale a spot in itself interesting." Hawthorne in his "Legends" is busy about giving tradition a hand. Henry James, writing in his *Hawthorne* about forty years after the first publication of the "Legends," sympathetically perceives that purpose and says in praise of it:

> There is no genuine lover of the good city of Boston but will feel
> grateful to him for his courage in attempting to recount the
> "traditions" of Washington Street, the main thoroughfare of
> the Puritan capital. . . . The Province House disappeared some
> years ago, but while it stood it was pointed to as the residence
> of the Royal Governors of Massachusetts before the Revolution.
> I have no recollection of it, but it cannot have been, even from
> Hawthorne's account of it, which is as pictorial as he ventures
> to make it, a very imposing piece of antiquity. The writer's
> charming touch, however, throws a rich brown tone over its
> rather shallow venerableness.

For that "rich brown tone" Hawthorne went to the Gothic convention. We remember that the Gothic was a recognized means for giving the recent and familiar romantic associations and an air of antiquity. Gothic associations pervade all four of the "Legends."

"HOWE'S MASQUERADE"

"Howe's Masquerade" is an exercise in the Gothic convention of the "explained supernatural," except that, as is characteristic of Hawthorne's use of the convention, the explanation is not quite complete. It is a compact little tale; it represents a half-hour at a masked ball given by Sir William Howe at the Province House "during the latter part of the siege of Boston."

To Sir William's amazement, there appears at his ball a "mysterious pageant," a procession of figures representing the governors of Massachusetts from Endicott on, figures who, one by one, descend the grand staircase of the Province House and go outside into the street, where an unseen military band is playing a funeral march. Among the guests at Sir William's ball are Colonel Joliffe, an old man of "known whig principles," and his granddaughter; they are—as the reader is allowed to infer from the beginning—cognizant of the origin of the mystery. For the figures of the first part of the procession, those representing the governors of the colony and the early governors of the province, Colonel Joliffe acts as a sort of chorus, identifying the persons represented and commenting on the careers of some of them.

The figures representing later governors—Shirley, Pownall, Bernard, and Hutchinson—have "succeeded in putting on some distant portraiture of the real personages," and are recognizable to some of the guests. The last figure has his face concealed, but he is wearing an old military cloak of Sir William's, and simulates his gait and bearing. Sir William challenges the figure, but when he reveals his face, Sir William recoils in consternation and drops his sword. As the figure is about to depart, he stamps his foot on the threshold and lifts his hands in despair, just as, we are told, Sir William Howe was soon to do at his final departure from the Province House. But what Sir William sees when the figure representing him reveals his face, we are never told.

Hawthorne, characteristically, endeavors to make the tale "a legend prolonging itself," and concludes it:

But superstition, among other legends of this mansion, repeats the wondrous tale, that on the anniversary night of Britain's discomfiture the ghosts of the ancient governors of Massachu-

setts still glide through the portal of the Province House. And,
last of all, comes a figure shrouded in a military cloak, tossing
his clinched hands into the air, and stamping his iron-shod boots
upon the broad freestone steps, with a semblance of feverish
despair, but without the sound of a foot-tramp.

The tale economically achieves its mystery and suspense; it is
technically a success. And it has a special interest for the student of
Hawthorne, since the procession of past governors represents so
much of the history with which he concerned himself in his fiction.
But the contriving of a continuing legend that should represent not
so much American ideals or achievement as British humiliation is
a sort of nationalism his work had not before displayed.

"EDWARD RANDOLPH'S PORTRAIT"

Of the four "Legends," it is the second, "Edward Randolph's Portrait,"
that seems particularly to require the attention of the student of
Hawthorne. A consideration of it is instructive because in it Hawthorne is unable to make an adequate use of striking event, and because
he fails relatively in his use of a Gothic device with which he elsewhere
succeeds. The source of the tale is Thomas Hutchinson's own account
of his dilemma about the garrisoning of Castle William. The
Gothic device is the well-worn one of the mysterious portrait.

The matter of the garrisoning of Castle William was important
among the events leading to Revolution. In 1770 the king ordered
a garrison of royal troops into Castle William in Boston Harbor.
The order was greatly resented by the citizens, for Castle William
had always been garrisoned by militia and supported by the province.
Benjamin Franklin made the order one of the "rules" in his ironic
satire "Rules by Which a Great Empire May Be Reduced to a Small
One" (1773):

> XVIII. If any colony should at their own charge erect a fortress
> to secure their port against the fleets of a foreign enemy, get
> your Governor to betray that fortress into your hands. Never
> think of paying what it cost the country, for that would look,
> at least, like some regard for justice; but turn it into a citadel to
> awe the inhabitants and curb their commerce. If they should

have lodged in such fortress the very arms they bought and used to aid you in your conquests, seize them all; it will provoke like *ingratitude* added to *robbery*. One admirable effect of these operations will be, to discourage every other colony from erecting such defences, and so your enemies may more easily invade them; to the great disgrace of your government, and of course *the furtherance of your project.*

And the Castle William affair seems to be alluded to in one of the "Facts . . . submitted to a candid world" in the Declaration of Independence: King George "has affected to render the Military independent of and superior to the Civil Power."

In Thomas Hutchinson's account of his conduct in the matter of the garrisoning of Castle William, Hawthorne had an excellent source. Hutchinson's account is manly and straightforward; although he had to decide the matter, he tries to write with a historian's objectivity. The implications of his account are very different from those of the tale Hawthorne draws from it.[3]

Hutchinson records a painful moral decision, and the distress of mind that had accompanied it shows through the historian's reserve. When the king's order came, Hutchinson, though nominally lieutenant-governor, had full responsibility, for Governor Francis Bernard was in England. Hutchinson had long been a loyal servant of the king through the greatest difficulties. Five years before, a mob had attacked his home and destroyed his property and papers, and his office was becoming increasingly onerous. But he was deeply identified with Massachusetts. He was born in Boston, a descendant of Ann Hutchinson. He was a graduate of Harvard; he had devoted himself for years to the history of the colony and province. He believed King George's order ill-advised and indeed unjust. Yet he was the royal governor, and he realized that he had no time to protest to his superiors or to temporize—he would lose the power of any action. He acted with decision, delivered the keys of Castle William to the appointed officer, and stood off the protests of the assembly. "This was one of the most difficult affairs to manage," he remarks mildly, "that happened during the lieutenant-governor's administration."

3. See Hutchinson, 3: 221–24.

Now here, one would suppose, is a moral dilemma that should have interested Hawthorne. If Hutchinson's statement of it is dispassionate, the dilemma is none the less real:

> The charter reserved to the governor the power, which constitutionally was in the king, over all forts and garrisons in the province. In the exercise of this power, there was no doubt that the governor was subject to the directions of the king, but it might well be doubted, whether, consistently with the charter, he could divest himself of the supreme command of any fort, by assigning it over to any other person.

Hutchinson did manage the transfer of the garrison in such fashion that he as governor kept at least a nominal control over the fort. But that did not at all satisfy the assembly, which sent him "a very angry message, signifying their opinion, that very false representations must have been made to their sovereign," and which conducted its own investigation of the manner of the transfer of the garrison.

Hutchinson had no course of conduct that could seem to him wholly good. His account of his own dilemma offers the opportunity for as sympathetic a representation of a moral problem as that Hawthorne had accomplished some years earlier in the first episode of "Roger Malvin's Burial." But in "Edward Randolph's Portrait" he recognizes no more of the moral problem in Hutchinson's decision than Franklin does in his satire.

Yet Hawthorne does not fail by inattention to his source. Even one of the touches of irony in the piece depends upon Hutchinson's account of the effort to force him "to appoint a day of solemn prayer and humiliation throughout the province." The venerable Selectman in the tale says: "We will strive against the oppressor with prayer and fasting, as our forefathers would have done. Like them, moreover, we will submit to whatever lot a wise Providence may send us,—always, after our own best efforts to amend it." And in general the tale is true to the historical circumstances, except that, for reasons of dramatic economy, the Province House and not Castle William is made the scene of the transfer of command. It is the moral essence of the source that does not come through in the tale.

Part of Hawthorne's difficulty may have been a feeling that a sympathetic representation of Thomas Hutchinson's dilemma would be unacceptable to his readers or—more probably—to the *Democratic Review*. The attitude in the tale toward Hutchinson as loyalist seems entirely ill-suited to Hawthorne. In *Grandfather's Chair*, when Grandfather's young auditors ask him about some loyalists, including Hutchinson, Grandfather is made to say:

> You must not think that there is no integrity and honor except among those who stood up for the freedom of America. For aught I know, there was quite as much of these qualities on one side as on the other. Do you see nothing admirable in a faithful adherence to an unpopular cause? Can you not respect that principle of loyalty which made the royalists give up country, friends, fortune, everything, rather than be false to their king? It was a mistaken principle; but many of them cherished it honorably, and were martyrs to it.[4]

Had the narrator of "Edward Randolph's Portrait" had Grandfather's enlightenment, we should have had a quite different tale.

But another part of Hawthorne's difficulty with the tale seems to be the necessity he felt to throw "the spell of hoar antiquity" over the action. He says in the frame that the tale has "a tinge of romance approaching to the marvellous," but the marvelous, such as it is, is more than a tinge; and the matter of the mysterious portrait of Randolph connects the tale with New England antiquity, for Randolph flourished more than a century and a half before the date of its publication. Hawthorne's readers would have remembered him as a personage in "The Gray Champion." Indeed, a sentence in that tale may be the germ of this one. When Hawthorne is describing the progress of Andros and his party, he writes, "At his right hand rode Edward Randolph, our arch-enemy, that 'blasted wretch,' as Cotton Mather calls him, who achieved the downfall of our ancient government, and was followed with a sensible curse, through life and to his grave." Hawthorne's use of Randolph as a sort of bogeyman is historically appropriate: he became, Caleb Snow says, "infamous and hated by the people as a spy upon their liberties; whose business it was, they said, to go up and down seeking to devour them."[5] Specifically, he incurred the colonists' hatred in his—not always

4. *Grandfather's Chair*, p. 602.
5. Snow, p. 168.

successful—attempts to collect the king's customs, and in his efforts to get the colony's charter annulled. Hawthorne may have remembered that Randolph had especially complained in England of his ancestor, Major William Hathorne, and of William's son, Colonel John Hathorne.[6]

Since Hawthorne knew well how worn and frayed the Gothic property of the mysterious portrait was, he labored to give the mystery of this one legendary connections. One is the legend that the portrait, too blackened to be recognizable, was "an original and authentic portrait of the Evil One, taken at a witch meeting near Salem." Another legend is that a familiar spirit "abode behind the blackness of the picture," appearing to the royal governors at times of public calamity. Hutchinson as historian, however, identifies the portrait as that of Randolph, and suggests that Randolph's evil reputation was largely the creation of Cotton Mather.

Hawthorne handles this mysterious portrait in the convention of the "explained supernatural." We are asked to suppose at the end of the tale that Hutchinson's niece, Alice Vane, has effected a temporary restoration of the portrait and then covered it with a black silk veil. (It had had the remnant of a black veil when it was first described—as if to make the Radcliffean connection unmistakable.)[7] Now to suggest that decades of grime can be cleansed away only temporarily in a restoration lasting less than a day is perhaps in the Radcliffean tradition of lame explanations. But for Hawthorne, who manages the explained supernatural in "The Gray Champion" and in "Drowne's Wooden Image" with so much more grace, the ineptness seems almost contemptuous.

In the denouement of the tale itself there is a like suggestion of contempt. As Hutchinson is about to sign the order giving over Castle William to the king's troops, Captain Lincoln, the commander of the militia at Castle William, points to the portrait, now covered by the black silk veil. When Hutchinson calls Alice, she snatches away the veil, and the portrait appears in all its horror, so that Hutchinson trembles to see the revealed visage of Randolph, with eyes of "a peculiar glare." But Hutchinson, putting aside the warnings of Alice and the old Selectman, says, "Away! Though yonder senseless

6. Loggins, pp. 86 and 105.
7. See *The Mysteries of Udolpho*, Pt. 1, chap. 19 and Pt. 2, chap. 55.

picture cried 'Forbear!'—it should not move me," and signs the order. Now when Hawthorne makes Hutchinson thus almost explicitly recognize the Gothic nature of the action and its literary antecedents,[8] he risks—and surely consciously—breaking the illusion he has seemed at some pains to build up.

It is as if Hawthorne were somehow impelled to an ironic recognition of how worn and conventional the whole matter of the portrait is, and impelled to deprecate its combination with a historical action that deserved a better treatment. The impression of a touch of contemptuous irony is made stronger by the extravagance of the concluding sentences of the tale, in which it is reported that Hutchinson complained on his death bed that "he was choking with the blood of the Boston Massacre," and that he had the frenzied look of Edward Randolph. It is difficult to believe that Hawthorne, who had celebrated Endicott's rending of the cross from the English colors with such complex ironic reservation, did not feel in some comparable fashion here.

"LADY ELEANORE'S MANTLE"

The third of the "Legends," "Lady Eleanore's Mantle," is in an American Gothic tradition; it stands between Charles Brockden Brown's *Arthur Mervyn* (1799), a story of the horrors of yellow fever, and Poe's "The Masque of the Red Death" (1842). "Lady Eleanore's Mantle" in its concern with smallpox has a historical inception. The time of the action is fixed as early in Governor Shute's administration (1716–1728). According to Caleb Snow's *History of Boston*, the smallpox was brought to Boston in 1721 "by the Sal Tortugas fleet, in April of that year. More than half of the inhabitants were probably liable to it."[9] The year 1721 is also the year of Dr. Zabdiel Boylston's introduction in Boston of inoculation for smallpox, a matter that Hawthorne describes in *Grandfather's Chair*. In the tale it is Lady Eleanore and not the Sal Tortugas fleet that brings the plague.

Lady Eleanore, a young Englishwoman of great beauty, is the guest

8. In Hawthorne's whimsical catalog of the most conventional of Gothic properties in "Dr. Heidegger's Experiment," it is recorded that when a chambermaid was about to dust a book of magic, a bust of Hippocrates said "Forbear!"
9. Snow, p. 218.

of Governor Shute in the Province House. She is the victim of an
inordinate pride of birth, wealth, and person. She is clearly intended to
be the representative of aristocracy and its evils; in an emblematic
scene she treads on Jervase Helwyse,[10] a young man driven mad by his
love for her and by her scorn. Yet she is hardly a successful symbol.
Her manifestation of the sin of pride seems more vulgar than aristocratic; and her pride is so obviously repellent that its melodramatic
representation seems gratuitous. It is as if one were to explain in great
detail and with portentous earnestness that—let us say—arson is un-
desirable. In Hawthorne's great tales on the sin of pride, pride devas-
tates persons potentially good.

Although "Lady Eleanore's Mantle" is an overt and obvious allegory,
it is everywhere interpreted—by the narrator, by a Dr. Clarke who
functions as chorus, and indeed by the title character herself. The
irony in the tale—which one supposes might have been effectively
handled—is so labored that it loses its effect as irony. It is Lady
Eleanore's embroidered mantle, which she wraps about herself as a sign
of her insulation from less fortunate mortals, that carries the contagion of the smallpox. If the reader were allowed to perceive for himself
that retribution is carried in the very fabric of the sin, there might
have been an effective irony. But the significance is labored out of the
symbol, and the irony turned to preachments. Dr. Clarke predicts
the catastrophe: "She seeks to place herself above the sympathies of our
common nature, which envelops all human souls. See, if that nature
do not assert its claim over her in some mode that shall bring her level
with the lowest!" When the catastrophe has come, the narrator
taunts Lady Eleanore: the contagion has been "traced back to a lady's
luxurious chamber—to the proudest of the proud—to her that was so
delicate, and hardly owned herself of earthly mold—to the haughty
one, who took her stand above human sympathies—to Lady Eleanore!"
And Lady Eleanore herself is made to say at last: "I wrapped myself
in PRIDE as in a MANTLE, and scorned the sympathies of nature; and
therefore has nature made this wretched body the medium of a dreadful
sympathy."

The mad lover carries a burden of secondary symbolism. Jervase

10. Hawthorne takes this name from that of an ancestral connection,
Gervais Helwyse, to whom Major William Hathorne left a farm in his will on
condition he come to New England to live. See Loggins, p. 95.

Helwyse steals a goblet of wine in the silver service of the Old South Church—"for aught that could be known, it was brimming over with the consecrated wine"[11]—and presses it upon Lady Eleanore, who only draws her mantle more closely around her, so as to shroud herself within it. And after Lady Eleanore is stricken, Helwyse imagines her triumphing over death itself. The introduction of a madman as a figure in moral allegory may add a certain Gothic terror, but it is not likely to make the allegory more meaningful. Although it was probably not Hawthorne's intention, the tale turns out to be more successful as a tale of terror than as an allegory: the horror of the plague does come though.

Yet the tale expresses convictions that Hawthorne seriously held and elsewhere impressively embodied. We are forced to ask why, when the tale is so close to the center of his belief and thought, it needs to be so labored and strident. The answer may be that the purposes of the "Legends" led him to give what was a moral conviction a political cast, and to seem to say what he could not have believed, that the sin of pride is a matter of class and aristocratic pretension to be countered by democratic dogma. A sentence early in the tale, as Lady Eleanore is being introduced to the reader, suggests a doubt on Hawthorne's part about his own intention: he writes: "Judging from many traditionary anecdotes, this peculiar temper was hardly less than a monomania; or, if the acts which it inspired were those of a sane person, it seemed due from Providence that pride so sinful should be followed by as severe a retribution." Since the retribution is so severe, Hawthorne seems to expect us to consider Lady Eleanore sane; but he has failed to make her representative.

"OLD ESTHER DUDLEY"

"Old Esther Dudley," the last of the four "Legends," is, but for a doctrinaire concluding passage, a fine tale.[12] It too has a flavor of the

11. Since Hawthorne is usually fairly careful with historical keeping in the detail of his stories, this matter in the tale is surprising. It seems impossible that in the early eighteenth century anyone would even suppose there was reserved Communion wine to steal in the Old South Church.

12. Hawthorne wrote in his notebook in 1837 this story suggestion: "A partially insane man to believe himself the Provincial Governor or other great official of Massachusetts. The scene might be the Province House" (*Passages,*

Gothic, but the Gothic elements in the tale come to the reader always in unvouched-for report, and they are whimsical and even wistful in their effect. The tale is the one tale "the old loyalist" tells; and even in the *Democratic Review* Hawthorne can allow a sympathy on the part of his readers for a loyalist in the person of a lady aged, infirm, and of no political importance.

The events of "Old Esther Dudley" follow shortly after those of "Howe's Masquerade." When Sir William departs from the Province House, he leaves behind old Esther, a poor gentlewoman who has been a sort of pensioner there. She is determined to stay until the king gets his own again and the royal governor returns. The new authorities are glad enough to allow her to stay in the empty mansion as caretaker; and she remains, loyal to her king and her convictions, almost able to make the past the present.

We learn of her life in the Province House mostly by report. The gossips whisper strange fables about her in all the chimney corners of the town:

> Among the time-worn articles of furniture that had been left in the mansion there was a tall, antique mirror, which was well worthy of a tale by itself, and perhaps may hereafter be the theme of one. . . . It was the general belief that Esther could cause the Governors of the overthrown dynasty, with . . . all the figures that ever swept across the broad plate of glass in former times—she could cause the whole to reappear, and people the inner world of the mirror with shadows of old life.

From this mirror, too, it is said, Esther summons a black slave of Governor Shirley's and sends him to invite guests from the tombs to meet with her at midnight, when Esther mingles with them "as if she likewise were a shade." More certainly, she sometimes entertains a few old tories left in Boston. And children, even children of the new time, become, under the spell of her stories, children of the past, and suppose they see Governor Belcher sitting in the Province House—only, when the story is ended, the governor seems to fade from his chair. Once she illuminates the Province House for the king's birthday.

Old Esther is always able to think of any British defeat she vaguely

---

p. 110). This suggestion, so unpromising in itself, seems to be the germ of the tale.

hears of as a British victory; and when she hears that a governor is again to live at the Province House, she supposes of course that he will be a royal governor. When John Hancock comes to take over, therefore, she greets him as a loyal servant rendering up her charge. Unhappily, before she dies, she recognizes Hancock as what is to her a usurper. And there the tale might have ended.

But this last of the four "Legends" is apparently intended to be in some sort a conclusion for them all, and the tale ends with an oration—Tudor would have called it a harangue—by the new governor:

> Alas, venerable lady! Your life has been prolonged until the world has changed around you. You have treasured up all that time has rendered worthless—the principles, feelings, manners, modes of being and acting, which another generation has flung aside—and you are a symbol of the past. And I, and these men around me—we represent a new race of men—living no longer in the past, scarcely in the present—but projecting our lives forward into the future. Ceasing to model ourselves on ancestral superstitions, it is our faith and principle to press onward, onward! Yet let us reverence, for the last time, the stately and gorgeous prejudices of the tottering Past!

As Hancock speaks, old Esther sinks down by one of the pillars of the mansion, murmuring, "I have been faithful unto death. God save the King!" And Hancock says solemnly, "We will follow her reverently to the tomb of her ancestors; and then, my fellow-citizens, onward—onward! We are no longer children of the Past!"

For any reader with a knowledge of Hancock's character and career, his claim to represent a new race of men will have some irony. But perhaps that is not important, for what his speech sounds like is the writings of John L. O'Sullivan, even like a passage in his introduction to his magazine:

> The eye of man looks naturally *forward*; and as he is carried onward by the progress of time and truth, he is far more likely to stumble and stray if he turn his face backward, and keep his looks fixed on the thoughts and things of the past. We feel safe under the banner of the democratic principle, which is borne onward by an unseen hand of Providence, to lead our race toward the high destinies of which every human soul contains the

God-implanted germ; and of the advent of which—certain,
however distant—a dim prophetic presentiment has existed,
in one form or another, among all nations in all ages. [1: 9]

Indeed, Hancock's speech, however much in accord with the idea of
manifest destiny and the spirit of the *Democratic Review,* is hardly
consonant with Hawthorne's essential attitudes.

For of all our early nineteenth-century writers, it is Hawthorne, as
"Earth's Holocaust" shows us, who is at bottom the most thoroughly
sceptical of the idea of progress.[13] And of all our writers it is he who, in
The House of the Seven Gables, has taught us most about the ways
in which we are inevitably children of the past. It is true that in the
romance Holgrave resents the pervasive influence of the past. "Shall we
never, never get rid of this Past?" he asks. "It lies upon the Present like
a Giant's dead body! . . . Just think a moment, and it will startle you
to see what slaves we are to bygone times" (chap. 21). Now since
Hawthorne is here taking up a notebook passage he wrote in 1844,[14]
we may suppose Holgrave's words to represent a feeling Hawthorne
could share. A passage in *The Ancestral Footstep,* too, resembles
Hancock's speech in some of its phrasing.[15] But Hawthorne could have
believed what he makes Hancock say only this far: we can neither live
in nor return to the past. He knew that we do not escape the past,
however we resent it or even if we deny it.

Hawthorne is much more likely than most fiction writers to indicate
his own discontent with his work. In the last sentence of the "Legends,"
he remarks that he is resolved "not to show my face in the Province
House for a good while hence—if ever." Perhaps he was not altogether
happy with his imaginative visits there.[16]

13. It may be significant that, at a time when Hawthorne was doing almost
all his writing for the *Democratic Review,* his "Earth's Holocaust" (1844)
appeared in *Graham's Magazine.*

14. *American Notebooks,* ed. Stewart, p. 106.

15. Hawthorne says that the moral of his account of Middleton's effort to go
back into the past and particularly of his search for ancestral wealth was to be
this: "Let the past alone: do not seek to renew it; press on to higher and
better things,—at all events, to other things; and be assured that the right
way can never be that which leads you back to the identical shapes that you
long ago left behind. Onward, onward, onward!" See *The Ancestral Footstep,*
pp. 488–89 and Edward H. Davidson, *Hawthorne's Last Phase* (New Haven,
1949), pp. 28–29.

16. For interpretations of the "Legends" different from mine, see Seymour

Hawthorne never returns to the Province House, but he does return to the vein of the "Legends" in *The House of the Seven Gables*. Although he does reuse other tales in the romance,[17] he returns to the "Legends" in an effort to solve what presented itself to him as a major problem. A romance writer, he wrote to Fields, "is always, or always ought to be, careering on the utmost verge of a precipitous absurdity, and the skill lies in coming as close as possible, without actually tumbling over."[18] It is Gothic absurdity that Hawthorne skirts in the romance; we find him reusing Gothic devices he had used in "Old Esther Dudley" and in "Edward Randolph's Portrait."

In the "Legends" Hawthorne had felt that a scene so close to his present required some "spell of hoar antiquity," and that it could be evoked by Gothic associations. Now that his scene is in his present, he returns to an expedient he had used in "Edward Randolph's Portrait." That tale has two imaginative centers, the time of Hutchinson and the time of Randolph. *The House of the Seven Gables* likewise has two imaginative centers, one in the time of the nineteenth-century Pyncheons and another in the time of their late seventeenth-century ancestors. The Gothic devices are used to evoke a sense of the evil persisting from that bygone time.

The Pyncheon house, it may be remembered, has something very like Esther Dudley's magic mirror, although its pictures are of the past, not as any Pyncheon chooses to remember it, but as it persists into the present, and as the evil that men do lives after them.

> A large, dim looking-glass used to hang in one of the rooms, and was fabled to contain within its depths all the shapes that had ever been reflected there; the old Colonel himself, and his many descendants, some in the garb of antique babyhood, and others in the bloom of feminine beauty, or manly prime, or saddened with the wrinkles of frosty age. Had we the secret of

L. Gross, "Hawthorne's 'Lady Eleanore's Mantle' as History," *Journal of English and Germanic Philology*, 54 (1955): 549–54; Robert H. Fossum, "Time and the Artist in 'Legends of the Province House,' " *Nineteenth-Century Fiction*, 21 (1967): 337–48; Julian Smith, "Hawthorne's Legends of the Province House," *Nineteenth-Century Fiction* 24 (1969): 31–44.

17. A striking example is the rewriting in chap. 11 of the account of the puppets on a barrel organ in "The Seven Vagabonds."

18. See Fields, pp. 55–56 for Hawthorne's letter.

that mirror, we would gladly sit down before it, and transfer its revelations to our page. But there was a story, for which it is difficult to conceive any foundation, that the posterity of Matthew Maule had some connection with the mystery of the looking-glass, and that—by what appears to have been a sort of mesmeric process—they could make its inner region all alive with the departed Pyncheons; not as they had shown themselves to the world, nor in their better and happier hours, but as doing over again some deed of sin, or in the crisis of life's bitterest sorrow.

Only this passage in chapter 1 deals substantially with the mirror—one wonders if Hawthorne had not originally intended some further use of it; he had remarked in "Old Esther Dudley" that her mirror "was well worthy of a tale by itself, and perhaps may hereafter be the theme of one." At any rate, the mirror stands there at the beginning of the romance, a symbol of the intrusion of the past into the present.

The paragraph that describes the magic mirror also introduces a major symbol in the romance: Colonel Pyncheon's portrait. "Those stern, immitigable features," Hawthorne writes, "seemed to symbolize an evil influence, and so darkly to mingle the shadow of their presence with the sunshine of the passing hour, that no good thoughts or purposes could ever spring up and blossom there." The portrait has two kinds of value: one is what we may call the inherent symbolism of old portraits; the other depends upon the Gothic associations of the mysterious portrait.

After looking at some old portraits belonging to the Essex Historical Society, Hawthorne had written in his notebook in 1837: "Nothing gives a stronger idea of old worm-eaten aristocracy—of a family being crazy with age, and of its being time that it was extinct—than these black, dusty, faded, antique-dressed portraits." This inherent portrait symbolism pervades the main story line of the book. There it gets a specifically Gothic connection only once, in chapter 7, when Clifford demands that the portrait be covered with "a crimson curtain, broad enough to hang in folds, and with a golden border and tassels"—very much the golden-tasseled curtain that was hung before the portraits in "The Prophetic Pictures."

The Gothic associations of the mysterious portrait Hawthorne uses cautiously; he says in his preface that the romance writer will be wise "to mingle the Marvellous rather as a slight, delicate, and evanescent flavor, than as any portion of the actual substance of the dish offered to the public." The portrait is treated as "the Marvellous" only in two digressions.

In "Alice Pyncheon," the tale Holgrave reads to Phoebe in chapter 13, Gothic associations can be used without requiring imaginative assent, on either Hawthorne's or the reader's part. In one portion of the reading, Hawthorne makes Holgrave's tale go this way:

> The wild, chimney-corner legend (which, without copying all its extravagances, my narrative essentially follows) here gives an account of some very strange behavior on the part of Colonel Pyncheon's portrait. This picture, it must be understood, was supposed to be so intimately connected with the fate of the house, and so magically built into its walls, that, if once it should be removed, that very instant, the whole edifice would come thundering down, in a heap of dusty ruin. All through the foregoing conversation between Mr. Pyncheon and the carpenter, the portrait had been frowning, clenching its fist, and giving many such proofs of excessive discomposure, but without attracting the notice of either of the two colloquists. And finally, at Matthew Maule's audacious suggestion of a transfer of the seven-gabled structure, the ghostly portrait is averred to have lost all patience, and to have shown itself on the point of descending bodily from its frame. But such incredible incidents are merely to be mentioned aside.

The passage is a self-parody—surely an entirely conscious one. It has the fiction Hawthorne had so often used of a chimney-corner legend behind the narrative. And his trick of the suggested preternatural is carried so far that the narrative proceeds by it alone.[19]

19. The quoted passage is an illustration of the danger of mistake in trying to tie any Gothic element in Hawthorne's work to any single source. One might naturally assume that Hawthorne was here remembering the behavior of the portrait of Manfred's grandfather in chap. 1 of *The Castle of Otranto*. But we happen to have evidence to the contrary: In 1857 he wrote in his notebook of a portrait of Lord Deputy Falkland that it was "a very stately, full-length figure in white, looking out of the picture as if it saw you. The catalogue says

Chapter 18, "Governor Pyncheon," is likewise apart from the narrative proper. As the narrator taunts the dead body of the Judge with the irony of death, he recalls "the ridiculous legend, that, at midnight, all the dead Pyncheons are bound to assemble . . . to see whether the portrait of their ancestor still keeps its place upon the wall, in compliance with his testamentary directions!" The narrator fancies a procession of Pyncheon specters, led by the specter of the Colonel himself, each trying the frame of the portrait to see if it be solidly affixed, while the specter of Matthew Maule "points his finger at the bearded Colonel and his descendants, nodding, jeering, mocking, and finally bursting into obstreperous, though inaudible laughter." Hawthorne, like his narrator, is "tempted to make a little sport with the idea," and to use the Gothic convention without quite accepting it.[20]

Whether or not "the Marvellous" in *The House of the Seven Gables* succeeds, its use there was almost inevitable. Hawthorne's literary habit had taken shape in a time when it was generally agreed that fiction could hardly deal effectively with the readers' own time and place. He used a skill gained in writing the tales to mitigate "this familiarity, which forever plays about present things."[21]

---

that this portrait suggested an incident in Horace Walpole's 'Castle of Otranto'; but I do not remember it" (*English Note-Books*, 2: 528).

20. Hawthorne's use of the magic mirror in chap. 18 is instructive. After the procession of Pyncheon specters has been described, he writes: "The fantastic scene just hinted at must by no means be considered as forming an actual portion of our story. We were betrayed into this brief extravagance by the quiver of the moonbeams; they dance hand-in-hand with shadows, and are reflected in the looking-glass, which, you are aware, is always a kind of window or doorway into the spiritual world." The magic mirror here is symbol for a febrile fancy, and "the spiritual world" in this context is a world of apparitions acting out a tableau of hereditary cupidity.

21. The quoted expression is from William Howard Gardiner's review of *The Spy*, in *North American Review* 15: 255.

8. TALES OF A NEW ENGLAND TRAVELLER

In prospect of one of his summertime vacations, Hawthorne wrote to Longfellow in 1837: "You . . . cannot imagine how much enjoyment I shall have in this little excursion"; and in his retrospective account of his life to 1853 in his letter to Stoddard he says: "Once a year, or thereabouts, I used to make an excursion of a few weeks, in which I enjoyed as much of life as other people do in the whole year's round." These excursions were also productive for him as a writer. In them he found material for rather different kinds of pieces: for that fine sketch "The Canal Boat"; for the North Adams journal; for "The Canterbury Pilgrims"; for one of his last tales, "The Great Stone Face" (1850); and for the three New Hampshire tales discussed in this chapter.

"THE SHAKER BRIDAL"

In August of 1831, during one of his summer excursions, Hawthorne visited the Shaker community at Canterbury, New Hampshire. As Catharine M. Sedgwick before him in her *Redwood* (1824), he found the Shakers good literary material, and two of his most interesting tales—very different tales—had their inception in this visit: "The Canterbury Pilgrims" and "The Shaker Bridal" (1837, in *The Token* for 1838). As soon as Hawthorne returned from his excursion, he withdrew from the Salem Athenaeum Thomas Brown's *An Account of the People Called Shakers* (1812), but neither tale seems to have specific dependence upon it, except perhaps for some detail in "The Shaker Bridal."

The Shakers, one of the most interesting of communal sects, flourished in Hawthorne's time; by 1826 there were some nineteen Shaker communities in the United States. The sect had its origin among English Quakers, but the American Shakers were disciples of Mother Ann Lee, an Englishwoman who, in obedience to a vision, came to this country in 1774. The Shakers had some beliefs in common with the Quakers, but they had special millennial doctrines and they enforced a strict rule of celibacy upon their membership, which was made up of both men and women. They were called Shakers in reference to characteristic physical manifestations of religious emotion. Their number was recruited from persons willing to leave the world and its affairs, and sometimes from orphaned children cared for by the community. Any member was free to leave the community at any time.

Hawthorne seems to have enjoyed his visit to the Canterbury community. He writes in a letter to his sister Louisa on August 17, 1831 of cheerful Shakers, of the prosperity of the establishment, of a heady draught of Shaker cider, of an excellent dinner. "On the whole," he says,

> they lead a good and comfortable life, and, if it were not for their ridiculous ceremonies, a man could not do a wiser thing than to join them. Those whom I conversed with were intelligent, and appeared happy. I spoke to them about becoming a member of their society, but have come to no decision on that point.[1]

As it seems to me, this letter has been taken far more seriously than Hawthorne intended it—his early letters to Louisa were usually playful, and the last sentence of the quoted passage certainly was. In a notebook record of a visit to another Shaker community in 1851 Hawthorne writes with some revulsion about the Shakers, "the most singular and bedevilled set of people that ever existed in a civilized land."[2] Of course at no time would Hawthorne have been attracted to Shaker asceticism. But neither "The Shaker Bridal" nor "The Canterbury Pilgrims" is primarily a consideration of Shaker belief or practice; in both tales Shaker communities are the scenes for the representation of larger themes.

"The Shaker Bridal" is an arresting, highly concentrated tale. It represents no more time than it would take to read it aloud, although it reaches back into the lives of its central figures, Adam Colburn and Martha Pierson. Adam and Martha, now in their middle years, had loved one another since childhood, but they had never married. Adam, a capable and ambitious man but unfortunate in all his efforts, had been unwilling to risk a marriage; Martha had remained single

1. Lathrop, pp. 144–45.
2. *American Notebooks*, ed. Stewart, pp. 229–30.

for his sake. Finally Adam despaired of worldly success, and persuaded Martha that they should together join the Shakers. In the Shaker community, Adam's abilities give him a kind of success, and Martha, too, finds a useful and respected place in it.

At the time of the tale, old Father Ephraim is ready to relinquish his leadership of the community, and he proposes to make Adam and Martha the Father and Mother of this Shaker village, according to the first form of Shaker government established by Mother Ann Lee. For Adam the post would fulfill ambitions for position and power that the world had denied him. He is able to say that his conscience is not doubtful in the matter, that he is ready to take on the new responsibility. Martha, when she is questioned about her willingness, at first can say only that her sentiments are like Adam's, and at last, when the elders eye her doubtfully, only this: "With what strength is left me by my many troubles, I am ready to undertake this charge, and to do my best in it." But she has little strength left to endure; and after Father Ephraim has bidden them join their hands as a symbol of their new function, she slips to the floor, heart-broken and unconscious.

Martha had been able to endure the community while there was yet a possibility—there was hardly a hope—of escape. But she cannot irrevocably renounce her woman's nature as the new position requires. She is unable even to indicate her real feelings; "had she attempted it, perhaps the old recollections, the long-repressed feelings of childhood, youth, and womanhood, might have gushed from her heart, in words that it would have been profanation to utter there." And she has no ambition, as Adam has, to substitute for love. This is an old story that repeats itself often enough in human experience. Euripides wrote it large in horror and violence in *Medea*; Hawthorne puts it in the ironically idyllic setting of a Shaker community whose members have come out from the world. But it is still the story of a man for whom love is but one motive, and of a woman for whom love is all of life. When Father Ephraim finishes his charge to the new appointees and all eyes are upon him, no one notices Martha's deathly pallor, not even Adam: "He, indeed, had withdrawn his hand from hers, and folded his arms with a sense of satisfied ambition."

"The Shaker Bridal" is an illustration of the remarkable technical skill of Hawthorne's early work. But, to realize fully Hawthorne's accomplishment in the tale, one needs to think of it historically, for fiction in the first half of the nineteenth century seldom achieved anything like its economy or its restraint. Poe, it is true, sometimes accomplished an effect in short compass, but he did not deal with representative men and women.

"THE AMBITIOUS GUEST"

In both "The Ambitious Guest" and "The Great Carbuncle" Hawthorne is busy about extending legends—although legends quite different from each other—and both tales are connected with Crawford's Notch in the White Mountains. When years later he had written "The Great Stone Face," he may well have thought of himself as having done for the White Mountains something of what Irving had done for the Catskills. "The Ambitious Guest" was first printed in the *New-England Magazine* in 1835; "The Great Carbuncle" in 1836 in *The Token* for 1837. Both tales seem to have come out of a summer excursion to New Hampshire in 1832; on September 16, 1832, Hawthorne, in a letter to his mother,[3] records his stay of "two nights and part of three days" at Ethan Crawford's inn at Crawford's Notch, an adventuresome horseback ride, beginning at four A.M., to the foot of Mt. Washington, and something of his experience in climbing it.

This stay at Crawford's inn Hawthorne made into two closely related sketches, "The Notch in the White Mountains" and "Our Evening Party Among the Mountains" (now parts of "Sketches from Memory" in *Mosses from an Old Manse*). These two sketches seem to have been originally part of the frame of "The Story-Teller." The legend of the Great Carbuncle is briefly told in "Our Evening Party," which seems to have been intended as an introduction to the tale. And "The Ambitious Guest" may also have been intended, as Professor Adkins thinks, for narration in connection with the sketches.[4] Certainly the first paragraph of "The Notch," which describes a journey along the valley of the Saco River and remarks the red pathways of avalanches "hardly to be effaced by the vegetation of ages," would have been preparation for it.

3. Quoted in *American Notebooks*, ed. Stewart, p. 283.
4. Adkins, "Early Projected Works of Hawthorne," pp. 141–42.

Toward the end of "The Ambitious Guest," when the fate of the family is clear, Hawthorne says, "Who has not heard their name? The story has been told far and wide, and will forever be a legend of these mountains. Poets have sung their fate." "The Ambitious Guest" is more literally a twice-told tale than any other in *Twice-Told Tales,* and Hawthorne wrote it with the assumption that virtually every one of his first readers would know the story of the Samuel Willey family and their annihilation on August 28, 1826. It is most unlikely that he heard the story for the first time on his visit to the Notch, although he probably did hear Ethan Crawford tell it then. Since he wrote the tale within a few years after the Willey House disaster, his sources were probably several newspaper or periodical accounts hardly to be identified now. We do have an account of the Willey disaster written by Samuel Willey's brother, Benjamin G. Willey, in his *History of the White Mountains,* first published in 1855. Since Benjamin Willey lived in the region and was a member of the party that searched for the bodies of the Willey family, contemporary newspaper and magazine accounts probably depended upon him primarily.

Although other Hawthorne tales have a quality of dramatic irony, it ordinarily depends—as in "The Prophetic Pictures"— on a fore-shadowing the narrative supplies. In "The Ambitious Guest" the dramatic irony for Hawthorne's first readers depended upon their sure knowledge of the outcome from the beginning of the tale. The dramatic irony for them was of the sort we know in Aeschylus' *Agamemnon.* In that play the effect for modern readers may be very much what it was for Aeschylus' first audience. We too know the story of Agamemnon's murder as it is told in the *Odyssey,* and when we read of Agamemnon strutting down that purple carpet, we have a sure knowledge of the humiliation and horror that await him within the palace doors. Likewise, Hawthorne's first readers, almost every one, would have realized by the time they had read the first paragraph of the tale that they were reading the story of the Willey family and that the family would be destroyed. The first paragraph begins and ends with references to avalanches, establishes the scene in the Notch, and describes the family happily gathered about their hearth. Most readers today who read "The Ambitious Guest" before they know the story of the Willeys, do indeed experience a comparable effect, but not quite the one Hawthorne intended for his first readers. The effect for readers without prior knowledge of the Willey House disaster may be roughly comparable to the effect of the dramatic irony in *Macbeth*, where the reader or spectator is made to foresee the outcome in part without sure knowledge of it.

Since Hawthorne not only is aware that his first readers know the story he is retelling, but is making use of their knowledge, he is careful to keep his version the standard story in its main outline. We may take this paragraph as an example:

> "The old mountain has thrown a stone at us, for fear we should forget him," said the landlord, recovering himself. "He some-times nods his head and threatens to come down; but we are old neighbors, and agree together pretty well upon the whole. Besides we have a sure place of refuge hard by if he should be coming in good earnest."

The Willey family had narrowly escaped an avalanche in June of 1826, and it was believed by some persons that the family were in a stable considered sturdier than the house when the avalanche overtook them, a belief Hawthorne seems to accept in his account. When Hawthorne says later in the tale that the avalanche divided into two parts, passing on either side of the house and leaving it standing, that is accurately the fact.[5]

Nor is the presence of the Ambitious Guest a departure from the probabilities of the legend. The Willey House was an inn and might well have had one guest or more on the night of August 28; since the bodies of three of the Willey children were never found,[6] the body of a guest might not have been found either. The one way in which Hawthorne departs from what is known of the disaster is in not mentioning the torrential rain that brought it on. Evidently he made a decision not to, for in the tale iterative mention of the sound of the wind is a device to evoke foreboding: "the dreary blast" of wind which heralded the approach of the Ambitious Guest, "and wailed as he was entering, and went moaning away from the door" sounds through the tale.

5. See Benjamin G. Willey, *History of the White Mountains* (New York, 1870), pp. 113–14, 123–24, 131.
6. Willey, p. 126.

The figure of the Ambitious Guest often has been supposed to be a projection of Hawthorne himself; the tendency to find Hawthorne's work self-portraiture—which has lately gone over into psychological criticism—has been strong from the beginning. Hawthorne may well have reflected on the way in which death cuts off achievement, as well as, say, Keats in "When I have fears." But Hawthorne is careful to generalize the figure of the Guest: there is no indication of the goal of his ambition, if indeed it has any clear goal. It is—Hawthorne chooses his terms carefully—"a high and abstracted ambition." To say that the Guest's ambition has some particular direction would be to limit his representativeness; and to make his ambition a literary ambition, which is so often entertained without any capacity for its fulfillment, would be to take away most of his significance.

Although "The Ambitious Guest" has been a favorite tale with the common reader, recent criticism (so far as I know) virtually ignores it—probably because it offers no great difficulty and no great opportunity for critical acumen. Indeed, most readers will be aware enough of the ironies of the tale without guidance, even if they do not trouble to identify them. The dramatic irony that makes the pattern of the tale carries with it ironies only a little more subtle. Perhaps the particular appeal the tale has had for young readers—who ordinarily recognize the fact of mortality only as a kind of abstraction —is that it suddenly makes that abstraction concrete and immediate for them.

The irony that inheres in the Guest's confession of his ambition just before his destruction is the irony of the discrepancy between intention and outcome that runs through all human experience, the irony that emerges so simply from one of the epigrams in the *Greek Anthology*: "I Brotachus of Gortyna, a Cretan, lie here, not having come hither for this, but for traffic." But to the discrepancy between the Guest's exalted intention and his destiny, there is a sort of converse; the simple hopes of the family have unlooked-for outcomes too. The old grandmother who has no ambition left but to lie neatly in her graveclothes will never do so. Samuel Willey, who would have been content to have his name on a slate grave stone, will achieve the fame he did not covet, and have a mountain called by his name. That the Willey family are never named in the tale was a good stroke so long as readers themselves were able to name them.

The quality of life of the family envisioned in the tale also helps to account for its persistence for generations of readers. The family represents, if not the reality of the lives of New England country people, at least the ideal that was potential in their lives. Barrett Wendell long ago described the family in Whittier's "Snow-Bound" in this way: "Simple with all the simplicity of hereditary farming folk, they are at the same time gentle with the unconscious grace of people who are aware of no earthly superiors." The sentence as well describes the host and his family. And since the reader knows this family, these representatives of an ideal, only while he foresees their destruction, he must be the more poignantly aware of their worth.

By the centrality of its concern with human experience, the tale deserves the currency it has had and may regain. And despite its insistent irony, it is told with compassion. It is not, to be sure, an example of Hawthorne's highest skill; indeed, it seems a little immature, as if it were the work of a young writer who has not learned to trust his reader quite enough, and whose effects are weakened by too much insistence upon them. That suggestion of immaturity is puzzling, for tales more subtle and controlled came as early in Hawthorne's career as this one.

"THE GREAT CARBUNCLE"

Toward the end of "Our Evening Party Among the Mountains," when Hawthorne has briefly recounted the legend of the Great Carbuncle, he remarks, "On this theme methinks I could frame a tale with a deep moral."[7] Even the most devoted of Hawthorne's readers could hardly think the tale he makes of the legend a complete success; and the moral, assuredly an important one, is not very successfully embodied. Hawthorne's struggle to make the legend substantiate his allegorical purpose is all too apparent. To the student of Hawthorne, "The Great Carbuncle" has an interest somewhat like that of "Edward Randolph's Portrait," for in both tales Hawthorne is working with such techniques and materials as elsewhere in his work come to better results.

In his note to the tale Hawthorne says: "The Indian tradition, on which this somewhat extravagant tale is founded, is both too wild and

7. *Mosses*, p. 483.

too beautiful to be adequately wrought up in prose. Sullivan, in his History of Maine, written since the Revolution, remarks, that even then the existence of the Great Carbuncle was not entirely discredited." The passage in James Sullivan's history, which is quoted in our note,[8] is doubtless connected with the tale. But it is not the only piece of source material Hawthorne had to work with. When he set about it to tell a story of a Great Carbuncle, he could hardly have helped remembering Norna's tale in chapter 19 of Scott's *The Pirate*. The physical phenomenon of a Great Carbuncle, and even the moral implications in Norna's description of it, are so closely paralleled in "The Great Carbuncle" that Andrew Lang says in his notes to *The Pirate*, "this must be the origin of Hawthorne's tale."[9] Hawthorne

8. The passage in Sullivan to which Hawthorne refers is this:

There was an early expectation of finding a gem, of immense size and value, on this mountain: it was conjectured, and is yet believed by some, that a carbuncle is suspended from a rock, over a pond of water there. While many in the early days of the country's settlement believed this report, each one was afraid that his neighbor should become the fortunate proprietor of the prize, by right of prior possession. To prevent this, credit was given to the tale of the natives, that the place was guarded by an evil spirit, who troubled the waters, and raised a dark mist, on the approach of human footsteps: this idea was necessary to those of avaricious credulity, who attempted in vain to obtain the prize, and were in hopes of a more fortunate adventure.

James Sullivan, *The History of the District of Maine* (Boston, printed by I. Thomas and E. T. Andrews, 1795), pp. 74–75. For an account of the phenomenon that seems to have given rise to the legend, see Raymond I. Haskell, "The Great Carbuncle," *New England Quarterly* 10 (1937): 533–35.

9. The passage in Norna's tale that seems to influence "The Great Carbuncle" is this:

In my childish courage, I was even but too presumtuous, and the thirst after things unattainable led me, like our primitive mother, to desire increase of knowledge, even by prohibited means. . . . Often when watching by the Dwarfie Stone, with mine eyes fixed upon the Ward-hill, which rises above that gloomy valley, I have distinguished, among the dark rocks, that wonderful carbuncle, which gleams ruddy as a furnace to them who view it from beneath, but has ever become invisible to him whose daring foot has scaled the precipices from which it darts its splendour. My vain and youthful bosom burned to investigate these and an hundred other mysteries.

Waverley Novels, The Highland Edition (Boston, 1892), 12: 299. For Lang's note, see p. 338.

would have been happy to follow Scott's example, as he did in "The Gray Champion" and "The Prophetic Pictures." But pretty clearly he had a much more immediate source. In "Our Evening Party Among the Mountains" Hawthorne says that the legend of the Great Carbuncle was recounted during his stay at Ethan Crawford's inn, and there is every likelihood that he did indeed hear the story there, as told by Ethan Allen Crawford himself.

Benjamin G. Willey tells us that Crawford, a giant of a man, "was nearly as well known to all the earlier visitors, and of almost as much interest, as Mount Washington itself."[10] He was a famous storyteller,[11] and one of his stories was of a search for the Great Carbuncle in which his father had taken part. Here is Mrs. Lucy Crawford's record of her husband's story:

> I recollect a number of years ago, when quite a boy, some persons had been up on the hills and said they had found a golden treasure, or carbuncle, which they said was under a large shelving rock, and would be difficult to obtain, for they might fall and be dashed to pieces. Moreover, they thought it was guarded by an evil spirit, supposing that it had been placed there by the Indians, and that they had killed one of their number and left him to guard the treasure, which some credulous, superstitious persons believed, and they got my father to engage to go and search for it. Providing themselves with everything necessary for the business and a sufficient number of good men and a minister well qualified to lay the evil spirit, they set out in good earnest and high spirits, anticipating with pleasure how rich they should be in coming home laden with gold; that is, if they should have the good luck to find it. They set out and went up Dry river, and had hard work to find their way through the thickets and over the hills, where they made diligent search for a number of days, with some of the former men spoken of for guides, but they could not find the place again, or anything that seemed to be like it, and worn out with fatigue and disappointment, they returned. Never since, to my knowledge, has any one found that wonderful place again, or been troubled with the mountain spirit.[12]

10. Willey, p. 80.
11. Willey, p. 83.
12. *The History of the White Mountains* (Portland, Me., 1886), pp. 103–4.

Hawthorne's "deep moral" may have been suggested by Norna's tale, and James Sullivan's account of the Great Carbuncle may have furnished a certain sanction for Crawford's story. But clearly Crawford's story suggests the action of the tale Hawthorne tells.

The time of the tale is fixed as about the middle of the seventeenth century by references to Captain John Smith as visiting the region some years before the action, the Great Fire of London as some years after, and to pine-tree shillings. Although Hawthorne probably felt that such an action ought to be developed in the far past, the time is not important, and the type figures who search for the Great Carbuncle might—except for minor details—have made their search a century or two later. These type figures are curiously ineffective. Now Hawthorne does sometimes have a felicity in the construction of types: in "The Canterbury Pilgrims" the type figures are impressive, and he is greatly successful, too, in the later "Earth's Holocaust" and "The Celestial Railroad." Yet most of the types in "The Great Carbuncle" would surely seem to a reader who had not read "The Notch" and "Our Evening Party Among the Mountains" to have been constructed out of literary convention.

But these types do have some relationship to persons Hawthorne had observed and describes in his two sketches. The type materialist, Ichabod Pigsnort, has a vague connection with a merchant at Crawford's inn. The mineralogist at the inn, "a scientific, green-spectacled figure in black, bearing a heavy hammer," comes over into the tale as Dr. Cacaphodel, a Gothic alchemist "from beyond the seas." The well-dressed young man at the inn, who turns out to be a poet, has his analogue in the poet who searches for the Great Carbuncle; the two "Georgian gentlemen" at the inn may have suggested the Lord de Vere of the tale. But the Cynic in the dark spectacles, who in the tale functions as an ironic chorus, has no parallel among the guests at the inn.

The one impressive figure among these types is the Seeker, who may have been suggested by Ethan Crawford's father. The Seeker seems intended to represent the frontiersman in quest of a not-fully-defined good, the pioneer who, throughout most of our history, has

---

The first edition of Mrs. Crawford's book was in 1845; there is a recent reprinting, edited by Stearns Morse, Dartmouth Publications, 1966. Willey, p. 45, quotes Crawford's story.

been in the van of American experience: "The pursuit alone," the
Seeker says, "is my strength." But the Gothic sort of curse he is alleged
to be under obscures rather than enhances his significance: "there
went a fable in the valley of the Saco, that for his inordinate lust
after the Great Carbuncle, he had been condemned to wander among
the mountains till the end of time, still with the same feverish hopes
at sunrise—the same despair at eve."

Hawthorne endeavors to use these types in making the legend into
an allegory, and for each there is an allegorical outcome. The
merchant gives up his quest, but as a rather remote consequence of
it, is ruined. Dr. Cacaphodel takes a chunk of granite as a substitute
for the Great Carbuncle, carries it home, analyzes it, and writes a
folio about it. The poet takes as his substitute for the gleaming
carbuncle a block of ice (the poet in "Our Evening Party" had written
for the inn album a "Sonnet to the Snow on Mount Washington,"
elegant lines but "cold as their subject"). The Lord de Vere goes
home to his ancestral hall—it was never likely that he would recognize
a splendor greater than his own. The Seeker finds; and dies at the
moment of his success. The Cynic, who has denied the existence of
the Great Carbuncle, is blinded when he takes off his cynic's darkened
spectacles and looks upon it.

But Matthew and Hannah, the young married couple and the
central persons in the action, are not developed as types; indeed,
Hawthorne as narrator remarks that they seem "strangely out of place
among the whimsical fraternity whose wits had been set agog by the
Great Carbuncle." We are invited to give them our fullest sympathy
and the narrative penetrates their minds and hearts, although for the
most part the type figures are done from the outside. In their innocence,
Matthew and Hannah do find the Great Carbuncle, but they are
"so simply wise as to reject a jewel which would have dimmed all
earthly things." "Never again," Matthew says, "will we desire more
light than all the world may share with us."

The moral is one that preoccupies Hawthorne in other tales. Aylmer
in "The Birthmark" and Ethan Brand have, each in his own way,
desired to step beyond the limits that belong to mortality. But of the
figures in this tale, only the Seeker has their kind of dignity in
destruction. Dr. Cacaphodel, Master Pigsnort, the poet, and Lord de
Vere do not understand what they aspire to and have reduced the

Great Carbuncle to the limits of their own conceptions. The Cynic, Hawthorne seems to be saying, has only the cheap wisdom that rests on denial. Yet the moral implications of the Cynic's blinding are not very clear; an unsympathetic reader might contend that the moral is that a cynic ought never to step out of character, as the Cynic allegorically seems to do when he takes off his cynic's darkened spectacles. Only the simple wisdom of Matthew and Hannah stands; and Matthew makes explicit one of Hawthorne's most important preoccupations. Yet its importance is obscured a little by its embodiment in a maladroit allegory.

The partial failure of Hawthorne's allegory here is not only a matter of the failure of imaginative energy in the construction of the types. To use a favorite nineteenth-century critical term, the tale fails in keeping, fails just where "The Minister's Black Veil" and "Dr. Heidegger's Experiment" so splendidly succeed. One evidence of Hawthorne's discomfort with the tale is the spots of "poetic" prose, for however wild and beautiful the legend, it demands simplicity of treatment. Another evidence is obvious trouble with shifts in narrative point of view. Sometimes Hawthorne indicates himself as omniscient narrator in such expressions as "it was observable that" or "the fourth whom we shall notice." Yet, as has been remarked, he proceeds one way with Matthew and Hannah and another way with the type figures, except that he finds it necessary to explain the Cynic and to comment on cynicism. With all this there is some effort to give the tale a legendary air, but the effort extends solely to what is outside the action, and depends upon such expressions as "it was told of him," and "some people affirmed," so that it is only in the next-to-last paragraph of the tale that the air and tone of legendary report is attained. Hawthorne's skill elsewhere is quite enough to manage inconsistencies in point of view so subtly that they do not intrude themselves upon the reader or at all lessen the effect of a tale. But in "The Great Carbuncle" there are problems in technique of which we are aware just because they are not solved.

The trouble with "The Great Carbuncle" is not that it is an allegory, but that it is a relatively poor allegory, in which satire and sentiment coexist unhappily. Hawthorne is not quite imaginatively at home with the legend he is using—as he seems to indicate even in his note to the tale. His materials, far from having "wrought themselves almost spontaneously, into a sort of allegory," have in the framing of this tale with a deep moral proved most intractable.

9. TWO SPECULATIVE TALES

The narratives in "Wakefield" and in "Fancy's Show Box" exist for the sake of sets of speculative moral ideas. Each piece explores a particular short passage in Hawthorne's reading: "Wakefield" an anecdote, "Fancy's Show Box" a passage in Jeremy Taylor's *Ductor Dubitantium*. The two pieces complement one another as examples of Hawthorne's allegorical method. The imaginative process in "Wakefield" starts with an anecdote that Hawthorne would invest with meaning. The imaginative process in "Fancy's Show Box," on the other hand, starts with moral ideas drawn from Taylor, ideas for which Hawthorne seeks an imaginative embodiment. Neither tale represents him at his best; but each represents his faculty for turning moral ideas about until their facets are all displayed.[1]

"WAKEFIELD"

"Wakefield" was first printed in the *New-England Magazine* in 1835. It has been compared to "Rip Van Winkle" and to "Peter Rugg, the Missing Man," and insofar as the title character in each of these tales loses his place among his fellows, there is a likeness—but rather a superficial one. Nor does Wakefield really belong among those Hawthorne characters separated from the rest of mankind by pride or sin—Wakefield's "long whim-wham" sets another sort of problem.

Hawthorne's source, he tells us in the first sentence of the tale, is "a story, told as truth, of a man . . . who absented himself for a long time from his wife," a story he had read "in some old magazine or news-

1. These two tales are discussed in the context of a consideration of Hawthorne's theological thinking in Henry G. Fairbanks, "Sin, Free Will and 'Pessimism' in Hawthorne," *PMLA* 71 (1956): 975–89.

paper." Wherever Hawthorne had read it, the story stems, as Sir Leslie Stephen remarked long ago, from Dr. William King's *Anecdotes of his Own Times*, 1818. King tells of a man named Howe, who inexplicably absented himself from his home for seventeen years and then as inexplicably returned—very much the story Hawthorne outlines in the first paragraph of his tale. King says of his acquaintance: "After he returned home, he never would confess, even to his most intimate friends, what was the real cause of such a singular conduct; apparently there was none."[2]

The genesis of Hawthorne's tale seems pretty clear. It must have occurred to almost everyone at some time that an actuality he knows about is so much an anomaly that, however true and however striking, it could hardly be used in fiction. In the anecdote, Hawthorne encountered such an actuality in a form that suggested an experiment. The anecdote was a coherent narrative. Could a character for its central figure be imagined? Could the practical and spiritual consequences of his act be so traced that they would seem convincing? The tale seems an exercise, even a kind of stunt.

The tale becomes more than a stunt, of course. What success it has depends to begin with on a narrative point of view that imaginatively involves the reader in the experiment—a very obvious form of a narrative point of view that Hawthorne uses subtly in some of his best tales. Here he overtly addresses the reader as a sort of collaborator, as if he could only display an action he had not devised, and indeed might not be fully informed about. The reader may, he says, "ramble with me through the twenty years of Wakefield's vagary." Yet it is not quite an action in the ordinary sense that is being represented; what the reader is being asked to share is an imaginative reconstruction of a character: "What sort of a man was Wakefield? We are free to shape out our own idea, and call it by his name"—and we will try to shape out an idea of a man for whom the facts of Wakefield's career are conceivable.

The man that Hawthorne posits seems such a man. His acquaintance would not have supposed him capable of anything unusual; his wife knows him better:

2. See *Nathaniel Hawthorne*, ed. Austin Warren (New York, 1934), pp. 364–65.

She, without having analyzed his character, was partly aware of a quiet selfishness, that had rusted into his inactive mind; of a peculiar sort of vanity, the most uneasy attribute about him; of a disposition to craft, which had seldom produced more positive effects than the keeping of petty secrets, hardly worth revealing; and, lastly, of what she called a little strangeness, sometimes, in the good man. This latter quality is indefinable, and perhaps non-existent.

This man, without any full resolve, intends at first only to puzzle his wife by an indefinite absence. He will take a room in the next street; he is curious to know how his absence will affect his little world: "A morbid vanity, therefore, lies nearest the bottom of the affair." The next morning, still with no clear resolve, he almost returns and then hurries away: "At that instant his fate was turning on the pivot."

Even in Wakefield, this man of vague resolve, there is a pivot on which fate turns. Or, as Hawthorne changes the figure two paragraphs later, "an influence beyond our control lays its strong hand on every deed which we do, and weaves its consequences into an iron tissue of necessity." The statement reminds us of Chillingworth's words to Hester in *The Scarlet Letter*: "By thy first step awry, thou didst plant the germ of evil; but, since that moment it has all been a dark necessity" (chap. 14). Now although Chillingworth does say that his old faith comes back to him "and explains all that we do and all that we suffer," his doctrine seems hardly Calvinistic, since he posits no necessity antecedent to Hester's first step awry. And in "Wakefield" Hawthorne is not stating a theological proposition, except as any statement about human destiny may have theological connections. Rather he is representing an idea somewhat like that represented in Robert Frost's "The Road Not Taken." The "I" of that poem may choose either of two roads; having chosen one, he must abide by its necessities—"way leads on to way"—the initial choice has made at last "all the difference." Hawthorne has taken the most difficult of illustrations, since Wakefield goes through no crisis of decision, never really faces a decision, acts almost in default of decision. But he has made enough choice to act—there is a deed—and he fails to make another choice when possibly he might still have made it, before he is quite caught up in necessity.

Yet perhaps Wakefield's predicament is therefore the more representative. Most of us are more like Wakefield than we are like Aylmer, say, or Ethan Brand. A man is fortunate if, looking back, he does not see that sometime or another he has been only a "crafty nincompoop," or does not wonder just how it has happened that he is caught in conditions he does not enjoy and yet does not—perhaps cannot—change. Hawthorne does fail, it seems to me, to make Wakefield's return to his wife convincing; and in that return, to be sure, the analogy to "The Road Not Taken" breaks down—for the "I" of the poem there was no return. But the happy event of Wakefield's return—"supposing it to be such," Hawthorne says—we do not follow, and how it may be affected by the initial choice and its twenty-year results we do not know.

Hawthorne's stated moral at the end of the tale is, he says, only a portion of the "food for thought" it offers; but he will shape that much "into a figure":

> Amid the seeming confusion of our mysterious world, individuals are so nicely adjusted to a system, and systems to one another and to a whole, that, by stepping aside for a moment, a man exposes himself to a fearful risk of losing his place forever. Like Wakefield, he may become, as it were, the Outcast of the Universe.

Too often this passage has been considered out of context and interpreted in connection with some other Hawthorne tale. It is true enough that Hawthorne is often concerned with persons who—by their volition—have separated themselves from their fellows. But Wakefield's is a separation of a different kind; and his vanity is only vanity and not pride. He has been able, we are told, "to retain his original share of human sympathies, and to be still involved in human interests, while he had lost his reciprocal influence on them." The tale considers that mystery of the interplay of choice and necessity in which even a momentary step aside may have consequences undesired and unlooked for. But there is no reason to suppose that it represents anything more final in Hawthorne's thinking than does, say, "The Prophetic Pictures," which embodies markedly different ideas about human destiny.

"FANCY'S SHOW BOX"

"Fancy's Show Box" was first printed in 1836 in *The Token* for 1837.
Hawthorne had withdrawn Jeremy Taylor's *Ductor Dubitantium:
or, The Rule of Conscience* (first published in 1660) from the Salem
Athenaeum in 1834. A passage from it becomes the core of "Fancy's
Show Box," and some years later he returns to the book in "Egotism; or,
the Bosom Serpent" (1843): on Roderick Elliston's table "lay that
bulky volume, the Ductor Dubitantium of Jeremy Taylor, full of
cases of conscience, and in which most men, possessed of a conscience,
may find something applicable to their purpose." It may have
influenced Hawthorne in ways that we cannot now trace. Emerson,
in "The Problem," called Jeremy Taylor "the Shakespeare of divines";
both Taylor's thought and the immediacy and power of his style
would have appealed to Hawthorne. Before he read *Ductor
Dubitantium,* he had withdrawn all three volumes of Taylor's *Discourses on Various Subjects,* apparently returning to two of the volumes
for a second reading. He refers to one of Taylor's sermons in "The
Wedding Knell."

"Fancy's Show Box" embodies Rule 3, in Part 2, Book 4, Chapter
1 of *Ductor Dubitantium.* Rule 3 is headed: "The act of the will
alone, although no external action or event do follow, is imputed to
good or evil by God and men."[3] These first sentences of "Fancy's
Show Box" are in clear connection with Taylor's statement of
Rule 3: "What is guilt? A stain upon the soul. And it is a point of vast
interest whether the soul may contract such stains, in all their depth
and flagrancy, from deeds which may have been plotted and resolved
upon, but which, physically, have never had existence." This "point
of vast interest" is illustrated "by an imaginary example . . . one Mr.
Smith." Old Mr. Smith's past is blameless so far as externals go.
But the personifications of "Fancy, Memory, and Conscience" recall
to him certain volitions. The allegory is of an eighteenth-century
"Eastern tale" sort. Fancy has a show box like the diorama of the

3. *The Whole Works of the Right Reverend Jeremy Taylor,* ed. Reginald
Heber and C. P. Eden (London, 1883), 10: 602. All quotations are from this
and the following page. Taylor is using or ultimately depending upon St.
Gregory the Great's *Pastoral Care,* Pt. 3, chap. 29. See *Pastoral Care,* trans.
Henry Davis, S.J., Ancient Christian Writers, no. 11 (Westminster, Md., 1950),
pp. 201–3.

traveling showman in "Ethan Brand," and in it presents to Mr. Smith "the semblances of living scenes," three of which are described. These scenes are not pictures of temptation or desire, but of what might have been the results of sinful volitions had they been carried out. Memory, carrying a great volume of records, points out to Mr. Smith what desires or passions might have resulted in the scenes Fancy has shown him. Conscience, when Mr. Smith has recognized what Memory has told him, stabs him in the heart with her dagger.

This allegorical action has a clear relationship to Taylor's discussion of Rule 3. According to Taylor, there are six steps in sinful volition; in all except the first the sin is actual. In summary, the six steps are these:

1. Inclination, which is not sinful unless habitual.
2. The step at which "the will stops and arrests itself upon the tempting object," consenting only so far as to consider and dispute it.
3. The will "is pleased with the thought of it."
4. The step at which there is desire to accomplish the action, and the action is prevented only by "something that lies cross in the way."
5. Final consent to the sin.
6. The action is "contrived within."

Through Memory's record, we can identify the steps in sinful volition of which Mr. Smith has been guilty.

The first of the three pictures described is of Mr. Smith as a young man scorning the appeal of a desperate girl. He recognizes himself and "his first love—his cottage love—his Martha Burroughs." He disclaims all guilt; but Memory searches her book and finds "a record merely of sinful thought, which was never embodied in an act." The youthful Mr. Smith's volition had not gone beyond the second step according to Taylor—or perhaps the third.

In a second picture, Fancy presents to Mr. Smith the likeness of a young man wounded in the temple and lying dead after a drinking party—Mr. Smith recognizes him as his friend Edward Spencer. But, he protests, Spencer was his friend for fifty years, and died his friend. Memory finds a most confused page in her book, but it seems to say that once Mr. Smith had flung a bottle at his friend's head, and missed his aim; so that, when the two dimly recalled the incident on the next day, they merely laughed about it. In this instance, although the youthful Mr. Smith was in drink, all steps of volition, as Taylor distinguishes them, were probably complete, and the sin was carried into action, though happily unsuccessful action.

The third picture is closer to Mr. Smith's present. It is of himself, "in the decline of life . . . stripping the clothes from the backs of three half-starved children." Mr. Smith considers the scene ridiculous; but Memory finds a page in her book that tells how Mr. Smith had been tempted to commence a lawsuit against the orphan heirs to a considerable estate, but had not carried it through because "his claims had turned out nearly as devoid of law as justice." Here volition had gone through the fourth step, and Mr. Smith had been prevented from carrying out his design only by a legal difficulty that lay "cross in the way."

In each of these three instances, Mr. Smith, according to Jeremy Taylor, has incurred the guilt of sin, for Taylor contends that "all the morality of any action depends wholly on the will, and is seated in the inner man," and that sinful action is worse than sinful volition only so far as an action presupposes "many precedent acts of lust." In the next-to-last paragraph of the tale, Hawthorne adduces two arguments against that contention.

The first argument depends upon an analogy between a "prospective sinner" who only plans evil and a fiction writer who fits out his villain with evil deeds. May they not "almost meet each other half-way between reality and fancy"? In neither has the sin, and therefore perhaps not the guilt, become actual. The analogy is not very convincing for its apparent purpose; one wonders if it implies a question about the spiritual health of the fiction writer's activities. The second argument is more pertinent. It is that a man's compunctions do not come into play when he merely contemplates an evil, and that no resolve is full and settled until the moment of the execution of a deed. "Let us hope, therefore," Hawthorne says as he ends the paragraph, "that all the dreadful consequences of sin will not be incurred, unless the act have set its seal upon the thought."[4]

4. Curiously, Hawthorne's second argument is close to Gregory but not to Taylor. Gregory says: "For often the merciful God absolves sins of thought the more readily, in that He does not allow them to issue in deed, and wickedness that is merely conceived is the more readily absolved, because it has not been

Nevertheless, Hawthorne's conclusion to his tale has an obvious relationship to the sentence with which Taylor concludes the discussion of Rule 3. Taylor says:

> But the sin begins within, and the guilt is contracted by what is done at home, by that which is in our power, by that which nothing from without can hinder. For as for the external act, God for ends of His own providence does often hinder it; and yet he that fain would, but cannot bring his evil purposes to pass, is not at all excused, or the less a criminal before God.

The last paragraph of "Fancy's Show Box" is this:

> Yet, with the slight fancy work which we have framed, some sad and awful truths are interwoven. Man must not disclaim his brotherhood, even with the guiltiest, since, though his hand be clean, his heart has surely been polluted by the flitting phantoms of iniquity. He must feel that, when he shall knock at the gate of heaven, no semblance of an unspotted life can entitle him to entrance there. Penitance must kneel, and Mercy come from the footstool of the throne, or that golden gate will never open!

It may not be quite kind to Hawthorne to put this paragraph, which is certainly not an example of his style at its best, next to a passage from Jeremy Taylor. But the present concern is the purport, not the style, of the passage; and the passage has considerable importance in the study of Hawthorne.

The passage is in no way especially Calvinistic. It expresses an idea about the nature of man at home in the thought of the Anglican Jeremy Taylor and common to the thought of many Christians, of all who believe that man is by his nature estranged from God and saved by grace. The idea that sin may inhere in volition without any outward act is no surprising idea in a Christian context: "the word of God . . . is a discerner of the thoughts and intents of the heart" (Heb. 4:12).

That "man must not disclaim his brotherhood, even with the guiltiest" is a central conviction in Hawthorne. Since he holds it, he can accept neither society's standards of respectability nor the

---

brought under the stronger bondage of the consummated deed" (*Pastoral Care*, p. 202).

Unitarian and Transcendentalist assumptions about the nature of man. The conviction is the basis for his compassionate representation of human frailty and human need.

10. THE MASTERPIECES IN TWICE-TOLD TALES

"The Gentle Boy," "The Minister's Black Veil," and "Dr. Heidegger's Experiment" stand out in the *Twice-Told Tales* with special distinctness. Technically, they are very different from one another; and in them Hawthorne's moral concern seems to have three tempers. Although they are of course comparable in some respects to other Hawthorne tales, no one of them is a companion piece to any other tale.

"THE GENTLE BOY"

"The Gentle Boy" was first printed in 1831 in *The Token* for 1832. As we have seen, it had been completed by December of 1829. We know, too, that Hawthorne withdrew William Sewel's *The History of . . . the Christian People Called Quakers*—"painful Sewel's ancient tome," Whittier calls it—from the Salem Athenaeum in January 1828 and October 1829, keeping it a month on the second withdrawal. The tale, therefore, seems to be one of the earliest-written Hawthorne tales that have come down to us.

"The Gentle Boy" has long been considered a sort of imaginative atonement on Hawthorne's part for the role the American progenitor of his family, William Hathorne, played in the persecution of the Quakers. His ancestor, Hawthorne writes in "The Custom House," "had all the Puritanic traits, both good and evil. He was likewise a bitter persecutor, as witness the Quakers, who have remembered him in their histories, and relate an incident of hard severity towards a woman of their sect, which will last longer, it is to be feared, than any record of his better deeds, although they were many." And there is a similar passage, with a reference to Ann Coleman by name, in "Main Street."

William Sewel, to whom Hawthorne refers in "The Gentle Boy" as "the historian of the sect" (his history was first published in English in 1722), writes that "Anne Coleman and four of her friends were whipped through Salem, Boston, and Dedham, by order of William Hawthorn, who before he was a magistrate, had opposed compulsion for conscience."[1] William Hathorne also presided over the court that tried Deborah Wilson—who had felt herself called to walk naked through the streets of Salem—and ordered her whipped at a cart's tail, although the court sometime later decided she was "distempered in the head."[2] Hawthorne, then, does have an ancestral connection with the persecution of Quakers he describes in "The Gentle Boy," and he must have considered the tale in some sense a recognition of a wrong in which his ancestor was much concerned. But we should not let the knowledge of that connection obscure or narrow—as evidently it can—the significance of the tale for us.

Rufus Choate, we remember, said that although the persecution of the Quakers was fact, it was just the sort of fact that the fiction writer in search of "the useful truth" ought to avoid. Now Hawthorne did, in "The Gray Champion" for instance, search for Choate's kind of useful truth. But he early discovered that American materials might yield another kind of useful truth, truth about the nature of man. We shall see something of the complex and detailed relationship "The Gentle Boy" has to history; but the purpose of the tale is far from nationalistic, and it has a significance far beyond the events it records.

The tale was a favorite in Hawthorne's family, and his fiancée, Sophia Peabody, made a sketch of Ilbrahim for an edition of "The Gentle Boy" dedicated to her and published at Hawthorne's expense in 1839. In his preface to that edition he writes:

> The tale, of which a new edition is now offered to the public, was among the earliest efforts of its author's pen; and, little noticed on its first appearance in one of the annuals, appears

1. *The History of . . . the Christian People Called Quakers*, 6th ed. (London, 1834), 1: 433–44.
2. Loggins, pp. 62–63.

ultimately to have awakened the interest of a larger number of
readers than any of his subsequent productions; . . . there are
several among the "Twice-Told Tales" which, on reperusal,
affect him less painfully with a sense of imperfect and ill-wrought
conception than "The Gentle Boy." But the opinion of many . . .
compels him to the conclusion that nature here led him deeper
into the universal heart than art has been able to follow.[3]

The appearance of the old distinction between nature and art in this
passage is curious, but the sense of an incomplete achievement it
represents is characteristic of Hawthorne.

If Hawthorne did not get the tale to satisfy him, he seems to have
made every effort. The best external evidence of his intention is in
his revisions of the tale. Seymour L. Gross in an excellent article
has shown that in revision Hawthorne worked toward representativeness, toward making the tale transcend any particular manifestation
of evil, toward making it touch "the universal heart."[4] And in that
revision Hawthorne did what is difficult for any writer to do: he
deleted passages good and effective in themselves for the sake of the
whole effect. The figures in the tale did not gather their import
without his conscious attention; and he must have realized that "The
Gentle Boy," although less overtly allegorical than many of his tales,
is in the end highly representative.

The representative quality of the tale, however, has its foundation
in the history of Puritan-Quaker relationships. G. Harrison Orians's
careful study shows that Hawthorne used several writers, the most
important to the tale certainly Sewel, with Hutchinson, on whom
Hawthorne so often relied, also among them.[5] The relationship of
the introduction to the tale and its sources is clear and direct. The
first three paragraphs of the tale—Hawthorne deleted one long
paragraph in revision—recount the general history of the Quaker
intrusion into the colony.[6] Hawthorne accepts Sewel's judgment that,

3. Quoted in the introductory note to *Twice-Told Tales*, p. 11.
4. "Hawthorne's Revision of 'The Gentle Boy,'" *American Literature* 26
(1954): 196–208. Hawthorne extensively revised the text that had appeared in
The Token for inclusion in the 1837 *Twice-Told Tales*.
5. "The Sources and Themes of Hawthorne's 'The Gentle Boy,'" *New
England Quarterly* 14 (1941): 664–78.
6. The deleted paragraph deals with the extenuations for the Puritan fear of

above all other persons involved, Endicott, then governor, must bear responsibility.[7] The next-to-last paragraph of the tale deals with the results of the "king's mandate to stay the New England persecutors." Within this frame the action may be dated. It begins on the evening of the day, October 27, 1659, that Marmaduke Stevenson and William Robinson (one of whom we are to take to be Ilbrahim's father) were executed, when Ilbrahim is about six years old. Ilbrahim dies at the time when the letters from Charles II ordering the end of the executions arrive in New England. The letters arrived September 9, 1661; Hawthorne makes them arrive somewhat later in the year.

Most of the figures in the tale, moreover, have historical connections. Tobias Pearson has precedents in New England Puritans converted to Quakerism as a kind of side effect of the persecution of the Quakers;[8] Orians cites six such persons, among them the well-known Lawrence Southwick. Pearson, once a soldier in Cromwell's army but disillusioned when he saw Cromwell's ambitions develop, had come to New England hoping to improve his fortunes. His imperfect sympathy with Puritanism he might never have realized fully had not his protection of Ilbrahim brought Puritan hate upon him. Ilbrahim's mother, Catharine, Orians thinks, is in her character and career largely patterned after Mary Dyer,[9] but after Mary Prince[10]

Quakers. Although it is historically sound, Hawthorne clearly decided that he was not discussing a historical controversy, but writing a tragic tale.

7. Sewel writes of Endicott's "blood-thirstiness" (1: 209), and of his being "drunk with blood" (1: 360). He says that Endicott disregarded the laws of England and listened to no appeal to them (1: 255), and that his death of a "loathsome disease" was appropriate to his life, "his name being like to give a bad savour through ages to come" (1: 442). Hawthorne's attitude toward the persecution of the Quakers differs markedly from the nineteenth-century nationalism of Bancroft's account, which says nothing about Endicott or about the order by Charles II that ended the execution of Quakers in the colony. See Bancroft, 1: 451–58.

8. Striking examples are Nicolas Upshal of Boston and Samuel Shattock of Salem. See Sewel, 1: 208 and 224.

9. See Sewel, 1: 292–303. Mary Dyer apparently left her children to go on missions as Catharine does in the tale. Sewel says: "I find also that she was of a comely and grave countenance, of a good family and estate, and a mother of several children: but her husband it seems was of another persuasion" (1: 301).

10. In the tale Catharine is identified as the "woman who had assaulted the Governor with frightful language as he passed the window of her prison."

and perhaps others too.[11] Mary Dyer was reprieved from a death
sentence and conveyed into banishment on the day Stevenson and
Robinson were hanged. But, like other Quakers, she returned from
banishment to incur the sentence of death that was the penalty for
return; likewise Catharine in the tale, as the Puritan minister reminds
her, is under sentence of death. Her invasion of the pulpit has
several historical parallels;[12] Hawthorne describes an invasion much
like it in "Main Street."

Figures less important to the tale are perhaps more completely
representative of historical persons. The old Quaker who offers his
comfort to Pearson on the evening of Ilbrahim's death has little function in the action, and exists primarily for his historical representativeness, for his combination of courage, fanaticism, and sweet-
ness. The Puritan minister who, although he has himself endured
persecution in England, preaches against the Pearsons' protection of
Ilbrahim has parallels, Orians thinks, in the famous John Wilson,
and in the apologist for the Quaker persecution, John Norton,[13] who
wrote *The Heart of N-England rent at the Blasphemies of the Present
Generation* (1659). But the passage on Quakers in "Main Street"
suggests that Hawthorne may have been thinking of the Salem
minister, Edward Norris.

Yet, although most of the figures in the tale have their historical
analogues, they have a more than historical representativeness, for
this is the story of the hate and pride that live always in human

---

Hutchinson says of Mary Prince that "as the governor was going from the
public worship . . . Mary Prince called to him from a window of the prison, railing
at and reviling him, saying, Woe unto thee, thou art an oppressor; and
denouncing the judgments of God upon him" (1: 168).

11. Catharine's name and her wide ranging career seem to be related to
Sewel's account of Catharine Evans, a remarkable woman to whom he gives
much space. The Turkish episode in Catharine's career is founded on an adventure of Mary Fisher, who also came to New England. See 1:332–33 and
378–414.

12. Sewel often mentions such preemption of pulpits by Quakers who speak
"a few words" after "the priest" has finished his sermon. For examples, see
1: 224 and 251.

13. Sewel says of Norton that it is no wonder the magistrates "were so cruel
in persecuting since their chief teacher thus wickedly encouraged them to it"
(1: 254) and holds him chiefly responsible for the law which banished Quakers
on pain of death if they returned (1: 257).

hearts, and assume their strange disguises in the righteous and well-meaning. And it is the story, too, of the love that lives in human hearts, so often despised and rejected.

"The Gentle Boy" leaves on the memory such an impression of continuity and wholeness that, when one returns to the tale to consider it closely, he may be a little surprised to find just how the action does develop. The structure of the tale deserves attention. After the first three-paragraph section of historical background, the action develops in four sections, separated by lines of suspension points, each section centering upon a single episode; and there is a short concluding section. Continuity is accomplished—except for a single decided time break—by passages of summary narration so skillful that one is hardly aware in ordinary reading of the transitions between them and direct representation. One has the illusion that a large part of the more-than-two-year time span of the action is represented. A consideration of structure, moreover, helps to make clear how much the tale is concerned with the spiritual changes in Pearson, and suggests that the episodes were designed to mark out those changes.

In the second section of the tale, at the outset of the action, Tobias Pearson finds Ilbrahim weeping at the newly-made graves of the two hanged Quakers. Pearson takes the boy home with him, and he and his wife, Dorothy, (who are childless) determine to care for him and "to afford him the instruction which should counteract the pernicious errors hitherto instilled into his infant mind"—their aversion to Quaker doctrines is at the beginning as great as that of their neighbors. But at once those neighbors subject the Pearsons to odium and insults, and their insults become for Pearson "imperceptible but powerful workers toward an end which his most secret thought had not yet whispered."

The third section of the tale represents an episode on the second Sunday of Ilbrahim's stay with the Pearsons. They take him to church, where the minister preaches of "the danger of pity, in some cases a commendable and Christian virtue, but inapplicable to this pernicious sect" of Quakers.[14] Before the congregation is dismissed, a Quaker

14. Hawthorne has a source for this sentence, curiously not in the words of a minister, but in a letter by Edward Rawson, secretary of the Court of Boston, written to English authorities defending the execution of Robinson and

woman, robed in sackcloth—whom Ilbrahim recognizes as his mother—
ascends the pulpit stairs and addresses the congregation. Her discourse
is evidence of "an imagination hopelessly entangled with her reason";
it is vague and incomprehensible; but it seems "to spread its own atmosphere round the hearer's soul, and to move his feelings by some
influence unconnected with the words."[15] In this scene, as later in
the tale, Catharine rises to an Aeschylean stature, and her denunciation
to a tragic grandeur. Hawthorne here rivals the great set speeches in
Scott, Meg Merrilees's speech beginning "Ride your ways, Laird of
Ellangowan" (*Guy Mannering*, chap. 8), for example, or that wonderful sermon of Ephraim Macbriar in *Old Mortality* (chap. 18).
Surely not often is a fiction writer able to provide with complete
convincingness an eloquence for a speaker of just the sort he affirms the
speaker has.

When Catharine's harangue is ended, Ilbrahim embraces her.
She has a momentary sense that she has failed him and her duty. But
Dorothy offers to care for the boy, and assures Catharine that "Providence has signally marked out my husband to protect him." It is
at this scene that Hawthorne, for the one time in the tale, points up
overtly the allegorical quality of his action: Dorothy Pearson is
"rational piety"; Catharine is "unbridled fanaticism"; and they form
a "practical allegory" as, each holding Ilbrahim by a hand, they seem
to contend for his heart. Elsewhere in the tale the imagery accomplishes
a more subtle sort of pointing-up.

Catharine, realizing Dorothy's simple goodness, and after narrowly
scrutinizing Pearson—who she sees is more likely to be influenced by
Ilbrahim than to influence him—agrees that Ilbrahim shall remain
with the Pearsons: "Even for his infant hands," she says, "there is a
labor in the vineyard." She goes thereafter on the missions to which
she believes herself called, "the apostle of her own unquiet heart."

The fourth section of the tale begins with summary narration in
which something like eight months of elapsing time are unobtrusively
indicated. The action had begun, we remember, in late October;

Stevenson. Rawson speaks of "pity and commiseration, a commendable and
Christian virtue, yet easily abused" (Sewel, 1: 350).

15. Hawthorne's sentence might describe two letters by Mary Dyer, addressed
to the General Court of Boston. See Sewel, 1: 296–301.

before the winter snows are melted Ilbrahim responds to the love the Pearsons give him, and to Dorothy's tact and understanding. Although he is over-sensitive and subject to fits of depression, he is often happy in their household. But the scorn of children of his own age and their rejection beforehand of the love he would bestow upon them are most grievous to him. As spring comes on, however, Ilbrahim comes to believe that he has found one friend among the Puritan children. A boy about two years older than he is injured in a fall from a tree near the Pearson house and is cared for by the Pearsons. He is not an attractive boy, but in his suffering he appeals to Ilbrahim's necessity to love, and there seems an affection between the two.

One pleasant summer afternoon, when this lad is enough recovered to get about with a staff, Ilbrahim—who, having manifested his love for one child, no longer fears the rest— tries to join a group of children at play. The scene is at the outset idyllic, and the men who pass by wonder why life cannot always retain this charm; "their hearts, or their imaginations" answer that "the bliss of childhood gushes from its innocence." The irony seems heavy-handed, but it underlines an irony inherent in experience.

When Ilbrahim joins the group, "all at once, the devil of their fathers" enters into "the unbreeched fanatics" and they attack him, displaying "an instinct of destruction far more loathsome than the bloodthirstiness of manhood." The boy Ilbrahim supposes his friend calls out encouragement to him; but when Ilbrahim struggles to "the foul-hearted little villain," he strikes Ilbrahim across the mouth with his staff. Ilbrahim thereupon gives up all effort to protect himself, and is beaten and trampled by the children. Severely injured, he is taken home by some neighbors, "who put themselves to the trouble of rescuing the poor little heretic." There is hardly a horror in nineteenth-century American literature so deep as this account of the Puritan children with the devil of their fathers in them; and certainly there is no more impressive symbol of the transmission of hate and ignorance.

Ilbrahim seems to recover in body, but never in spirit, and indeed the attack of the children is the beginning of a decline in which he feels the absence of his mother as never before. In the meantime, the change in Pearson—the change the reader has been led to expect—

becomes apparent to Pearson himself. Hawthorne's account of it seems both psychologically and historically convincing, the what-must-have-been that turned more than a few Puritans to the numbers of the persecuted.

> The incident with which this tale commences found Pearson in a state of religious dulness, yet mentally disquieted, and longing for a more fervid faith than he possessed. The first effect of his kindness to Ilbrahim was to produce a softened feeling, and incipient love for the child's whole sect; but joined to this, and resulting perhaps from self-suspicion, was a proud and ostentatious contempt of all their tenets and practical extravagances. In the course of much thought, however, for the subject struggled irresistibly into his mind, the foolishness of the doctrine began to be less evident, and the points which had particularly offended his reason assumed another aspect, or vanished entirely away. The work within him appeared to go on even while he slept, and that which had been a doubt, when he laid down to rest, would often hold the place of a truth, confirmed by some forgotten demonstration, when he recalled his thoughts in the morning. But while he was thus becoming assimilated to the enthusiasts, his contempt, in nowise decreasing towards them, grew very fierce against himself; he imagined, also, that every face of his acquaintance wore a sneer, and that every word addressed to him was a gibe. Such was his state of mind at the period of Ilbrahim's misfortune; and the emotions consequent upon that event completed the change, of which the child had been the original instrument.

To find as skillful an analysis of an inner life in all Hawthorne's work, we should have to go to *The Scarlet Letter*.

At the end of the fourth section of the tale there is a decided time break: "And now the tale must stride forward over many months." Since the fifth section includes the news of the arrival of the letters from Charles II but begins "A winter evening . . . ," it seems clear that Hawthorne has extended the historical time of the arrival of the king's letters to the winter in order to have a winter storm surround the last action. The tale strides forward something like seventeen months.

As the fifth section begins Pearson and the old Quaker are represented together in Pearson's house. Their conversation lets us know how Pearson has fared in the long interval. We see a most unhappy Pearson, who has suffered much for his faith, who is desolate and rebellious in his suffering, and who feels the imminent death of Ilbrahim the crown of his sorrows: "Now he too must die," Pearson says, "as if my love were poison." The communing of the two men is interrupted by a knock on the door and Catharine appears. The action of the tale ends with what Aristotle calls a reversal.

Catharine returns exalted by the news she bears—the news that the king had ordered an end to the New England executions[16]—exalted as if the tidings were those of her own victory. But she returns also to devastating sorrow for herself. It falls to the old Quaker, who has been in his way comforting Pearson, to inform her: "Sister," he says, "thou tellest us of His love, manifested in temporal good; and now must we speak to thee of that selfsame love, displayed in chastenings." But Catharine, who has long mistaken her own will for the will of God, is far from submission to any chastening she has not herself desired. Hawthorne points up the dramatic quality of her speech—here as elsewhere one thinks of the tale as like a play—by indications of its increasing emotional intensity. In the second sentence of the speech, the ironic reminiscence of St. Paul in 2 Cor. 11:23–27 seems calculated:

> "I am a woman, I am but a woman; will He try me above my strength?" said Catharine very quickly, and almost in a whisper. "I have been wounded sore: I have suffered much; many things in the body; many in the mind; crucified in myself, and in them that were dearest to me. Surely," added she, with a long shudder, "He hath spared me in this one thing." She broke forth with sudden and irrepressible violence. "Tell me, man of cold heart, what has God done to me? Hath He cast me down, never to rise again? Hath He crushed my very heart in his hand? And thou, to whom I committed my child, how hast thou fulfilled thy trust?

16. When in 1661 Edward Burrough informed Charles II of what was happening to Quakers in New England and the king ordered that executions be stopped and accused persons sent to England for trial, Burrough also persuaded the king to allow his letters to be carried by Samuel Shattock of Salem, then in England, banished from the Bay Colony on pain of death if he returned. The ship that carried Shattock was captained by a Quaker and Shattock was accompanied by a number of Quakers. See Sewel, 1: 361–64.

Give me back the boy, well, sound, alive, alive; or earth and
Heaven shall avenge me!"

Ilbrahim has the comfort of his mother's presence at his death; if his
last words—"Mourn not, dearest mother. I am happy now"—comfort
her, they do not change her.

Hawthorne's tact is too acute to suggest any such change. Indeed,
in the concluding section for the tale we are told that after Ilbrahim's
death Catharine's fanaticism becomes the greater, and that she seeks
out every lifted scourge and casts herself on the floor of every dungeon.
Not until the persecutions finally end is her nature softened, and at
last her neighbors in some sense accept her. Hawthorne's account
of that acceptance seems as bitter a comment on Puritans—or perhaps
just on human nature—as he ever made, for he ascribes to Catharine's
neighbors the spiritual effrontery of a patronizing pity for her; she
becomes "a being on whom the otherwise superfluous sympathies
of all might be bestowed."

"The Gentle Boy" is quite different from "My Kinsman, Major
Molineux" and from "Roger Malvin's Burial," written about the same
time but passed over by Hawthorne in the selection for *Twice-Told
Tales.* He had no hesitation about "The Gentle Boy." It has nothing
of the ambiguity we think characteristic of him.[17] Its irony, but for the
reversal at Catharine's return, is only the pointing-up of the irony that
inheres in its historical substance, and irony of a verbal sort, when
Hawthorne allows himself the wry casting of a phrase or sentence.
With "Young Goodman Brown" it has in common only Hawthorne's
ancestral connection with its materials and the highly representative
quality of its action.

Possibly these differences from the favored early tales account for the
lack of any great interest in "The Gentle Boy" in the criticism written
within the last twenty years. Hyatt H. Waggoner remarks paren-
thetically that "The Gentle Boy" "is in fact a very fine story. We need

17. "The Gentle Boy" has, however, an enigmatic passage. In the description
of the boy who betrays Ilbrahim's trust, Hawthorne says, "The disposition of
the boy was sullen and reserved, and the village schoolmaster stigmatized him
as obtuse in intellect; although, at a later period of life, he evinced ambition
and very peculiar talents." The sentence suggests that Hawthorne was thinking
of some historical personage. The boy would have been in his middle years in
the witchcraft time.

to reread it." Now it may be that the pathos of the tale has repelled critics. Yet the pathetic gentle boy is properly the title character, the passive center of the tale with all its disparate passions. And if critics feel the pathos embarrassing or unrewarding to discuss, they must feel the scenes of passive suffering in Shakespeare or Dostoevski equally so.

But "The Gentle Boy" has a quality beyond pathos. We recognize in the tale the ineluctable flaw in our nature, and apprehend that we can name but never fully understand human motives, that our experience, despite sages, scholars, and scientists, remains for us opaque.

Horatio Bridge had not read "The Gentle Boy" until it was collected; then he wrote to Hawthorne that the tale had made him weep and that he thought it the best in the volume. Bridge was no sentimentalist; and perhaps he read "The Gentle Boy" better than we do. Our forebears used to like to quote Virgil's *Sunt lacrimae rerum et mentem mortalia tangunt*. We have not lost our humanity but we are confused about our norms of feeling. And we may be sure that at some passages in the tale, Bridge did not weep; for some there is no relief in tears.

On the night in which Ilbrahim dies, the voice of the wind comes "as if the Past were speaking." The Past speaks in this tale, as it does in other Hawthorne tales with other voices; we may again listen to this voice as attentively as we listen to others.

"THE MINISTER'S BLACK VEIL"

Since Hawthorne included "The Minister's Black Veil: A Parable" in the first edition of *Twice-Told Tales*, he apparently did not think it a difficult tale—rather one that "may be understood and felt by anybody who will give himself the trouble to read it." Yet his critics have by no means agreed about its purport; and although we do not ordinarily think of a parable having multiple meanings, this tale has been read in very different fashions. Since it was first printed in 1835 in *The Token* for 1836, it seems not to have been one of the pieces for the projected "Story-Teller" volume, and it may have been written not long before its first printing.

"The Minister's Black Veil" has two kinds of importance in Hawthorne's development. He uses American materials in the tale, but he uses them to his own purposes; the tale stands in considerable contrast to, say, "The Gray Champion," first printed in the same year. In the second place, the tale is an early example of Hawthorne's way of "turning different sides of the same dark idea to the reader's eye,"[18] exploring its every nuance, exhausting its suggestion. This is the technique that distinguishes *The Scarlet Letter* and seems less satisfactory in the other three romances. We see something of it in other tales, notably in "The Birthmark," but it appears in no marked fashion earlier than "The Minister's Black Veil." One looks far to find a comparable success in this technique in other writers: Tolstoy's *The Death of Ivan Ilych* is one; perhaps Albert Camus' *The Fall* is another. But a writer attempting this persistent and minute manipulation of an idea risks an intolerable repetitousness that he can avoid only through finish of style and perfection of pattern. Hawthorne achieves both in "The Minister's Black Veil."

Since the minister preaches an election sermon during Governor Belcher's administration (1730–1741), years after he had put on his black veil, the time of the action is fixed as the first part of the eighteenth century. The narrator of the tale seems a citizen of Milford; we may suppose him in the latter part of his life a deacon in Mr. Hooper's church. He has been acquainted with Mr. Hooper through the many years the tale spans and, with one exception, he reports only what he could have heard and seen, and, of course, his inferences therefrom. And even the interview between Mr. Hooper and his fiancée he might have known through some account of it by Elizabeth. Throughout his story he considers the meaning of what he has to tell, and by implication invites the reader to consider it with him. He emerges clearly: a likable, shrewd man who views Mr. Hooper and his parishioners sympathetically or, on occasion, with a wry amusement. He moves his story with remarkable skill from the time Mr. Hooper was "about thirty" through his "long life."

The narrator begins with an account of Mr. Hooper's congregation gathering on a Sunday morning in their various ages and conditions, for all are to be affected by the mysteries of the veil he has donned for the first time. The account of this first Sunday occupies about two-fifths of the narrative. It includes the Sunday morning service, the funeral of a young lady following the afternoon service, and an evening

18. The quoted expression is from a letter of Hawthorne's to James T. Fields concerning *The Scarlet Letter*. See Fields, p. 51.

wedding—the rituals for what is really important in human experience. The next day Mr. Hooper's parishioners talk of little but his black veil, and their preoccupation with the veil grows so that at length it is "found expedient to send a deputation of the church, in order to deal with Mr. Hooper about the mystery." The narrator's amused remark about its result is a fine touch: the deputies pronounce the matter "too weighty to be handled, except by a council of the churches, if, indeed, it might not require a general synod."

When the deputies have failed, Elizabeth endeavors to discover the secret of the veil. Her interview with Mr. Hooper is directly reported at some length. But if we are to suppose that Elizabeth has been able "to penetrate the mystery of the black veil" (and there is a suggestion that she has), we must suppose that she has not communicated her knowledge to the narrator, and he moves into summary narrative with a single sentence of transition: "From that time no attempts were made to remove Mr. Hooper's black veil, or, by a direct appeal, to discover the secret which it was supposed to hide."

The summary narrative records what is commonly thought and said about Mr. Hooper and his veil, and it is often interpretive, but it leaves the mystery unresolved. It brings us—at long last, as we feel under its spell—to Mr. Hooper's deathbed. The illusion of elapsing time is complete; the adroit transitions sustain our feeling of continuity and wholeness. When the narrator has recorded what is said to Mr. Hooper at his deathbed and what Mr. Hooper replies, he has done, we feel, all he can toward his and our understanding of the veil his clergyman has felt himself bound to wear through almost a lifetime.

Hawthorne doubtless assumed that Mr. Hooper's deathbed speech would be accepted as a sufficient interpretation of the tale—had he not, it is most unlikely that he would have included "The Minister's Black Veil" in *Twice-Told Tales*. When the clergyman attending Mr. Hooper pleads that he remove his veil, and then insists that he do so, Mr. Hooper gathers his last strength to say what he had meant by the symbol he had worn so long:

"Why do you tremble at me alone? Tremble also at each other! Have men avoided me, and women shown no pity, and children screamed and fled, only for my black veil? What, but the mystery which it obscurely typifies, has made this piece of crape so awful? When the friend shows his inmost heart to his friend; the lover to his best beloved; when man does not vainly shrink from the eye of his Creator, loathsomely treasuring up the secret of his sin; then deem me a monster, for the symbol beneath which I have lived, and die! I look around me, and, lo! on every visage a Black Veil!"

So far as Mr. Hooper is an allegorical figure, he seems to have interpreted his own significance.

Hawthorne's note to the tale indicates its inception and seems to suggest the direction of its interpretation:

> Another clergyman in New England, Mr. Joseph Moody, of York, Maine, who died about eighty years since, made himself remarkable by the same eccentricity that is here related of the Reverend Mr. Hooper. In his case, however, the symbol had a different import. In early life he had accidentally killed a beloved friend; and from that day till the hour of his own death, he hid his face from men.

As *The Scarlet Letter* seems to have had its inception in Hawthorne's reflection on the spiritual result of an enforced and continual confession by the wearing of a symbol, so, in something the same way, "The Minister's Black Veil" seems to stem from speculation about the spiritual import of a symbol of concealment voluntarily worn. And since the Reverend Mr. Moody wore his veil as a self-imposed penance and Mr. Hooper's veil has "a different import," Hawthorne seems to be saying that the reader's primary concern need not be to identify the nature of some guilt in the minister. But that has often enough been the concern of critics of the tale.

Edgar Allan Poe's interpretation of the tale in his 1842 review of *Twice-Told Tales* may be the first effort on the part of a critic to identify Mr. Hooper's guilt:

> "The Minister's Black Veil" is a masterly composition, of which the sole defect is that to the rabble its exquisite skill will be *caviare*. The *obvious* meaning of this article will be found to smother its insinuated one. The *moral* put into the mouth of the dying minister will be supposed to convey the *true* import of the narrative; and that a crime of dark dye (having reference to

the "young lady") has been committed, is a point which only minds congenial with that of the author will perceive.

Poe has apparently seized upon a preternatural suggestion the narrator records without assenting to it—a suggestion such as we learn to expect from Hawthorne. At the funeral of the young lady, as the minister bends over the coffin and his black veil hangs straight from his forehead, he hastily pulls it back, as if he feared the corpse might see his face. A witness affirms that at this moment "the corpse had slightly shuddered." "A superstitious old woman," the narrator remarks amusedly, "was the only witness of this prodigy." Another preternatural suggestion seems to point in a different direction. As the mourners are leaving, a woman who had looked back at Mr. Hooper remarks, "I had a fancy that the minister and the maiden's spirit were walking hand in hand." Her husband confesses to the same fancy, but it is a fancy that hardly suggests "a crime of dark dye."

Nevertheless Poe points to a problem: there is an ambiguity in the tale that does not depend upon half-playful preternatural suggestion. The narrator speaks of "an ambiguity of sin or sorrow, which enveloped the poor minister"; and when Elizabeth warns Mr. Hooper that "there may be whispers that you hide your face under the consciousness of secret sin," he answers, "If I hide my face for sorrow, there is *Ambise* cause enough, and if I cover it for secret sin, what mortal might not do the same?" Even his dying speech does not preclude his having treasured up "the secret of his sin"; nor does anything the narrator says preclude it.

It is perhaps no wonder, then, that writers on the tale have tried to identify some sort of guilt or guilt feeling in the minister. Of late it has been insisted that it is a guilt Mr. Hooper—or perhaps Hawthorne himself—does not consciously recognize.[19] The tale seems to invite such attempts, but they run into trouble.

Discussion of Hawthorne's work should never proceed, it seems to

19. Here is a selection of recent interpretations: William Bysshe Stein, "The Parable of the Antichrist in 'The Minister's Black Veil,' " *American Literature* 27 (1955): 386–92; Thomas F. Walsh, Jr., "Hawthorne: Mr. Hooper's 'Affable Weakness,' " *Modern Language Notes* 74 (1959): 404–6; E. Earle Stibitz, "Ironic Unity in Hawthorne's 'The Minister's Black Veil,' " *American Literature* 34 (1962): 182–90; Frederick C. Crews, *The Sins of the Fathers* (New York, 1966), pp. 106–111.

me, as if his characteristic ambiguity were not ambiguity really, but
a sort of puzzle set for critical acumen to solve. Hawthorne's
ambiguity is one of his ways of representing his pervasive sense of
mystery, a kind of humility in him. Even in a children's story, "The
Minotaur," he remarks that "the heart of any ordinary man . . . is
ten times as great a mystery as the labyrinth of Crete." He will not
presume to solve the mystery, nor can he forget it. If one reads a
Hawthorne tale recognizing the ambiguity, but accepting it as really
ambiguous, he is reading the tale, it is safe to say, as Hawthorne
intended it to be read, and to that extent reading it well.

This consideration applies in a special way to "The Minister's Black
Veil." The narrator does not know what the veil conceals, and it
conceals perhaps a "dreadful secret." A reading of the tale that dis-
closed the secret—could it do so—either as a sinful act or a psychological
quirk would destroy the impressiveness of the symbol, destroy the very
quality for which the tale exists. From time to time a "faint, sad smile"
glimmers or flickers on Mr. Hooper's lips, but always in the same context, always when some one or more of his fellowmen seek an explanation of the veil. It is as if he smiles in the realization that what the
questioners seek to know is at once simpler and far more complex than
they can think. That faint smile lingers yet.

The central concern of the tale, indeed, is not the minister but the
effect of the black veil on all of Milford. The narrator records its effect
on the minister, on his ministry, on his fiancée, on the deputation of
the church, on the officials who listen to his election day sermon, on
the citizens of Milford, down to the "imitative little imp" who covers
his face and is, as the narrator thinks the minister may be, "affrighted
by himself." By the effect of the veil, Mr. Hooper becomes "a man
of awful power over souls that were in agony for sin." Dying sinners
shudder at the veil, but will not yield their breath without its wearer.
The gloom of the veil enables him "to sympathize with all dark affections." And the veil has its effect not because Mr. Hooper's fellows
do not recognize its meaning as a symbol, but because they do recognize
it. "What," the minister asks at last, "but the mystery which it obscurely typifies, has made this piece of crape so awful?"

The citizens of Milford recognize, as everyone at least in some of his
experience recognizes, how far alone each man and woman is. They
do not put their recognition into words; few of us have been able to say

what all mankind know. Sometimes a poet has said it for us; Matthew
Arnold in "To Marguerite" has. And in a poem by Hawthorne's
contemporary, Christopher Pearse Cranch, there seems almost an echo
of Hawthorne's tale:

> We are spirits clad in veils;
>   Man by man was never seen;
> All our deep communing fails
>   To remove the shadowy screen.

> Heart to heart was never known;
>   Mind with mind did never meet;
> We are columns left alone
>   Of a temple once complete.

Of this human burden Mr. Hooper has vowed to make himself, and
does make himself, the "type and symbol." "The Minister's Black
Veil" is a parable just in its representation of that burden.

If the tale is read as a parable, it touches us nearly. "Always the
struggle of the human soul," Don Marquis once wrote, "is to break
through the barriers of silence and distance into companionship.
Friendship, lust, love, art, religion—we rush into them pleading, fight-
ing, clamoring for the touch of spirit laid against our spirit." If the
tale is read as a parable, some passages become, not indications of a
morbid condition in Mr. Hooper, but allegorical representations of
human need. "It is but a mortal veil—it is not for eternity!" the minister
says to Elizabeth. "O! you know not how lonely I am, and how frightened, to be alone behind my black veil."

To neglect what Poe calls "the *moral* put into the mouth of the
dying minister" is to neglect what the narrative has proceeded toward.
The "ambiguity of sin or sorrow, which enveloped the poor minister,"
is an ambiguity in his person and his past; his last words concern us all,
and they are unambiguous. An interpretation of the tale that dis-
regards or depreciates its next-to-last paragraph is rather like an interpretation of Robert Frost's "Desert Places" which should disregard
the last stanza of the poem. And such interpretation of the tale neglects
Hawthorne's preoccupation with the need of men for their fellows
and, therefore, obscures the place of "The Minister's Black Veil" in a
pattern that his takes make.

"The Minister's Black Veil" has also an important relationship to *The Scarlet Letter*; it becomes part of the fabric of the romance and a means to the development of the character of the Reverend Mr. Dimmesdale. Mr. Hooper, Sir Leslie Stephen remarks, is "a kind of symbolic prophecy of Dimmesdale"; but more than that, Dimmesdale has attributes nearly identical with some of those of Mr. Hooper. The narrator of the tale assures us that the black veil had made its wearer "a very efficient clergyman": converts and dying sinners both found in him a peculiar spiritual power. Now the clerical efficiency of Mr. Dimmesdale is of the same kind as that of Mr. Hooper. Both, set apart from their parishioners, have yet by a secret sharing with them a special insight. Mr. Hooper inspires in his people a strange mixture of dread, confidence, and dependence. Mr. Dimmesdale has a power denied to the "true saintly fathers" among his brother clergy of reaching common men, "of addressing the whole human brotherhood in the heart's native language." We are strangely reminded of Mr. Hooper's "ambiguity of sin or sorrow" when the narrator in the romance says of Mr. Dimmesdale: Ambiguity.

> The burden, whatever it might be, of crime or anguish, beneath
> which it was his doom to totter . . . gave him sympathies so inti-
> mate with the sinful brotherhood of mankind; so that his heart
> vibrated in unison with theirs, and received their pain into
> itself, and sent its own throb of pain through a thousand other
> hearts, in gushes of sad, persuasive eloquence. Oftenest persuasive,
> but sometimes terrible! The people knew not the power that
> moved them thus. [chap. 11]

The gloom of the black veil enables Mr. Hooper "to sympathize with all dark affections"; Dimmesdale has "sympathies so intimate with the sinful brotherhood of mankind." Mr. Hooper has "an awful power" over souls in agony for sin; Dimmesdale's eloquence is "sometimes terrible." We cannot suppose Hawthorne unconscious of Dimmesdale's spiritual descent from Mr. Hooper.

Nor can we suppose Hawthorne unconscious of another return to "The Minister's Black Veil" in the romance. In the last chapter the narrator presents us with a version of Dimmesdale's career and death quite different from that of the central narrative, but one which is like a new version of "The Minister's Black Veil" in little. Some of

Dimmesdale's parishioners reject entirely any idea of his guilt with Hester, and deny that his dying words acknowledge or imply it; he has, they believe, "made the manner of his death a parable, in order to impress on his admirers the mighty and mournful lesson, that, in the view of Infinite Purity, we are sinners all alike." As Mr. Dimmesdale's loyal parishioners see him, he has, like Mr. Hooper—but to use the words of "Fancy's Show Box"—claimed "his brotherhood, even with the guiltiest."

"DR. HEIDEGGER'S EXPERIMENT"

"Dr. Heidegger's Experiment" seems not to have much interested Hawthorne's critics; it is usually dismissed as perhaps charming but certainly slight. Yet the tale has multiple suggestion; one is likely, at each return to it, to find some touch he had not noticed before. It was first printed (under the title "The Fountain of Youth") in the *Knickerbocker Magazine* in January 1837 and collected in the same year in the first edition of *Twice-Told Tales*.

The tale is Hawthorne's first use of the elixir of life motif. Neither the time nor the place of the action is made quite clear. Dr. Heidegger remarks that Ponce de León sought the elixir of life "two or three centuries ago"; since he did discover Florida in 1513, that seems to indicate the eighteenth century, as does the attire of the men. But the names of the figures in the tale—and what evocative names they are!—suggest the seventeenth century, or at least Wycherly and Killigrew do. We may take the place to be somewhere in New England; as we have seen, there were alchemists and students of the occult in seventeenth-century New England, indeed in Salem. This intentional obscurity about time and place puts the action of the tale in a world of playful Gothic parable appropriate to its timeless concern.

Dr. Heidegger's study is furnished with all the most familiar small properties of Gothic romance. The long list of them in the third paragraph of the tale is a set of literary allusions, but even for the reader who hardly recognizes them as such, they establish an atmosphere playfully portentous, and imaginatively convincing for the action that is to be represented. Here, we are told, when the doctor's book of magic once had been disturbed by a chambermaid, "the skeleton had rattled in its closet, the picture of the young lady had stepped one foot upon the floor, and several ghastly faces had peeped forth from the mirror; while the brazen head of Hippocrates frowned, and said,—'Forbear!' "

The narrative point of view is complex and—as often in Hawthorne —eludes precise definition. The beginning of the tale seems to establish it as a story current in the narrator's society: the narrator can say of the doctor's study, "If all the stories were true," and hint that the community thinks the doctor's four friends a little mad. Dr. Heidegger's "eccentricity had become the nucleus for a thousand fantastic stories," some of which might be traced to the narrator's "veracious self." Even toward the end of the tale, he reports what the mirror "is said to have reflected." Yet the behavior of Dr. Heidegger and his four friends is minutely reported, as if by a witness present at the experiment. The narrator seems to report what he sees and hears and such inference therefrom as is natural to an observer who knows the past lives of the five. But he tells his story with full confidence in his readers' perceptiveness, and allows a delicate thread of irony to run through the tale. The technique in "Dr. Heidegger's Experiment" is far more subtle than that of some Hawthorne tales more often discussed.

The action is a simple one. It begins on a summer's afternoon and ends at sunset. Old Dr. Heidegger invites four friends of his to experiment with an elixir from the Fountain of Youth. The friends are Mr. Medbourne, once "a prosperous merchant . . . now little better than a mendicant"; Colonel Killigrew, who "had wasted his best years . . . in the pursuit of sinful pleasures"; Mr. Gascoigne, "a ruined politician"; and the Widow Wycherly, who had been "a great beauty in her day," and with whom the three men had all been in love. The elixir effects a temporary restoration of their youthful spirits, if not perhaps of their youthful persons. But the influence of the elixir lasts but an hour or so. During that time Dr. Heidegger's four friends are, in their desires, attitudes, and propensities, exactly what they had been in their prime.

At the end of the tale, therefore, the doctor says that if the Fountain of Youth gushed at his doorstep, "I would not stoop to bathe my lips in it—no, though its delirium were for years instead of moments. Such is the lesson ye have taught me!" If that be the "lesson" of the tale, the implications are of greater importance. And they are the more disturbing because they arise from a comic action.

Dr. Heidegger's lesson is only the confirmation of his expectation by his experiment. His four friends learn nothing from the experiment, as they have learned nothing from their experience. They are, it is true, amused at the doctor's warning before they drink the elixir, for it is ridiculous to suppose that "knowing how closely repentance treads behind the steps of error, they should ever go astray again." But their repentance—as so often in the rest of us—has not been contrition, only unhappiness. They take the same road they took so long before; their destiny seems the result of their own natures, their misdirection inevitable. Moreover, although each of the men has misdirected his life after his own fashion, they are equally prey to the calculating sexuality of the widow, who neither grants nor withholds her favors. It is their struggle over her that spills the remainder of the elixir, and destroys even their illusion of happiness. Dr. Heidegger, it is twice suggested, seems an embodiment of Time, "whose power had never been disputed, save by this fortunate company." But his four friends, in their illusion, feel "like new-created beings in a new-created universe," as we have lately and often been told was the characteristic American feeling. Their version of the Adamic myth, at least, is quickly destroyed.

Two of the moral ideas that emerge from "Dr. Heidegger's Experiment" Hawthorne had represented before, much less effectively. "The Wedding Knell" concerns the effort to deny or to ignore the power of time. The widow in that tale disputes the power of time in her way, as the doctor's friends dispute it in theirs, and accepts her defeat. And as we have seen, "The Prophetic Pictures," in a way quite different from that of "Dr. Heidegger's Experiment," represents the idea that character is or may be destiny. But these tales, perhaps because they are so explicit, are far less disturbing than the story of the old doctor's magic potion. "Dr. Heidegger's Experiment" does not seem to us to be the contrived illustration of a proposition; we accept its assumptions, and along with the doctor foresee the upshot of his experiment.

But the tales with which it is most natural to compare "Dr. Heidegger's Experiment" are "The Birthmark" and "Ethan Brand," since each of the three has as a central figure a scientist conceived and handled in the Gothic tradition. (Dr. Heidegger is a not-very-sinister Gothic scientist.) He does not have the spiritual pride of Aylmer nor is he guilty, as Ethan is, of invading the person of another—Dr. Heidegger's friends, even under the conditions of his experiment, act according to their own natures. Yet in Hawthorne's moral scheme (perhaps Dr. Heidegger is not quite guiltless, for the motive of his experiment can be little other than a curiosity about the natures and reactions of his friends.[20])

Artistically, the two later tales seem far less mature than "Dr. Heidegger's Experiment." In "The Birthmark" Hawthorne's effort to establish a setting in which the action can go on with imaginative convincingness is apparent, indeed intrusive.[21] "Ethan Brand" is disfigured by the almost desperate authorial interpretation in which Hawthorne struggles to justify his theme. The artistic problems in the three tales are not wholly different in kind; the degree of failure in the two later tales is just the degree of the reader's awareness of the problem in each.

Indeed, "Dr. Heidegger's Experiment" is (as it seems to me) a little masterpiece, without fault of taste or failure in tone. And it is pleasant to find that, at least this time, one of Hawthorne's editors recognized the essential excellence of a tale. In a congratulatory letter to Hawthorne about "Dr. Heidegger's Experiment," Lewis Gaylord Clark, the editor of the *Knickerbocker Magazine* wrote: "I have rarely read anything which delighted me more. The style is excellent, and the *keeping* of the whole excellent."[22]

Hawthorne probably would have thought of the tale as an allegory, but it does not have "the pale tint of flowers that blossomed in too retired a shade." The figures in the tale, although they are types, are lively ones. The vigorous tableau in which (they take their parts is but an allegorical condensation of their lives, for their hearts have always

20. See Coverdale's self-analysis at the beginning of chap. 9 of *The Blithedale Romance*.

21. This effort in "The Birthmark" is curiously like—and no better than—Poe's effort in "Ligeia" to make Lady Rowena's chamber in the former abbey an appropriate place for his action to go on.

22. *Hawthorne and His Wife*, 1:133. Poe's praise for the tale is very like Clark's; the tale is, Poe says, "exceedingly well imagined and executed with surpassing ability."

been given to what cannot endure.)The more or less nefarious bents of the widow's lovers emerge clearly;(the widow looms in our imaginations in her "buxom prime.")Dr. Heidegger's special powers and knowledge are established so disarmingly that we accept both them and the efficacy of his elixir. Although the mirror reflects only "withered grandsires ridiculously contending for . . . a shrivelled grandam," their illusion is, as we read, ours. We do not—willingly or unwillingly—suspend our disbelief: we have none to suspend.

Perhaps the special effect of the tale depends most of all on the restrained playfulness of its use of the Gothic. Without the Gothic tradition, the assumptions of the tale would have been imaginatively unconvincing; with the Gothic elements used in the ordinary Gothic fashion, the tale could only have been commonplace. And the balance is yet more delicate. Hawthorne achieves a tension between the comic surface and the somber implications of the tale, so that this least pretentious tale may disturb us more than either his "blackness" or his exhortation elsewhere. In no work is his control more sure.[23]

11. EARLY TALES IN MOSSES FROM AN OLD MANSE

Hawthorne said in "The Old Manse" that he was writing the piece as his appointment to the Salem Custom House was being announced. The Salem *Advertiser* announced the appointment on April 22, 1846. "The Old Manse," then, charming as it is, was written in Salem to plump out *Mosses from an Old Manse.* In it Hawthorne confessed his disappointment with his production in the three years and more that he had lived in Concord:

> All that I had to show, as a man of letters, were these few tales and essays, which had blossomed out like flowers in the calm summer of my heart and mind. . . . With these idle weeds and

23. For a discussion of the ill-considered note Hawthorne added to the tale in 1860, see Victor E. Gibbens, "Hawthorne's Note to 'Dr. Heidegger's Experiment,'" *Modern Language Notes* 60 (1945): 408-9.

withering blossoms I have intermixed some that were produced long ago,—old, faded things, reminding me of flowers pressed between the leaves of a book,—and now offer the bouquet, such as it is, to any whom it may please. These fitful sketches, with so little of external life about them, yet claiming no profundity of purpose,—so reserved, even while they sometimes seem so frank,—often but half in earnest, and never, even when most so, expressing satisfactorily the thoughts which they profess to image,—such trifles, I truly feel, afford no solid basis for a literary reputation.

This characteristic deprecation probably does not much affect the feeling of most readers that *Mosses* contains some of Hawthorne's best, and some of his weakest, work. But the reader today may not realize how small Hawthorne's production at the Old Manse really was.

The Riverside edition of *Mosses* contains three titles added in the 1854 edition: "Passages from a Relinquished Work" (1834), "Sketches for Memory" (1835), and Hawthorne's last tale, "Feathertop," first printed in 1852. The 1846 *Mosses* was made up of twenty-three pieces (counting "The Old Manse"); four of them were first printed early enough so that they might have been collected in the 1837 *Twice-Told Tales*: "Roger Malvin's Burial," "Young Goodman Brown," "Monsieur du Miroir," and "Mrs. Bullfrog." "A Virtuoso's Collection" was first printed in 1842, before Hawthorne's marriage. For reasons that will be advanced in a discussion of the tale, we may conclude that "Drowne's Wooden Image" was also written early. No more, then, than sixteen or seventeen of the twenty-six titles in *Mosses* as we now have it designate pieces written at the Old Manse.

Properly to add to these pieces to make an acceptable collection must have seemed to Hawthorne an important matter. From our point of view, his selection of the four pieces first printed before 1837, pieces that he had twice passed over in making his collections, poses two problems. In considering them, we cannot assume that he was holding anything back: in "The Old Manse" he says that *Mosses* is "the last offering, the last collection, of this nature which it is my purpose ever to put forth. Unless I could do better, I have done enough in this kind." Doubtless he meant the statement when he made it.

The first problem—to explain Hawthorne's choice of "Monsieur du

Miroir" and "Mrs. Bullfrog"—is the more difficult. Few readers can have much enjoyed them, and Hawthorne himself seems to have valued them very little. He wrote to Sophia Peabody in 1841:

> I do not very well recollect Monsieur du Miroir, but, as to
> Mrs. Bullfrog, I give her up to the severest reprehension. The
> story was written as mere experiment in that style; it did not
> come from any depth within me,—neither my heart nor mind
> had anything to do with it. I recollect that the Man of Adamant
> seemed a fine idea to me when I looked at it prophetically; but
> I failed in giving shape and substance to the vision which I saw.
> I don't think it can be very good.[1]

"The Man of Adamant" Hawthorne passed over for a third time in collecting the pieces for *Mosses*; it was finally collected in *The Snow-Image*.

If "Monsieur du Miroir" has any interest for us now, it is as an example of Hawthorne's preoccupation with reflecting surfaces. But apparently it had no special interest for him, and when read in and for itself, it may seem only a much-labored fancy. In the sketch Hawthorne plays for thirteen pages with an idea he had set down in his notebook in 1835: "To make one's own reflection in a mirror the subject of a story." There is probably some intention of representing the mystery that a man is to himself, but the sketch is not concentrated enough for a sense of mystery to emerge in any impressive fashion. Emerson records in his journal a remark by Ellery Channing, who thought that "he is the lucky man who can write in bulk forty pages on a hiccough, ten pages on a man's sitting down in a chair, like Hawthorne, etc. that will go."[2] But that facility was as often a misfortune for Hawthorne as it was a strength; and it is a facility that in this sketch he clearly does not trust, for in its last pages he endeavors to load his fancy with much more moral significance than it will sustain. Still, "Monsieur du Miroir" will bear one reading.

Reading "Mrs. Bullfrog" can only be an embarrassment to anyone with a respect for Hawthorne's work. It is quite as uncharacteristic as he said it was in his 1841 letter. His humor at its best is whimsical

---

1. *Passages*, pp. 239–40. This letter of September 10, 1841, is printed entire in *Love Letters of Nathaniel Hawthorne*, 2: 40–43.
2. *Journals* (Boston, 1914), 8: 257.

and wry; "Mrs. Bullfrog" is an attempt to use a farcical action.[3] The newly-married Mr. Bullfrog, a clerk in a dry goods store and "a very ladylike sort of gentleman"—he is the "I" narrator of the tale—discovers, partly as a result of the overturn of the coach in which the married pair are riding, a number of things about his bride. He discovers that she has false teeth and false hair, that she carries her private brandy bottle, that she can be a terrifying sort of virago, and that she has been the successful plaintiff in a breach-of-promise suit, and gained a judgment of five thousand dollars. She is willing to use it to stock a dry goods store for Mr. Bullfrog, and that, he concludes, is happiness enough. Hawthorne might have left this sort of thing, one feels, to Nathaniel Parker Willis.

At best, "Monsieur du Miroir" and "Mrs. Bullfrog" are feeble companions for either "Young Goodman Brown" or "The Celestial Railroad." Hawthorne had much better pieces still uncollected, and one can suppose only that these two were chosen for *Mosses* in an effort to fulfill a design for the collection. They are in some contrast to the eight satirical allegories in *Mosses*, and they add an innocuous variety. Hawthorne seems to have proceeded on the same principles of balance and variety he had used in *Twice-Told Tales*.

The other problem Hawthorne's selection for *Mosses* sets us is to explain the belated collection of "Young Goodman Brown" and "Roger Malvin's Burial." Hawthorne may not really have changed his mind about them since their exclusion from *Twice-Told Tales*. It is true that he had a feeling, perhaps intensified by family attitudes, that his work was over-somber. But that feeling had not prevented him from collecting somber tales, and these two presented to Hawthorne a somewhat more complex problem than just somberness.

In an article Hawthorne very much admired, his friend Edwin P. Whipple wrote, years after the publication of *Mosses*: "Young Goodman Brown and Roger Malvin are not persons; they are the mere loose, personal expression of subtile thinking."[4] Although our own

3. When in 1835 Hawthorne set down in his notebook an idea for a tale that should represent "the process by which sober truth gradually strips off" a young man's illusions about a woman, he specified: "This to be done without caricature, perhaps with a quiet humor interfused, but the prevailing impression to be a sad one." See *Passages*, pp. 22–23.

4. "Nathaniel Hawthorne" in *Character and Characteristic Men* (Boston,

time is interested in such a figure as Goodman Brown just because he has a larger reference than himself—because he is not merely a person— Hawthorne was conscious of the taste and judgment of his time, of which Whipple is an excellent representative. Hawthorne's public might be counted upon to deal with an overt allegory; if he thought that it could not be counted on to deal with such figures as Goodman Brown and as Reuben Bourne in "Roger Malvin's Burial," that would have been reason enough for passing over the tales when he was selecting for *Twice-Told Tales*. He might have reasoned in the same way, to be sure, when he came to make up the *Mosses* volume. But by that time he had won his way, and felt sure of a loyal public. And in selecting for *Mosses* he was somewhat pressed for material.

For *Mosses* Hawthorne clearly needed more pieces of narrative interest than had come out of his stay at the Old Manse. These two early tales are the only tales in *Mosses* with a firm substantiation in colonial history—where his greatest success had been—although "The Birthmark" and "Drowne's Wooden Image" have some background in it. Indeed, besides "Young Goodman Brown" and "Roger Malvin's Burial," only "The Birthmark," "Rappaccini's Daughter," and "Drowne's Wooden Image" have much narrative interest. The two early tales gave a needed balance to a volume largely made up of satirical allegories, apologues, and essay-like sketches.

Nevertheless, "Young Goodman Brown" and "Roger Malvin's Burial" may well have given Hawthorne pause. However much Hawthorne's ambiguity is a part of his genius, it was not, apparently, a quality that he expected readers to admire. His ambiguity, indeed, may not have been always calculated; we may too easily assume that it was.

"DROWNE'S WOODEN IMAGE"

"Drowne's Wooden Image" was first printed in 1844 in *Godey's Lady's Book*, during a time when most of Hawthorne's work was going to the *Democratic Review*. It has been thought that the tale was written

---

1866), p. 226. This critique first appeared in the *Atlantic* in May 1860. Hawthorne wrote to Fields that it was "a really keen and profound article" (Fields, p. 89). In the quoted sentence, I take "Roger Malvin" to be a slip for Reuben Bourne.

at the Old Manse, but it is quite unlike the work we know to have been written there. And it is difficult to see why anyone should suppose a tale of an unconsummated love especially appropriate to the Old Manse period. Moreover, this tale of "a modern Pygmalion in the person of a Yankee mechanic" seems to stem from the early impulse in our literature to naturalize an old story originally foreign to America. In it Hawthorne is doing much the same thing that Irving had done in "The Storm-Ship" and that Austin had done in "Peter Rugg." The period of Hawthorne's residence at the Old Manse seems too late a time for the tale; there is no hint of it in his notebooks for the period,[5] nor any other external evidence about it. It looks as if in conception and probably in composition the tale came early in Hawthorne's career.

In the afterword to "The Three Golden Apples," Hawthorne makes his narrator say that the classical myths and legends "are the common property of the world, and of all time. The ancient poets remodelled them at pleasure, and held them plastic in their hands; and why should they not be plastic in my hands as well?"[6] Certainly Hawthorne manipulated Ovid's story, and he manipulated his historical materials as well. The scene of his tale is Boston; the action must be supposed to go on a little before 1774, for in that year John Singleton Copley, whom Hawthorne makes a character in the tale, left Boston to live in England. Since Copley was a well-known figure, Hawthorne must have assumed that his presence in the tale would date the action. Copley is used, however, in no particular relation to his career or achievement; rather his function in the tale is to represent the view of the skillful and informed professional.

The title character takes his name from Deacon Shem Drowne, coppersmith and prominent citizen of Boston.[7] Deacon Drowne was born in 1684 and died in 1774; the historical Drowne was therefore in his late eighties at the time of the action of the tale. Apparently

5. There are notebook suggestions for many of the pieces written at the Old Manse. See *American Notebooks*, ed. Stewart, p. xxiv.

6. *A Wonder-Book*, p. 135.

7. Drowne, according to Samuel G. Drake, was "often employed in Town affairs, especially in the management of the Fortifications." *The History and Antiquities of Boston* (Boston, 1856), p. 615. The American Antiquarian Society of Worcester, Massachusetts, has Drowne's daybook for 1720–21 and 1754–68.

Hawthorne uses his name for that of his hero because all his first readers, at least, would have recognized it as that of a Boston artisan whose skill and gifts were untutored.

The historical Drowne is probably best known for his famous grasshopper weather vane on Faneuil Hall. In Hawthorne's time, many of his readers would have known the Indian weather vane, made of two sheets of hammered copper, on the old Province House, which is described in the next-to-last paragraph of the tale as a gilded woodcarving.[8] In the same paragraph, Hawthorne describes a shop sign of a mariner and his quadrant which once existed at the designated corner, but there seems no evidence that it was Drowne's work, and it probably represented a British naval officer, Admiral Vernon,[9] certainly not Captain Hunnewell. The title character of the tale, indeed, has little in common with his namesake, and may be as much related to Joseph True, a woodcarver of Salem and a contemporary of Hawthorne.[10] But the names Copley and Drowne both are a kind of allusion, a way of helping to make an ancient story at home in eighteenth-century Boston.

Hawthorne's skillful adaptation of Ovid's story results in a simple story line. Drowne is commissioned by Captain Hunnewell to carve a figurehead for his brig. The captain communicates a secret to Drowne, who starts to work forthwith. The figure of a beautiful woman that emerges from the log he works on far surpasses anything

8. The Province House weather vane is now in the museum of the Massachusetts Historical Society. Hawthorne is at least consistent, for in the frame of "Howe's Masquerade" he describes the Province House weather vane as the work of "good Deacon Drowne, a cunning carver in wood." He must have known that the Province House vane was not a woodcarving; if he could not tell by looking at it, he had read in Caleb Snow's *History of Boston*: "Upon the cupola on the roof a pedestal supports a figure of bronze, an aboriginal native holding in his hand a bow and arrow, well executed by Dea. Drowne, formerly an ingenious artist in the town" (p. 245 n.). It looks as if Hawthorne were consciously making the reference in "Howe's Masquerade" consistent with the Drowne of "Drowne's Wooden Image," and as if "Drowne's Wooden Image" had been written before "Howe's Masquerade."

9. See E. G. Porter, *Rambles in Old Boston* (Boston, 1887), pp. 60–62. In the course of the tale, Hawthorne mentions two figures representing Admiral Vernon.

10. See *American Folk Art, the Art of the Common Man in America, 1750–1900* (New York: Museum of Modern Art, 1932), p. 20; Henry W. Belknap, *Artists and Craftsmen of Essex County, Massachusetts* (Salem, 1921), p. 20.

the carver has ever done before. Drowne, it is reported, kneels at the feet of the figure and gazes passionately at its face. He has fallen in love, seemingly with his own handiwork. Copley is amazed and enchanted by the new powers of his artisan friend, and Drowne's achievement becomes the talk of Boston. One morning Captain Hunnewell escorts a beautiful young lady through the streets of Boston and into Drowne's shop—they are at the point of embarking on a voyage. The lady seems Drowne's wooden image come to life, and they walk through a gathering of astounded citizens of Boston.

Hawthorne makes every effort to fit the Pygmalion story into its Boston habitation. Woodcarvers were, of course, the only sculptors indigenous in early America, and ships' figureheads their most impressive work. The narrator says that he is retelling "one of the most singular legends that are yet to be met with in the traditionary chimney corners of the New England metropolis." References to witchcraft as it was still remembered in oral tradition are carefully spaced in the latter part of the tale. And when the "image, or the apparition" that is so like Drowne's woodcarving appears on the street of Boston, the narrator records that the aged shake their heads and hint that their forefathers "would have thought it a pious deed to burn the daughter of the oak with fire." The location of Drowne's shop, and even the pattern of Boston streets over which the apparition walks to it, are identified with a care comparable to William Austin's care with topography in "Peter Rugg."

A "rumor in Boston," recorded in the last paragraph of the tale, explains the apparent animation of Drowne's carving. Captain Hunnewell had under his protection a beautiful young woman, a Portuguese from Fayal in the Azores: the original of Drowne's carving must have been she. The inspiration of Drowne's masterpiece is thereby accounted for; but, as often in Hawthorne's tales, the reader may, if he likes, hold to an alternative suggestion. As the beautiful guest of Captain Hunnewell—if that is what the "airy image" is—walks toward Drowne's shop, she breaks her fan. When Copley, anxious to see her, enters the shop, he finds only Drowne standing "beside his creation mending the beautiful fan, which by some accident was broken in her hand." He finds no woman, "nor even the witchcraft of a sunny shadow that might have deluded people's eyes as it flitted along the street." Copley hears, but the reader need not attend to, Captain Hunnewell's voice, off stage as it were, saying, "Sit down in the stern sheets, my lady," and directing his men at the oars.

We recognize in the tale, of course, one of Hawthorne's pre-occupations: the enlargement of the sympathies and understanding by the experience of love. Ovid's story furnishes Hawthorne a better embodiment for it than do the apologues he contrives, the singularly inept "Egotism; or, the Bosom Serpent," or the negative representation in "The Man of Adamant." The brief portion of Drowne's life devoted to the fair stranger is, we are willing to believe, the portion in which he truly lived. But his love does not, apparently, illumine the rest of his career, however successful and respected he becomes.

It is tempting to see also something of Hawthorne's concept of the artist and his art in the tale. For example, Copley is made to say of Drowne's image, "It is as ideal as an antique statue, and yet as real as any lovely woman whom one meets at a fireside or in the street." Arlin Turner remarks that Hawthorne is here stating his own "ideas of fusing the real and the ideal in a romance," and it may well be that he was thinking of his own aims as he wrote. Yet the sentence given Copley condenses five lines of Ovid's story and tones them down a bit.[11] Indeed, a good deal of what is said about art in the tale is implied in the myth as Ovid tells it, or is an easy extension therefrom.

To be sure, there is in the tale a kind of doctrine of inspiration. Copley is made to say: "No wonder that she inspired a genius into you, and first created the artist who afterwards created her image." But the fair stranger is gone. Drowne turns to Copley a tear-covered face, from which "the light of imagination and sensibility, so recently illuminating it, had departed"; and Drowne never again produces a work of real merit. The narrator asks us if Drowne was not "more consistent with himself when he wrought the admirable figure of the mysterious lady, than when he perpetrated a whole progeny of

11. See Arlin Turner, *Nathaniel Hawthorne* (New York, 1961), p. 114. Lines 247–51 of *Metamorphoses* X are these:

> Interea niveum mira feliciter arte
> sculpsit ebur formamque dedit, qua femina nasci
> nulla potest, operisque sui concepit amorem.
> virginis est verae facies, quam vivere credas,
> et, si non obstet reverentia, vella moveri.

blockheads?" Doubtless he was; yet the inspiration of Drowne's love does not go beyond the representation of its object.

But there is another artistic principle in the tale that seems to have little connection with this doctrine of inspiration but considerable connection with Hawthorne's practice. As Drowne is beginning to develop his carving, the narrator remarks: "It seemed as if the hamadryad of the oak had sheltered herself from the unimaginative world within the heart of her native tree, and that it was only necessary to remove the strange shapelessness that had incrusted her, and reveal the grace and loveliness of a divinity." And later, when the carving is well along, Copley asks: "What inspired hand is beckoning this wood to arise and live? Whose work is this?" Drowne replies: "No man's work. The figure lies within that block of wood, and it is my business to find it." This statement of the traditional idea that the design of an artist's work is implicit in his materials—to which Copley is made to assent fervently—has an application to Hawthorne's own fiction.

In the tales that come out of historical materials, Hawthorne endeavors to find an inherent significance—to remove the shapelessness of history, and let the hidden shape reveal itself. The concept of the artist and his art represented in "The Artist of the Beautiful"—a tale we know to have been written at the Old Manse—is quite different. That tale embodies Hawthorne's doubts about the validity of the artist's function, and his feeling, implicit so often in his remarks about his work, that the aims of the artist are neither fully understood by his public nor, indeed, realized for himself in his own work.

Of course we are bound to be interested whenever an important writer of fiction deals with an artist or the artistic process in a story and to consider how far it may represent his own thinking about his art. But whatever we may derive from "Drowne's Wooden Image," the tale is not a treatise in aesthetic theory. It is best regarded as a successful exercise in the naturalization of a classical story in just the time and place one would have supposed least congenial for it. To be sure, Ovid's story cannot be taken over entire; in a scene in Boston about 1770 there can be no Venus to bless "the nuptials she has formed," and Drowne's experience concludes quite differently from Pygmalion's. Hawthorne's adaptation shows his literary tact, and it has its own poignancy. It is the quality of myth that new meanings and new feeling will grow out of it, not of course at each repetition, but at each new telling.

"ROGER MALVIN'S BURIAL"

"Roger Malvin's Burial" seems to have been written about the same time as "The Gentle Boy" and "My Kinsman, Major Molineux"; it probably was one of the tales intended for the projected "Provincial Tales." It was first printed in 1831 in *The Token* for 1832. The tale offers peculiar difficulties in interpretation;[12] once the tale is fully considered, one sees why Hawthorne passed it over twice when he was collecting *Twice-Told Tales*, and why he may have thought it failed to fulfill his intention.

The first section of the tale is based upon an incident in the history of Lovewell's Fight. In 1725 Captain John Lovewell led an expedition of forty-six men from Dunstable, Massachusetts, to attack the Pequawket Indian tribe. They encountered the Indians near Fryeburg in southwestern Maine close to the New Hampshire border, and suffered a severe defeat. In the last sentence of his first paragraph Hawthorne suggests that he is working in oral tradition. The story of Lovewell's Fight was indeed well known, and the young Longfellow had written two poems concerning it. But, as we are aware, the suggestion that he is using a chimney-corner legend is a frequent device of Hawthorne's. Here as elsewhere he is using printed sources.

In a 1938 article G. Harrison Orians pointed out some of the sources

12. There are difficulties even in the introductory paragraph, but perhaps they do not much affect the interpretation of the tale. Hawthorne says he is dealing with "one of the few incidents of Indian warfare naturally susceptible to the moonlight of romance," but one hardly knows the intention of the statement in the context of this tale. His reference to certain circumstances about Lovewell's Fight that might be cast judicially in the shade can hardly be a reference to the desertion of one member of the little band, who, when he arrived where a reserve garrison was stationed, frightened it away, for the desertion is mentioned in the tale. He may mean that one has to overlook many circumstances of the warfare between white men and Indians as matter humiliating to recall. He would have read in Hutchinson, just before the brief account of Lovewell's Fight, this episode in Captain Lovewell's career: "He discovered ten Indians round a fire, all asleep. He ordered part of his company to fire, who killed three, the other seven, as they were rising up, were sent to rest again by the other part of the company reserved for that purpose. The ten scalps were brought to Boston 3d of March [for the bounty]" (Hutchinson, 2: 238).

of "Roger Malvin's Burial" in John Farmer and Jacob B. Moore, *Collections, Topographical, Historical, and Biographical* (Concord, N. H., 1822–1824), all three volumes of which Hawthorne drew from the Salem Athenaeum in 1827, returning to the third volume a second time in 1829.[13] The *Collections* includes a ballad written soon after Lovewell's Fight, another ballad by Thomas C. Upham (a professor at Bowdoin), and, more important, the *Historical Memoirs of the Late Fight at Piggwacket* by the Reverend Thomas Symmes. In Symmes's work there are the stories of the four wounded men who were left behind in the forest, and particularly that of Lieutenant Farwell and Eleazer Davis, on which the first episode of Hawthorne's tale is based.

But David C. Lovejoy has discovered that a passage in an article in the second volume of Farmer and Moore, an article called "Indian Troubles at Dunstable" by "J. B. H.," is closer to the first episode in the tale than anything in Symmes. Since it furnishes a striking example of how intimately a tale may be related to a source in Hawthorne's work, it is here copied:

> Farwell was afterwards engaged as Lieutenant in Lovewell's fight, and in the commencement of the action was shot through the belly. He survived the contest two or three days, and with one Eleazer Davis, from Concord, attempted to reach home. . . . Though his case was hopeless, Davis continued with and assisted him till he became so weak as to be unable to stand, and then, at Farwell's earnest entreaties that he would provide for his own safety, left him to his fate. Previous to this he had taken Farwell's handkerchief and tied it to the top of a bush that it might afford a mark by which his remains could the more easily be found. After going from him a short distance, Farwell called him back and requested to be turned upon the other side. This was done, and was the last that was known of him. Davis reached Concord in safety.[14]

In the first episode of the tale, Hawthorne follows this account point by point, and it provides for an important symbol in the last episode.

13. "The Source of Hawthorne's 'Roger Malvin's Burial,' " *American Literature* 10 (1938): 313–18.
14. Quoted in David S. Lovejoy, "Lovewell's Fight and Hawthorne's 'Roger Malvin's Burial,' " *New England Quarterly* 27 (1954): 530.

As the tale begins, Roger Malvin, severely wounded, urges young Reuben Bourne, himself painfully but not dangerously wounded, to save himself. "I have loved you like a father, Reuben," Malvin says; "and at a time like this I should have something of a father's authority. I charge you to be gone that I may die in peace." Reuben has expected to marry Malvin's daughter, Dorcas, and Malvin does not fail to urge her happiness as a consideration in Reuben's return: "Hasten away, if not for your own sake, for hers who will else be desolate." Reuben is faced with the most difficult of moral problems; whatever he does he will have some cause to blame himself. To leave the wounded man to die alone will seem or be heartless and disloyal. To stay and sacrifice himself and Dorcas's happiness when it is clear that Malvin will die is, as Malvin urges, futile. When he also urges that possibly he will survive and Reuben be able to send help in time for a rescue, the narrator says that Reuben's "wishes seized on the thought," and Reuben consents to go. As in the source passage, he marks the spot with a handkerchief bound to a sapling. Malvin exacts a promise that Reuben will return to bury him. As Reuben is leaving, Malvin, like Farwell in the source passage, calls him back, and asks that he be turned over with his face toward home. Reuben leaves with "a sort of guilty feeling, which sometimes torments men in their most justifiable acts." But, the narrator asks at the end of the episode, who shall blame him for shrinking from a useless sacrifice?

So far Hawthorne has followed his source passage closely; for the rest there seems to have been no source. So far we have a clear and consistent narrative. We are disturbed by Reuben's moral dilemma, but we can understand it and sympathize with him. What seems to be foreshadowed is a future feeling of guilt on Reuben's part—a suspicion that the basis of his action was after all just selfishness.

The end of this episode is marked by a line of suspension points, as are the other divisions of the narrative, so that the tale has four clearly marked sections. Since the long time span offered Hawthorne difficulties, it will be well to mark out the structure of the tale in our discussion of it.

The second section introduces a set of moral and spiritual problems rather different from those of the first. On Reuben's return, he finds himself unable to acknowledge to Dorcas that he has left her father alive. She assumes, and of course the community assumes, that Reuben had stayed with Roger Malvin until his death, buried him, and then returned. Dorcas is in a measure comforted to believe that her father has had a proper burial. Reuben is taken as a hero; he experiences "from every tongue the miserable and humiliating torture of unmerited praise"—as does Dimmesdale in *The Scarlet Letter*. Reuben's problems are complex and appalling, but they have developed—at least as it seems to him—almost inevitably out of his antecedent decision to leave Malvin. For that he does not blame himself: he feels—or thinks he feels—"that for leaving Roger Malvin he deserved no censure."

Reuben's unhappy spiritual state has two separable causes. He suffers under his undeserved reputation for heroism. And he is most painfully conscious of his unredeemed vow to bury Malvin. Hawthorne had carefully prepared for this consideration in the first section of the tale:

> An almost superstitious regard, arising perhaps from the customs of the Indians, whose war was with the dead as well as the living, was paid by the frontier inhabitants to the rites of sepulture; and there are many instances of the sacrifice of life in the attempt to bury those who had fallen by the "sword of the wilderness." Reuben, therefore, felt the full importance of the promises which he most solemnly made to return and perform Roger Malvin's obsequies.

Now, since Reuben has allowed his acquaintances to think Malvin buried, he cannot ask help in the burial; and "superstitious fears, of which none were more susceptible than the people of the outward settlements," keep him from going alone.

We are reminded of the plea for proper burial by the shade of Elpenor in the *Odyssey* or, in the *Iliad*, of Achilles' dream in which the shade of Patroclus appears to him. We are to think of an importance attached to burial of much the same kind that we know in the Homeric poems. It is Reuben's failure to fulfill his vow for Roger Malvin's burial that is spiritually devastating to him.

The last two paragraphs of this second section of the tale are rapid summary narration. They recount the decay in Reuben's material fortunes that forces him to take up new land on the frontier. But they also recount his spiritual state as it has developed over almost eighteen years. His life is now centered on his only son, Cyrus, a promising boy of fifteen, whom Reuben loves "as if whatever was good and happy in his own nature had been transferred to his child, carrying his affections with it." Beyond his love for the boy with whom he identifies himself, and some feeling for Dorcas, Reuben's feelings are all turned inward on himself: "Reuben's secret thoughts and insulated emotions had gradually made him a selfish man, and he could no longer love deeply except where he saw or imagined some reflection or likeness of his own mind."

So far the reader is in a moral and spiritual world that he recognizes as Hawthorne's; he may feel that for the rest of the tale, Hawthorne's control is not so sure. Yet the third section of the tale is impressive. On the surface of the journey to the frontier, Reuben, his wife, and his son are pioneers, adventuring into the future. Dorcas is content to adventure in company with those she loves; Cyrus realizes something of his father's compulsion; Reuben travels to a destination that he does not know.

The second paragraph of this third section is an elaborate statement of the pioneer's dream of the great good place over the western horizon. We are interested to know that Hawthorne could imaginatively share that dream, since in general his tales are unaffected by it (there is, of course, the Seeker in "The Great Carbuncle"). But the reader's foreboding is strong; he can believe in no future for Reuben undetermined by his past. And the journey is a curious one. Reuben and Cyrus had explored the region and know the way; indeed they had cleared the land for their new home the autumn before. Cyrus is therefore troubled to find that his father keeps bearing north, out of his direct way. Cyrus suggests to his father more than once that his direction is mistaken, but when he finds that Reuben temporarily corrects his course and then resumes his northerly direction, Cyrus forbears to say anything further. On the twelfth of May, the eighteenth anniversary of the day on which Reuben left Roger Malvin to die, Reuben, Dorcas, and Cyrus are still on their journey.

Reuben realizes that he is under a strong compulsion; apparently he is aware that he is near the spot where he had left Malvin so long ago. But he is unable "to penetrate to the secret place of his soul" where his motives lie hidden. He trusts that he will now have an opportunity to expiate his sin of a broken vow, to give Malvin the burial he had so long ago promised. As these reflections are going through his mind, he is roused by a rustling some distance away in the forest. This is the account of the next incident:

> Perceiving the motion of some object behind a thick veil of undergrowth, he fired, with the instinct of a hunter and the aim of a practised marksman. A low moan, which told his success, and by which even animals can express their dying agony, was unheeded by Reuben Bourne. What were the recollections now breaking upon him?

With this passage we come to the crux of the tale.

And with this passage, as it seems to me, something has gone wrong in the narrative. We expect to believe the narrator—but he tells us that it is "the *instinct* of a hunter" to fire at any movement he becomes aware of (and this hunter knows his wife and son are in the immediate neighborhood). Moreover, the narrator tells us, Reuben can fire with "the *aim* of a practised marksman" at "the *motion* of some object behind a thick veil of undergrowth." The statement hardly makes sense.[15] Possibly there is some ironic intention; what seems more likely is a failure in technique. Hawthorne seems to have tried to achieve the ambiguity or the mystery he achieves in other tales by subtle but legitimate means. But in this tale he tries for it by a merely bewildering statement. It is a wrong narrative tack, for it does not move the reader's mind toward any understanding of the event, nor does it suggest a choice among possibilities.

As the section concludes, we find that Reuben is or seems quite

15. We cannot just assume that Hawthorne did not know any better. He had hunted as a boy (*Hawthorne and His Wife*, 1: 95–96) and while he was in college (Bridge, p. 46). But for Reuben's random shot there is a kind of literary antecedent in Irving's "Dolph Heyliger" (*Bracebridge Hall*). In that story Antony Vander Heyden shoots at a movement on the cliff above him and nearly hits Dolph. Vander Heyden, the narrator says,

> "had fired at the place where he saw the bushes move, supposing it to be the sound of some wild animal. He laughed heartily at the blunder, it being what is considered an exceeding good joke among hunters: 'But faith, my lad,' said he, 'if I had but caught a glimpse of you to take sight at, you would have followed the rock. Antony Vander Heyden is seldom known to miss his aim.'"

We do note, however, that even Vander Heyden has to see his target in order to aim at it.

unaware of what he has done (nor are we told specifically), but that he does recognize the very spot in which he had left Roger Malvin eighteen years before. And he sees that the sapling to which he had bound a handkerchief has grown to a substantial oak, with its top blighted, and its topmost branch dead. "Whose guilt had blasted it?" On this question the section ends.

The last section of the tale begins with a kind of dramatic irony that is at least as old as the song of Deborah in Judges. Dorcas, happy in her journey toward a new life, sings a little song of domestic content, and when she hears the report of a gun, goes forth singing, confident that she will meet Cyrus, her "beautiful young hunter." As she comes round a rock, she sees her husband, "apparently absorbed in the contemplation of some object at his feet," his face pale, his features rigid, and his son lying dead. When he finally speaks he says, "This broad rock is the gravestone of your near kindred, Dorcas. Your tears will fall at once over your father and your son." Dorcas faints away; she is as it were out of our immediate consideration. As the tale ends, the dead topmost branch of the oak falls in fragments over the dead boy, his unconscious mother, his father, and the bones of Roger Malvin. The last sentences are these:

> Then Reuben's heart was stricken, and the tears gushed out like water from a rock. The vow that the wounded youth had made the blighted man had come to redeem. His sin was expiated,— the curse was gone from him; and in the hour when he had shed blood dearer to him than his own, a prayer, the first for years, went up to Heaven from the lips of Reuben Bourne.

We are left to realize, if we can, what has been expiated and what the expiation is.

We need to consider first Hawthorne's allegorical procedure in this tale. Commonly, we have seen, his allegory takes one of two directions. It sometimes starts with a concrete event or set of events, often historical, and invests the action with moral or spiritual significance. In other tales, the moral idea seems the inception of the tale, and Hawthorne works to find an imaginative substantiation of it. In this tale there is something of both procedures. The tale begins with a historical incident—it might have made an allegory, one would suppose, quite by itself. But, apparently, it would not have worked out to represent the spiritual problem Hawthorne was impelled to concern himself with, and he continued the historical story in a further action he trusted would represent that problem.

One difficulty surely is that the spiritual concern on which Hawthorne fixed his interest required more scope than he allowed himself. The tale deals with the spiritual life of Reuben Bourne over eighteen years. We are told that Reuben has been unable to confess that he left Malvin unburied; that he is therefore unable to redeem his vow; that he must live a lie, and be falsely esteemed; that his spiritual troubles not only make him an unsuccessful man in all his outward endeavors and relationships, but also turn him inward on himself. He has become almost completely self-centered. He can love only himself; for his love for Cyrus is that he sees himself, or his potential self, repeated in the boy. But we are told all these things in the second section of the tale, and some of them in the rapid summary narration of its last two paragraphs. None of them is in any full sense represented; and there is none of the minute analysis that we find, say, in Hawthorne's concern with Dimmesdale's comparable problem in *The Scarlet Letter*—for Reuben, too, has "one secret thought" which becomes "like a chain binding down his spirit and like a serpent gnawing into his heart."

If (as it seems to me) "Roger Malvin's Burial" does fail—however interestingly—and if the tale does not fulfill Hawthorne's intention, it may not be possible to state that intention. The tale seems to start out to be a parable which should embody in an action our Lord's words: "For whosoever will save his life shall lose it; but whosoever will lose his life for my sake, the same shall save it" (Luke 9:24). In a quite literal way, Reuben in the first section of the tale saves his life. In saving it, he finds himself caught in traps of deceit, secrecy, fear, and finally a self-love that isolates him from his fellows spiritually and indeed in every relationship. He has lost the life he saved. But there the clarity of the parable ends.

Since the suggestion that for Reuben his son Cyrus is the surrogate for his own self-love is so strong, critics have been able to maintain rather persuasively that the tale ends in a kind of psychological symbolism in which Reuben destroys a guilt in himself. But what

Reuben confesses is the slaying of his son and the abandonment of Malvin so long ago. The one identifiable spiritual change in Reuben is that he has confessed his guilt—guilt which he fully recognizes himself and which soon will be apparent to all the world. The dead topmost branch of the oak, the symbol of his spiritual death during these many years, falls in fragments about him; he is able to weep, and for the first time in years to pray.

But much about the tale remains troubling. Not perhaps Reuben's compulsive return to the scene of his first failing—his long consciousness "that he had a deep vow unredeemed, and that an unburied corpse was calling to him out of the wilderness" accounts for that. But whether or not the slaying of Cyrus was a part of that compulsion we can hardly determine. And there is a greater difficulty. Although the tale seems, to begin with, so much in a Christian context, the concept of Cyrus's death as somehow a necessary sacrifice is certainly in no way Christian;[16] at the center of Christian belief is the assurance of a full, perfect, and sufficient sacrifice once offered for the sins of the whole world.

The critical problems in "Roger Malvin's Burial" are problems of conscious intention and of the coherence and the imaginative acceptability of the narrative itself. In no other Hawthorne tale in the period of our concern are the difficulties so great.

"YOUNG GOODMAN BROWN"

When one approaches the discussion of "Young Goodman Brown," a passage in Montaigne's "Of Experience" comes all too insistently to mind. Montaigne is deploring the multiplication of commentaries and he asks, "When do we agree and say: 'There has been enough about this book; henceforth there is nothing more to say concerning it'?" Of course we are in the habit of saying that the multiplicity and diversity of the interpretations of "Young Goodman Brown" are only evidence of its suggestiveness, subtlety, and richness of texture, even

16. Nor can I see any significant analogy between this tale and the story of Abraham and Isaac in Genesis. And the biblical analogues W. R. Thompson finds for the tale, though interesting, seem not to help very much in interpreting it. See his "The Biblical Sources of Hawthorne's 'Roger Malvin's Burial,'" *PMLA* 77 (1962): 92–96.

though we may recognize that with this tale interpretation has bred interpretation. Yet when a work has been turned over and over in critical discussion, the most obvious things about it are what gets lost, and perhaps they may be usefully insisted upon. And in "Young Goodman Brown," as in other Hawthorne tales, we need to distinguish as clearly as possible between Hawthorne's materials and his use of them.

"Young Goodman Brown" was first printed in the *New-England Magazine* in April 1835. It was one of the batch of manuscripts sent to the editor, Joseph T. Buckingham. "The Gray Champion" was also among these manuscripts; the two tales, apparently written about the same time, are markedly different uses of American materials. Indeed, "Young Goodman Brown" seems to us now more mature than any of the other tales sent to the *New-England Magazine*. But it is a tale that may be misunderstood.

When misunderstandings of the tale arise, they arise primarily from the inability of readers to follow the tale as an exercise of the historical imagination. In "Witches, and Other Night-Fears," Charles Lamb asks, "When once the invisible world was supposed to be opened, and the lawless agency of bad spirits assumed, what measures of probability, of decency, of fitness, or proportion . . . could [our ancestors] have to guide them in the rejection or admission of any particular testimony?" A reader needs to remember that, as Lamb says, "We do not know the laws of that country"; for if a reader's preconceptions about witchcraft inhibit his realization of what witchcraft felt like to the seventeenth century, they will also inhibit his understanding of the tale. A good background study for the tale is Hawthorne's own account of the witchcraft years in "Main Street"; since its assumptions are those of witchcraft times, one gets some imaginative realization of what it may have been like to believe that one's neighbors were pledged to the devil's service.

Hawthorne had an ancestral connection with Salem witchcraft. As William Hathorne had been active in the persecution of Quakers, so his son John in his generation was active in the pursuit of witches. In "The Custom House" Hawthorne says that John Hathorne "inherited the persecuting spirit, and made himself so conspicuous in the martyrdom of the witches, that their blood may fairly be said to have left a stain upon him." The statement may be misleading, for, although John Hathorne took part in the preliminary examinations of scores of persons accused of witchcraft, he seems not to have exercised his right to sit on the court of oyer and terminer which tried them.[17] But Hawthorne, as he pored over witchcraft history, would often have found his ancestor's name signed to records of examinations, records that may have influenced his tale. For "Young Goodman Brown" holds in solution a great deal of witchcraft history. The historical connections may be illustrated from several sources, and bits of the tale tied to particular sources, but Hawthorne, who as we have seen once thought of writing a history of witchcraft, is drawing on a wide knowledge of the records.

The action of "Young Goodman Brown" goes on near Salem Village, probably in 1691, the year before the witchcraft trials, for it cannot be during them. The names Goody Cory, Goody Cloyse, and Martha Carrier are names of women who were tried in 1692; Martha Cory and Martha Carrier were hanged; Sarah Cloyse was in prison when the witchcraft persecution was brought to an end. The witch-meeting which is the scene of the central action has parallels in the records. At an examination conducted by John Hathorne and John Corwin, Abigail Williams testified that she had, with about forty others, attended a diabolical communion service, at which Goody Cloyse was one of the deacons. In "Young Goodman Brown" an initiation is represented, and the diabolical service is a profane parody of baptism, but that too appears in the records: Mary Osgood confessed (before John Hathorne) to having been baptized by the devil.[18] Cotton Mather laments in his *Wonders of the Invisible World* the "Hellish *Randezvouzes,* wherein the Confessors do say, they have had their Diabolical Sacraments, imitating the *Baptism* and the *Supper* of our Lord."[19]

It is to such a witch-meeting that Young Goodman Brown intends to go, and his intention is made perfectly clear. His wife, Faith, is a

17. Loggins, p. 131.
18. Examinations quoted in Hutchinson, 2: 21–22 and 24.
19. 3rd ed., 1693, as reprinted in *Salem Witchcraft,* ed. Samuel P. Fowler (Salem, 1861), p. 395.

blessed angel upon earth, he says, and he is a wretch to leave her on such an errand; he resolves that "after this one night I'll cling to her skirts and follow her to heaven." He will, he thinks, for this once give himself wholly to evil; then he will come back to his ordinary, well-conducted life. If he has been tempted to go to the wood of evil, the temptation is antecedent to the action; at any rate he knows where he is going, and he goes with the full consent of his will.

The emphasis on the sexual side of witchcraft rites in some recent writers on the tale is not beside the point, for witchcraft had its sexual side (although there is surprisingly little evidence of it in the Salem records). And it is true that the devil's sermon particularly promises insight into sexual sin. The unfortunate implication of emphasis on the sexuality of the tale is that Goodman Brown leaving his wife for a night in the forest becomes only a kind of seventeenth-century parallel to a young married man today leaving his wife for a night on the town. But Brown has made a compact with the traveler he meets in the forest to go to a witch-meeting—to take part in a diabolical sacrament. When he has met the traveler, he does indeed have some scruples—but we know what his intent was, and that he continues in it. What the tale is about is the spiritual results of Brown's resolve.

Although the tale is worked out allegorically, it seems to have had its inception in what C. S. Lewis calls a supposal. Suppose that a young man thinks he can temporarily subject himself, give himself, to evil, and then resume his ordinary decency and uprightness, and suppose that he tries it, what would happen to him? Hawthorne could hardly have reflected upon such a supposal without remembering two sobering and enigmatic passages in the New Testament:

> For if we sin wilfully after that we have received the knowledge of the truth, there remaineth no more sacrifice for sins, but a certain fearful looking for of judgment and fiery indignation, which shall devour the adversaries. [Heb. 10:26–27]

> If any man see his brother sin a sin which is not unto death, he shall ask, and he shall give him life for them that sin not unto death. There is a sin unto death: I do not say that he shall pray for it. [1 John 5:16]

Now it is made quite clear that we are to think of Goodman Brown as one who has received the knowledge of the truth, that he is a Christian fallen into willful sin.

"Goodman" is of course a title of civility for, say, a small farmer; Brown's surname is one of the commonest. He is always "Goodman Brown" in the tale; we are to think of him having been to the time of the tale a quite ordinary, righteous young man. He has been recently married to Faith, who is literally his wife, but who stands also for his faith: "My love and my Faith," he addresses her, and it is only when he calls upon Faith that he can be released from the witch-meeting. The allegorical meaning of these names is perhaps too obvious to need this pointing out; it seems, however, to get confused in some readings of the tale.

Goodman Brown leaves both his love and his faith. When he meets the traveler with whom he has an appointment, he explains, "Faith kept me back a while," and his new experience begins. The narrative point of view is complex, even for Hawthorne. The narrator can get well into Brown's mind and heart, and he knows Brown's perceptions; but he does not affirm their truth to any external reality. Goodman Brown believes that he recognizes the figure of a hobbling old woman as Goody Cloyse; Goodman Brown is almost sure he recognizes the voices of the minister and Deacon Gookin; when something flutters down through the air and catches on the branch of a tree, Goodman Brown beholds a pink ribbon and believes it to be one of Faith's.

The narrator is not precluded, however, from comment in his own person. The staff the traveler carries seems a snake, but that must be "an ocular deception, assisted by the uncertain light." There is some suggestion of legendary report: "Some affirm that the lady of the governor was there."[20] The narrator may take up into his account a portion of the witchcraft record: there is "Martha Carrier, who had received the devil's promise to be queen of hell. A rampant hag was she."[21] Yet the narrator resolves for the reader none of Goodman

20. This sentence reflects a passage in Robert Calef, *More Wonders of the Invisible World* (1700). The lady was the wife of Sir William Phips. See *Narratives of the Witchcraft Cases 1648–1706*, ed. George Lincoln Burr (New York, 1914), p. 201 n.

21. This passage reproduces part of Cotton Mather's "Memorandum" at the

Brown's doubts or confusions. His occasional comment, sometimes ironic and sometimes reflective, is distinct from his account of Brown's perceptions. It is as if the narrator, with all his knowledge, yet does not fully understand the action he records; he and the reader must work out its meaning together.

The narrator does not, therefore, identify the traveler with whom Goodman Brown has an appointment. The figure of Goody Cloyse recognizes him as the devil, and he nearly identifies himself so. But he is a good deal more urbane and subtle than the devil the confessors in the witchcraft trials seem to have known. And there are complex suggestions about him. He looks like an older and more sophisticated Goodman Brown. After Goodman Brown has been with him a while, his arguments seem "rather to spring up in the bosom of his auditor than to be suggested by himself." When Brown, thinking he sees such a pink ribbon as his wife wears, and taking it as evidence of her presence at the witch-meeting, cries out, "Come, devil; for to thee is this world given," no devil appears, but Brown is given over to blasphemous despair. "The fiend in his own shape," the narrator comments, "is less hideous than when he rages in the breast of man."

Nevertheless the figure that Goodman Brown meets in the forest is at first distinct from him. The figure answers Goodman Brown's scruples by an account of his influence in New England. He, as well as Goodman Brown's forebears, has had a hand in the persecution of the Quakers and in King Philip's War, and the influential and the great have been his intimate acquaintance. Goodman Brown answers that he is but a simple farmer, and that if he continued his journey, he could not meet the eye of his minister. His companion only laughs at that, but when Goodman Brown says, "Well, then, to end the matter at once, there is my wife, Faith," his companion tactfully seems willing to give up his design: "I would not," he says, "for twenty old women like the one hobbling before us that Faith should come to any harm." The figure hobbling before them seems to be Goody Cloyse, who, Goodman Brown later says, had taught him his catechism. "There was," the narrator remarks, "a world of meaning in this simple comment."

---

end of his record of the trial of Martha Carrier. See *Wonders* as reprinted in *Narratives of the Witchcraft Cases*, p. 244.

Now the allegory of the tale turns on this question: what did Goodman Brown see in the figure of Goody Cloyse and in the multitude of other figures at the witch-meeting? As David Levin shows in a fine article, Hawthorne has taken the question of "spectral evidence," so troubling to the witchcraft judges, and made it the substantiation of his allegory.[22] Everyone who has read *Hamlet* is familiar with one form of the question. When Hamlet has had time to reflect on his interview with the ghost, he realizes that what had seemed to be a specter of his father

> May be a devil; and the devil hath power
> T' assume a pleasing shape; yea, and perhaps
> Out of my weakness and my melancholy,
> As he is very potent with such spirits,
> Abuses me to damn me.
>
> [2.2.627–31]

For the examiners and judges in witchcraft cases, the question took a somewhat different and a bewildering shape. When they heard testimony that a specter of an accused person had "afflicted" a witness, or urged him to sign the devil's book, how were they to take it? In the first trials, spectral evidence was evidence against the accused.

Thomas Hutchinson writes: "Mr. [William] Stoughton, the lieutenant-governor, upon whose judgment great stress was laid, had taken up this notion, that although the devil might appear in the shape of a guilty person, yet he would never be permitted to assume the shape of an innocent person." This official position was nevertheless in doubt. Cotton Mather in his *Wonders of the Invisible World* remarks "the Great and Just Suspicion, that the *Dæmons* might impose the *Shapes* of Innocent Persons in their *Spectral Exhibitions* upon the Sufferers."[23] And the accused themselves, who had learned from the magistrates and the clergy, argue the question. Here is a part of Mary Osgood's confession:

---

22. "Shadows of Doubt: Specter Evidence in Hawthorne's 'Young Goodman Brown,'" *American Literature* 34 (1962): 344–52. Professor Levin uses historical materials other than those I adduce.
23. Hutchinson, 2: 18; *Salem Witchcraft*, ed. Fowler, p. 390.

She confesses further, that she herself, in company with Goody
Parker, Goody Tyler, and Goody Dean, had a meeting at Moses
Tyler's house, last monday night, to afflict, and that she and
Goody Dean carried the shape of Mr. Dean, the minister,
between them, to make persons believe that Mr. Dean
afflicted.
Q. What hindered you from accomplishing what you intended?
A. The Lord would not suffer it so to be, that the devil should
afflict in an innocent person's shape.[24]

But Susanna Martin, who pled not guilty, and who had another belief
about the nature of specters, answered the magistrate with great
cogency:

Magistrate. Well, what have you done toward this?
Martin. Nothing at all.
Magistrate. Why, tis you or your Appearance.
Martin. I cannot help it.
Magistrate. Is it not Your Master? How comes your Appearance
    to hurt these?
Martin. How do I know? He that appeared in the shape of
    Samuel, a Glorify'd Saint, may Appear in any ones shape.[25]

Susanna Martin was executed, but opinions on this matter like hers
finally prevailed. In June of 1692 a group of influential clergymen, in a
formal statement probably written by Cotton Mather himself, asserted
that "it is an undoubted and a notorious thing, that a dæmon may, by
God's permission, appear, even to ill purposes, in the shape of an
innocent, yea, and a virtuous man."[26] In 1693 the courts decided not to
give weight to spectral evidence in further trials.

    "What shall be done," Cotton Mather asks in *Wonders*, "as to those
against whom the *Evidence* is chiefly founded in the *dark World?*" All

    24. Quoted in Hutchinson, 2: 25. This testimony may explain a detail in
"Young Goodman Brown": the appearance of Faith at the witch-meeting is
"led *between*" Goody Cloyse and Martha Carrier.
    25. Cotton Mather's record in *Wonders* as reprinted in *Narratives of the
Witchcraft Cases*, p. 230.
    26. Quoted in Hutchinson, 2: 38.

the evidence Goodman Brown has is so founded. He sees convincing appearances of respected persons well known to him, and finally stands beside what indeed seems to be Faith herself. He hears a diabolical sermon given by one who bears "no slight similitude, both in garb and manner, to some grave divine of the New England churches."[27] In this dark world the appearance of Deacon Gookin, for instance, might indeed be Deacon Gookin in the flesh. But all the appearances might be the specters of the persons they resemble—by one theory as good evidence of their wickedness as their appearance there in the flesh. Or all of them might be merely "the devil's legerdemain" and the devil be abusing Goodman Brown to damn him. Even if Goodman Brown were fully acquainted with all the theories of spectral appearances—and in 1691 he could hardly have been—his knowledge would have been little protection. "The Devil improves the *Darkness* of this Affair," Cotton Mather says, "to push us into a Blind mans Buffet."[28]

The sermon by him who bore a similitude to a grave divine horribly interprets what has arisen in Brown's mind through his night's experience:

> There are all whom ye have reverenced from youth . . . all in my worshipping assembly. This night it shall be granted you to know their secret deeds. . . . Far more than this. It shall be yours to penetrate, in every bosom, the deep mystery of sin. . . . And now, my children, look upon each other. . . . Depending upon one another's hearts, ye had still hoped that virtue were not all a dream. Now you are undeceived. . . . Welcome . . . my children, to the communion of your race.

During the sermon Goodman Brown and the appearance of his wife stand together, Brown awaiting his baptism and believing that Faith awaits hers. In a shudder of revulsion, Brown cries out, "Faith! Faith! look up to heaven, and resist the wicked one." And when he calls upon

27. The devil also took the role of a clergyman and mocked Christian rites in Scottish witchlore. Sir Walter Scott records testimony in Scottish trials that "the Devil . . . used to rebaptise the witches with their blood, and in his own great name," and that "the devil appeared to his servants in the shape of a black man occupying the pulpit." *Letters on Demonology and Witchcraft* (London, 1830), pp. 290 and 312.

28. See *Salem Witchcraft*, ed. Fowler, pp. 399–400.

his Faith, he is released from the witch-meeting. But he is not then or ever in this life released from its effects.

After Goodman Brown's return home, in the next-to-last paragraph of the tale, the narrator asks, "Had Goodman Brown fallen asleep in the forest and only dreamed a wild dream of a witch-meeting?" The narrator seems to allow that possibility: "Be it so if you will; but, alas! it was a dream of evil omen for young Goodman Brown." The passage used to be taken as the significant ambiguity in the tale (although no one ever takes the tale as "only a dream"). But the passage has little effect either upon our apprehension of Goodman Brown's experience, closely tied as his adventure in the forest is with the records of witchcraft times, or upon the interpretation of the allegory. Even if Goodman Brown's experience be taken as a dream, it is a dream in the dark wood to which he has gone—fully awake and aware of his intention—to take part in a diabolical sacrament. It is the spiritual consequences of such a decision that are represented allegorically by Goodman Brown's night in the forest.

In a first reading of "Young Goodman Brown," the more receptive the reader, the less he is likely to realize the tale as allegory; the witch-meeting as witch-meeting will preempt his interest, as surely Hawthorne intended. The allegory may come clear in the account of Brown's return home and his life thereafter in the last paragraphs of the tale—but perhaps not then, perhaps not until a second reading.

For Brown's inability really to believe in any virtue all the rest of his life long is an extension of the confusion of his horrible night. He lives his life under the same sort of delusion he suffered then, a delusion the more insidious because it has some admixture of truth—of course some apparent virtue, some respectability, is hypocrisy. Hawthorne has taken the historical matter of spectral evidence to represent appallingly a truth that everyone knows of his own experience and observation. In Goodman Brown's experience that truth is written very large, for Brown thought he could embrace evil and then escape from it—most men only touch it, impelled not so much by pride as by desire or envy.

But we know clearly enough that the person who discovers only a part of his potentiality for evil loses in proportion his assurance of the virtue of others. The man who cheats in little ways—on his income tax, his expense account—is likely to be miserably sure that everyone else is out to cheat him. The promiscuous woman is pretty sure that most other women are promiscuous in inclination if not in fact. The intellectually dishonest scholar expects a complementary dishonesty in his colleagues. Young Goodman Brown, who put himself in the way of discovering his whole potentiality for evil, can have no assurance of good in anyone. He has neither humility nor sympathy; he can feel only revulsion from his neighbors. He had not believed the sermon preached by the Father of Lies, he had recognized him and escaped from him, but he had listened—and that was enough.

"Young Goodman Brown" is a tale of terror in a special way, for if it has some quality of Gothic terror, it has more of the horror of an evil almost tangible. In this regard there was nothing like it before it; and it had no rivals after it until Robert Louis Stevenson's great witchcraft tale, "Thrawn Janet," and Henry James's "The Turn of the Screw."

In *The Scarlet Letter* Hawthorne strikingly returns to the major concern of "Young Goodman Brown." His reflections on Goodman Brown's spiritual predicament stayed in his mind, and twice in the romance he goes over the same speculative ground, once in reflective exposition, and once representationally. The passages are important in the romance, impressive in themselves, and interesting as partial interpretations of "Young Goodman Brown."

In chapter 5 Hester struggles not to suspect her own sin in others, struggles against the conviction that her sin has given her insight into breasts other than her own. In analyzing her condition, Hawthorne has written the best commentary on "Young Goodman Brown":

> She felt or fancied . . . that the scarlet letter had endowed her with a new sense. She shuddered to believe, yet could not help believing, that it gave her a sympathetic knowledge of the hidden sin in other hearts. She was terror-stricken by the revelations that were thus made. What were they? Could they be other than the insidious whispers of the bad angel, who would fain have persuaded the struggling woman, as yet only half his victim, that the outward guise of purity was but a lie, and that, if truth were everywhere to be shown, a scarlet letter would blaze forth on many a bosom besides Hester Prynne's? Or, must she receive those intimations—so obscure, yet so distinct—as truth? In all her miserable experience, there was nothing else so awful and

so loathsome as this sense. . . . Such loss of faith is ever
one of the saddest results of sin.

This passage is explicit and analytical; the same concern is represented
in chapter 20 ("The Minister in a Maze") in a narrative that is so
curiously like "Young Goodman Brown" that it seems almost another
version of the tale.

In the preceding action Dimmesdale had encountered Hester in the
forest and agreed to flee to England with her; he had, the narrator tells
us, "yielded himself with deliberate choice, as he had never done before,
to what he knew was deadly sin." On his return from the forest, he
experiences inexplicable impulses toward evil, and asks himself, "What
is it that haunts and tempts me thus? Am I mad? or am I given over
utterly to the fiend? Did I make a contract with him in the forest, and
sign it with my blood? And does he now summon me to its fulfillment,
by suggesting the performance of every wickedness which his most foul
imagination can conceive?" As if in answer, Mistress Hibbens, the
governor's sister and reputed witch,[29] seems to appear—at least she "is
said to have been passing by." She assumes Dimmesdale has been to the
forest to seek the "yonder potentate" they both know, and merely
smiles at his protestations, "like one willing to recognize a secret
intimacy of connection." The minister asks himself again, "Have I then
sold myself to the fiend?" and the narrator answers for him, "He had
made a bargain very like it! . . . And his encounter with old Mistress
Hibbens, if it were a real incident, did but show his sympathy and
fellowship with wicked mortals and the world of perverted spirits."

"If it were a real incident." Just as in "Young Goodman Brown," the
doubt of actuality is the sign of allegorical significance, and witchcraft
the sign of the will to evil with its concomitant spiritual delusions.
Dimmesdale, like Goodman Brown in his homecoming, returns from
the forest another man, "with a knowledge of hidden mysteries which
the simplicity of the former never could have reached." The narrator
exclaims, "A bitter kind of knowledge that!"

Hawthorne's return to "Young Goodman Brown"—and to "The

29. Just as Hawthorne used the names of women tried for witchcraft in 1692
in "Young Goodman Brown," so he uses the name of the historical Ann
Hibbens, who was said to be Governor Bellingham's sister. She was executed for
witchcraft in 1656.

Minister's Black Veil"—in *The Scarlet Letter* goes far to explain a puzzling quality of the romance. Edward H. Davidson says that in it "Hawthorne unwittingly warped history for the purpose of his narrative and his moral aim," and that, although the span of the action is 1642–1649, the Puritan temper represented is the "gloom, the somber duskiness, and the morbid sense of human iniquity" of a later period of history, the period in which, for the most part, Hawthorne had worked in his tales.[30] Now it is certainly true that, although 1642–1649 is the time of the first-generation emigrants, when, to use Hawthorne's own expression, "the zeal of a recovered faith burned within their hearts," the Puritans and the Puritan temper in the romance seem to belong to a later and less happy period. That this warping of history was on Hawthorne's part unwitting seems to me not so sure. Whatever had been his intention at the outset, as the romance grew under his hand he must have been quite aware that he was reworking materials from tales that dealt with times appreciably later than the span of its action.[31] And for that matter he had done some warping of history even in "Endicott and the Red Cross," which represents an incident of 1634.

The debt of *The Scarlet Letter* to the tales does not, to be sure, make it the less Hawthorne's masterpiece, but the realization of that debt shows how much of his ability had manifested itself before 1839; and perhaps we may conclude that if the romance is greater than its sources in the tales, it is so only in sustained effect.

30. "The Question of History in The Scarlet Letter," *The Emerson Society Quarterly*, no. 25 (1961), pp. 2–3.

31. Hawthorne was surely aware of the anachronism in chap. 6, where he has the Puritan children playing "at scourging Quakers." Of course he knew that the first Quakers to arrive in Boston came in 1656.

12. EARLY TALES IN
THE SNOW-IMAGE

When Hawthorne wrote his preface to the 1851 *Twice-Told Tales* (it is dated January 11, 1851), he seems to have had no intention of collecting any more of his early work. "Much more, indeed, he wrote," Hawthorne remarks of himself; "and some very small part of it might yet be rummaged out (but it would not be worth the trouble) among the dingy pages of fifteen-or-twenty-year-old periodicals, or within the shabby morocco covers of faded souvenirs." But within the year he did make a new collection, *The Snow-Image and Other Twice-Told Tales*. In his prefatory letter to that collection, addressed to Horatio Bridge and dated November 1, 1851, he promises that this will be his last collection—a promise that this time he kept. He speaks of turning back upon his path, "lighted by a transitory gleam of public favor, to pick up a few articles which were left out of my former collections," and thereby implies that he and his publishers were anxious to ride on the success of his two great romances.

Hawthorne gathers together rather a curious collection of pieces for this last offering. "Some of these sketches," he says, "were among the earliest that I wrote, and, after lying for years in manuscript, they at last skulked into the Annuals or Magazines, and have hidden themselves there ever since. Others were the productions of a later period; others, again, were written recently." Only four were recent: "The Snow-Image," "The Great Stone Face," "Main Street," and "Ethan Brand." Two were first printed in the early 1840s; they had been passed over when Hawthorne made his selection for *Mosses from an Old Manse*. The other nine were all first printed in the 1830s, and had been passed over two or three times in his previous collections.

Some of these nine pieces would have appeared, no doubt, in the abortive collection that Hawthorne and Evert A. Duyckinck were planning in 1842. And some of them, apparently, Hawthorne planned to use in "Old-Time Legends: Together with Sketches, Experimental and Ideal," the volume which he was planning just after he lost his position in the Salem Custom House, and which would have included

The Scarlet Letter in its first version.[1] Nevertheless, these nine pieces are pieces of which Hawthorne had spoken most disparagingly in both "The Old Manse" and in the 1851 preface to *Twice-Told Tales*, and which, had it not been for the exigency of the new collection, he might willingly have let die. Now of course Hawthorne's preferences are not binding upon us; we may consider, for instance, "My Kinsman, Major Molineux" a great tale even if he did not. But his preferences are of considerable importance in the study of Hawthorne, and in the effort to understand his intention as a writer. And the fact does remain that in collecting this early work when a volume of short pieces became expedient, Hawthorne violated a twice publicly-stated intention not to do so.

At the close of the prefatory letter for *The Snow-Image*, Hawthorne implies the existence of pieces he would not wish to acknowledge:

> The public need not dread my again trespassing on its kindness, with any more of these musty and mouse-nibbled leaves of old periodicals, transformed, by the magic arts of my friendly publishers, into a new book. These are the last. Or, if a few still remain, they are either such as no paternal partiality could induce the author to think worth preserving, or else they have got into some very dark and dusty hiding-place, quite out of my own remembrance, and whence no researches can avail to unearth them. So there let them rest.

We know what some of these unacknowledged pieces are. We have noted that some were later unearthed and added to *Mosses* in its 1854 edition.[2] The biographical sketches like "Mrs. Hutchinson" Hawthorne

1. Fields, pp. 49–52. And see William Charvat's introduction to the Centenary Edition of *The Scarlet Letter*, pp. xx–xxv. The plan for a collection persisted almost to the publication of *The Scarlet Letter*. Hawthorne writes in "The Custom House": "Some of the briefer articles, which contribute to make up the volume, have likewise been written since my involuntary withdrawal from the toils and honors of public life, and the remainder are gleaned from annuals and magazines of such antique date that they have gone round the circle, and come back to novelty again." He attaches a footnote to say that the projected collection has been deferred. "The Custom House" must have been in type before the decision to publish it and *The Scarlet Letter* alone was made. "A new volume of tales" by Hawthorne was advertised in January of 1850 (Charvat, p. xxi).
2. See *Letters of Hawthorne to William D. Ticknor*, 1: 44–45 and 48–49.

did not collect for reasons which, as we have seen, are pretty clear. "Alice Doane's Appeal" may well be one of the pieces that Hawthorne in 1851 warned Fields not to rummage out, and that no paternal partiality could have induced him to acknowledge.

Of the nine early pieces in *The Snow-Image*, four will be here discussed. In time of composition, "The Wives of the Dead" and "The Man of Adamant" stand at either end of the period in which Hawthorne wrote the pieces he had at hand when he made his selections for the 1837 *Twice-Told Tales*. In both temper and technique they are in decided contrast to one another. "The Canterbury Pilgrims" and "My Kinsman, Major Molineux" offer problems not only in the understanding of Hawthorne's attitude toward them, but in the interpretation of the tales themselves.

"THE WIVES OF THE DEAD"

"The Wives of the Dead" was first printed in 1831 in *The Token* for 1832. It is apparently one of the tales Hawthorne sent to Goodrich in December of 1829, and may have been once intended for the "Provincial Tales." It is the development of an anecdote, and its virtue is the restraint of that development. The tale begins apologetically: "The following story, the simple and domestic incidents of which may be deemed scarcely worth relating, after such a lapse of time, awakened some degree of interest, a hundred years ago, in a principal seaport of the Bay Province." The simple incidents may be briefly recounted.

Two sisters-in-law, the recent brides of two brothers, share the same house. They are now sisters in a "mutual and peculiar sorrow." On successive days, Mary, who had married the sailor brother, has heard of his death in a shipwreck, and Margaret, who had married the landsman brother, has heard of his death in a frontier skirmish. The narrator begins on the evening of a day in which they have had many sympathetic callers; they are at last alone to support one another in their sorrow. When they have gone to bed, but before Margaret's grief has allowed her to sleep, the innkeeper knocks at the door with the news that the death of her husband has been a false report, that he is alive and well. Margaret is of course overjoyed, but she refrains from waking Mary lest Mary find her sorrow sharpened by Margaret's happiness.

Hours later, after Margaret has gone to sleep, there is another knock at the door, which Mary answers. She finds there a young man, a former suitor, with the news that her husband has escaped the wreck in which it had been supposed he was drowned. She too intends to refrain from waking her sister, but as she straightens the disarrayed bedclothes over Margaret, Margaret awakes. And there the tale ends.

For a story written in the 1820s, such an ending is most unusual. It allows the reader's imagination to move out beyond the confines of the text, to construct for itself a completion of the domestic incidents and relationships of the tale. Of course some other of Hawthorne's tales do move the mind of the reader beyond the tales themselves. The young lovers in "The Maypole of Merry Mount" and in "The Canterbury Pilgrims" take their difficult paths into the future, paths which in a general way the reader may envision. In "Wakefield," "Roger Malvin's Burial," and "My Kinsman, Major Molineux," the mind is impelled to go beyond the limits of the narratives, but it moves uncertainly, into mystery, perhaps into bafflement. In "The Wives of the Dead" this completion carries itself out into imaginative satisfaction. The tale is more like the best *New Yorker* short fiction of the 1940s than it is like the fiction of Hawthorne's time. It seizes upon that short portion of its characters' lives that implies what is significant in their pasts and in their futures.

Hawthorne's control in this very early tale is remarkable. Mary and Margaret are sufficiently distinguished; we realize Mary as the more self-disciplined and therefore the more naturally capable of generosity, Margaret as the more impulsive, the more inclined to passion and bitterness. Yet because they love one another, their sympathetic realizations of each other's sorrow are almost identical, so that the tale develops by a sort of incremental repetition, and ends in a pleasant dramatic irony as we regard Mary refraining from waking her sister in ignorance that Margaret has a happiness parallel to her own. The narrative point of view has a subtlety which for the most part eludes analysis. The narrator gives the young women his full sympathy in their sorrow and in their joy without quite intruding himself in either. His perceptions are not quite identified with theirs, however, and sometimes the distinction is pointed up, as in this passage, which comes just after the innkeeper has delivered his message to Margaret:

So saying, the honest man departed; and his lantern gleamed
along the street, bringing to view indistinct shapes of things,
and the fragments of a world, like order glimmering through
chaos, or memory roaming over the past. But Margaret stayed
not to watch these picturesque effects. Joy flashed into her heart,
and lighted it up at once; and breathless, and with winged steps,
she flew to the bedside of her sister. She paused, however, at the
door of her chamber, while a thought of pain broke in upon her.

Indeed the tale transcends the perceptions of its two characters.
Without moralizing and despite its happy outcome, it embodies a
somber recognition of the precariousness of human happiness.[3]

One can imagine this anecdote being as well developed by Sarah
Orne Jewett at the end of the century; one can hardly imagine any
writer of Hawthorne's time doing as well with it as he did, and going so
far outside the taste and literary habit of the day. Yet apparently
Hawthorne did not much value this tale. It has none of the faults he
finds with some tales in *Twice-Told Tales*, and all of the virtues he
claims for the pieces therein. But in collecting *Twice-Told Tales* he
gave preference to—for instance—"David Swan" and "The Lily's
Quest."

We have, then, a difficult question in Hawthorne's values: Did he
three times pass over it because it led to no explicit moral conclusion,
because it seemed to him not quite a serious work? He had said of Scott

3. H. J. Lang's reading of the tale also makes it a recognition of the precariousness of human happiness, but his reading is quite different from mine.
Professor Lang contends that we are to read the tale as a dream—or, apparently,
a pair of dreams—and that the husbands are dead. His argument turns on an
ambiguity in the last sentence of the tale: "But her hand trembled against
Margaret's neck, a tear also fell upon her cheek, and she suddenly awoke." We
should read the "she," Professor Lang thinks, as standing for Mary. The objection to this reading, as it seems to me, is that we should have to assume an
entirely dishonest narrator, a narrator who—to take one instance—distinctly tells
us that, although Mary had been dreaming, she awakes and realizes the knocking at the door (*Snow-Image*, pp. 603–4). And one might note that in the
passage quoted in the discussion of the tale above, the narrator reports effects of
the lantern light that do not come through Margaret's perceptions. But see H. J.
Lang, "How Ambiguous is Hawthorne?" from *Geist einer freien Gesellschaft*
(Heidelberg, 1962) as reprinted in *Hawthorne: A Collection of Critical Essays*,
ed. A. N. Kaul (Englewood Cliffs, N. J., 1966), pp. 86–89.

that the world nowadays requires "a more earnest purpose, a deeper moral, and a closer and homelier truth," than Scott supplied. If Hawthorne undervalued his own achievement in the close and homely truth of "The Wives of the Dead"—if he did not fully realize the moral integrity of the tale—it would seem that he was equating earnestness with express moral purpose. It is clear enough that his quest for explicit significance, for the "deep moral," led him to "The Man of Adamant."

"THE MAN OF ADAMANT"

"The Man of Adamant" was first printed in 1836 in *The Token* for 1837; it was written in 1835 or early in 1836, for the suggestions for it appear in Hawthorne's notebook of 1835. Of this tale, the reader will remember, Hawthorne wrote to Sophia Peabody that it "seemed a fine idea to me when I looked at it prophetically; but I failed in giving shape and substance to the vision which I saw. I don't think it can be very good."

We have only the tale, and it will not tell us what Hawthorne envisioned. But we can see that the tale does attempt to embody a fine idea. That idea is stated positively in the first Epistle of John: "No man hath seen God at any time. If we love one another, God dwelleth in us, and his love is perfected in us" (4:12). Hawthorne characteristically represents the idea negatively—by the penalty of isolation that falls upon self-love and pride. So he does in this tale, although the good spirit that would save the Man of Adamant tells him what will heal him: "Come back to thy fellow-men; for they need thee, Richard, and thou hast ten-fold need of them."

Hawthorne labels the tale "An Apologue"; its fable is a simple one: Richard Digby, whose "plan of salvation was so narrow . . . it could avail no sinner but himself," retires from the world of men and into a cave, a cave in which stalactites hang from the roof. He already suffers from a "a deposition of calculous particles within his heart"; but ignoring the beautiful spring of water near by, he drinks the drippings of the stalactites and aggravates his malady. He enjoys his spiritual isolation, until the spirit of a former love appears to him and pleads with him to return to the world of men, offering him a cup of water from the spring as a sort of sacrament. Digby rejects both the sacramental cup and the heaven-sent messenger, and dies saying,

"What hast thou to do with my Bible?—what with my prayers?—what with my heaven?" A century later his petrified body is found, an enduring symbol of his isolation.

Although the apologue promises more interest than we ever find in it, there are still a number of things to be interested in. It has some effect of satire: one wonders if, in the figure of Digby, there is an intent to ridicule the Calvinistic doctrine of Election, for Digby has reduced the number of the Elect to one. He is "well pleased that Providence had intrusted him alone, of mortals, with the treasure of the true faith." His life in the cave removes him from any necessity of "communion with those abominable myriads which [Heaven] hath cast off to perish."

Digby seems himself a comic figure in his complete spiritual self-satisfaction, and some of the detail has a comic effect: we are twice assured, for instance, that Digby reads his Bible amiss because he cannot see it clearly in the half-light of his own cave. His speeches are given a second, ironic meaning. When he says, "Of a truth, the only way to heaven leadeth through the narrow entrance of this cave,—and I alone have found it!" he absurdly perverts Matt. 7:14—"Because strait is the gate, and narrow is the way, which leadeth unto life, and few there be that find it." When the good spirit pleads with him, he puts her off with these words: "Leave me, earthly one; for the sun is almost set; and when no light reaches the door of the cave, then is my prayer-time." Of course Digby as a comic figure is hardly consonant with the figure of the ethereal messenger who comes to save him. Yet we have noted a somewhat like inconsonance in the figures in "The Great Carbuncle."

If Digby rejects man, he also rejects nature, and the symbolism is striking. In nature, we are told in Acts, God "left not himself without witness" (14:17), but Digby rejects both light and the spring of water, and accepts only the least beneficent of the gifts that nature offers, indeed only the cave and the stalactites, which seem hardly intended for the use of man. The light symbolism is insistent, and the spirit-messenger materializes out of the light of the setting sun and melts back into its last rays.

This spirit-messenger, whose name on earth was Mary Goffe, is a somewhat surprising figure. She is perhaps the only symbol of grace in all Hawthorne's tales; the supremely self-satisfied Richard Digby is the only character in them to whom grace is clearly offered within the confines of a tale. Mary Goffe seems more like a figure from medieval allegory than any other in the tales. Indeed in conception—although not in interest or in awe—she is like Dante's Beatrice. She had known and loved Richard Digby in England, before his bigotry had come upon him; she comes to him now in spirit. Like Beatrice she stands for human and for divine love, and for the essential oneness of the two manifestations of love.

"The Man of Adamant," then, has interests in itself. And it has a special significance in the context of Hawthorne's work, for it makes explicit a conviction that informs several of his tales. But one may wonder as he reads the tale if the label "An Apologue" is not an apology for an allegory without substantiation. "I don't think it can be very good," Hawthorne says. We are likely to accept his own estimate. To say why this potentially good or great tale is not very good is merely to develop Hawthorne's own judgment that he failed to give the tale substance.

From two story suggestions we know something about the inception of "The Man of Adamant." Hawthorne put this down in his notebook in 1835:

> The story of a man, cold and hard-hearted, and acknowledging no brotherhood with mankind. At his death they might try to dig him a grave, but, at a little space beneath the ground, strike upon a rock, as if the earth refused to receive the unnatural son into her bosom. Then they would put him into an old sepulchre, where the coffins and corpses were all turned to dust, and so he would be alone. Then the body would petrify; and he having died in some characteristic act and expression, he would seem, through endless ages of death, to repel society as in life, and no one would be buried in that tomb forever.[4]

Apparently somewhat later in the same year, Hawthorne returns to the idea of the petrified man: "It might be stated, as the closing circumstance of a tale, that the body of one of the characters had been petrified, and still existed in that state."[5] In both passages, the petrified man is the dominant image, although the first sentence of the first

4. *Passages*, p. 24.
5. *Passages*, p. 24.

passage leads in another way to "The Man of Adamant." That the cold-hearted man would also be a man with his private theology, who believed that he alone was saved, must have been the next conceptual step. If it was, the allegorical outline was almost complete, and the tale never gets much beyond it.

It may seem odd that the tale should so lack imaginative substantiation. Hawthorne evidently thinks of Richard Digby as coming out of American Puritanism, as being an absurd extreme of a Puritan direction. He is, we are told in the first sentence of the tale, "the gloomiest and most intolerant of a stern brotherhood," an expression which, applied to Digby, will make sense if he has something in common with a recognizable group, if only the extreme of their worst traits. He has no other attributes of "brotherhood." He had been a minister in England before he emigrated to America. As the Puritan emigrants went into the wilderness to worship in their own way, so he goes into the wilderness to worship in his—but farther into it.

Now one would think that such a figure might easily have been substantiated from the history of American Puritanism. No sooner had the Puritans established their Holy Commonwealth than there were dissenters from it, and not only famous ones like Roger Williams, Ann Hutchinson, and Thomas Hooker, but scores of less well-known persons. Hawthorne's reading included many accounts of minor doctrinal and ecclesiastical quarrels. Of course it is true that had Richard Digby been constructed out of Puritan history, he would have been a somewhat different figure. But perhaps he needs to be, for he cannot seem to many readers representative enough to be important. Puritanism did not breed anchorites; and persons with private illuminations in the Bay Colony seem to have been much more likely to try to impose their convictions on others than to nurse them in their own bosoms.

Of course Hawthorne knew all that. And since he did, we can wonder whether, as he looked at the idea for "The Man of Adamant" prophetically, he did not think of Richard Digby as representing a spiritual peril more characteristic of his own time than of Puritanism. Later Hawthorne tales—"The Birthmark," "Rappaccini's Daughter," and "Ethan Brand"—are oblique representations of the dangers of the spiritual self-reliance taught in his New England. Perhaps one may think of "The Man of Adamant" as a study for them.

But whatever Hawthorne intended, whatever he saw prophetically in "The Man of Adamant," did not come out, for him or for us. Perhaps a comparison with a later, more successful tale will suggest the reason. "Ethan Brand" seems to have had an inception comparable to that of "The Man of Adamant." In 1844 Hawthorne wrote in his notebook two suggestions for it, a few days or weeks apart.[6] In these entries the development of the tale may be a little farther along than the development of "The Man of Adamant" is in the 1835 notebook entries, but not much farther. Hawthorne did not write "Ethan Brand" until he found a way, about four years after he put down the notebook suggestions, of substantiating his allegory from his notebook account of a North Adams vacation in 1838, so that in "Ethan Brand" the allegorical action goes on in what seems a real world.

This last stage in the genesis of "Ethan Brand" has no parallel in the genesis of "The Man of Adamant." In this tale the allegorical action remains just allegory when it is developed, and goes on in an allegorical world. Hawthorne turns neither to his observation nor to his reading to find a substantial world in which the ideas of the tale might be developed. His apologues, so far as they are failures, are perhaps not so much failures of imagination as of effort.

"THE CANTERBURY PILGRIMS"

"The Shaker Bridal" Hawthorne was willing to include in *Twice-Told Tales*. The other tale that seems to have come out of his visit in 1831 to the Shaker community at Canterbury, New Hampshire, he rejected for that collection. "The Canterbury Pilgrims" was first printed in 1832 in *The Token* for 1833. The tale does have an intricate texture, and if Hawthorne made a choice between the two tales concerned with Shakers, he probably chose "The Shaker Bridal" as the more accessible to "anybody who will give himself the trouble to read it."

"The Canterbury Pilgrims" is a tale of a sort not easily defined. Toward the close of the tale, it is remarked that "the varied narratives of the strangers had arranged themselves into a parable." Now H. W. Fowler says in his *Modern English Usage* that "allegory" and "parable" are "almost exchangeable terms." "The Canterbury Pilgrims" is an

6. See *American Notebooks*, ed. Stewart, p. 106.

instance in which the terms are not exchangeable (as indeed they are not always exchangeable in reference to New Testament parables).[7] The pilgrims who tell their stories, although they are types, are not allegorical figures, not at all like the Giant Despair, or Acrasia, or Mary Goffe, or even Young Goodman Brown. The stories they tell, although they are exemplary, are not allegories. Yet if we call the tale a parable, we should see that it is a parable of rather a special sort. And perhaps at its very end, it does become allegory.

The implications of the title are realized fully only after the tale is read, but the title clearly fixes the scene at the Shaker community at Canterbury. It is a summer night; the tale begins: "The summer moon, which shines in so many a tale, was beaming over a broad extent of uneven country." If this is the moonlight of romance of which Hawthorne often speaks, it illuminates some real and recognizable human foibles and human burdens. But of course we know what it shines for; it is to light up "a neutral territory," as Hawthorne calls it in "The Custom House," "somewhere between the real world and fairy-land, where the Actual and the Imaginary may meet, and each imbue itself with the nature of the other." The experiences of the figures in the tale are actual; they meet in imaginary circumstances controlled by the maker, and recount their experiences as they would not and could not in actuality. It is, indeed, the figure of the poet who arranges the revelations.

In the moonlit scene, by the Shaker spring, appear first Josiah and Miriam, young persons who have been brought up by the Shakers, but who, as Josiah later explains, "have a gift to love each other, and . . . are going among the world's people, to live after their fashion." They encounter at the spring a little group of persons on their way to join the Shakers; and the poet among them, when he has understood the intention of the young lovers, asks his companions, "Shall we tell our stories, here by this pleasant spring, for our own pastime, and the benefit of these misguided young lovers?" There follow the stories of the poet, of the merchant, and of the farmer, with his wife's complementary story.

Hawthorne uses a type poet and a type merchant in "The Great

7. The parable of the Sower, for instance, is a parable *and* an allegory; the parable of the Good Samaritan is a parable—an illustrative story—without being an allegory.

Carbuncle," but far less successfully than he uses the types here. It is
tempting to suppose that "The Great Carbuncle" is the earlier-written
tale, but what indications we have are otherwise. Of course the poet
and the merchant in this tale do not have to fit into an allegorical
action, as the poet and the merchant in "The Great Carbuncle" do; and
all the figures in "The Canterbury Pilgrims" are handled from the same
narrative point of view. Perhaps these differences are enough to explain
the contrast between the flat type-figures in "The Great Carbuncle"
and the carefully observed and trenchantly portrayed types in "The
Canterbury Pilgrims." Hawthorne's satirical wit is well displayed in
the figures of the merchant and, particularly, the poet.

"In me," the poet begins, "in me, you behold a poet." He is, he says,
a neglected genius, whose great gifts have brought him only despair:
"O Fate! why hast thou warred with Nature, turning all her higher and
more perfect gifts to the ruin of me, their possessor? What is the voice
of song, when the world lacks the ear of taste? . . . Have I dreaded scorn
like death, and yearned for fame as others pant for vital air, only to find
myself in a middle state between obscurity and infamy?" This poet
may be a type romantic poet, but if he is, his is a romanticism that has
carried over into our time. He represents, and pretty well, those among
our own poets who demand our recognition without showing the
slightest concern for our needs and interests. This poet's revenge on a
public unaware of his existence will be to join the Shakers and cease to
be a poet; posterity, he feels sure, "will cry shame upon the unworthy
age that drove one of the fathers of American song to end his days in a
Shaker village!" The narrator remarks that, so impassioned the poet
grew, "there appeared reason to apprehend his final explosion into an
ode extempore," but that he was really a gentle, harmless fellow whom
Nature "had sent into the world with too much of one sort of brain,
and hardly any of another."

Now, in order to show what sort of mind the poet does have,
Hawthorne recounts his reverie, and the passage is a surprising one.
It is not more a burlesque of romantic reverie than it is self-parody on
Hawthorne's part.[8] The graceful fancy and shallow ideality of the poet's
thought as it is set down here is unmistakably like passages in

8. For examples of Hawthorne's prose that have the qualities he here
parodies, the reader might use the first paragraph of "Sights from a Steeple" and
the first paragraph of "Snow-Flakes," both in *Twice-Told Tales*.

Hawthorne's sketches, even to the straining for an emblem. Nor can we suppose Hawthorne unconscious of the likeness—for we cannot suppose him insensitive to language and sentence pattern—although he may not have expected the parody to be noticed. But it is the best stroke in his satiric portrait of the poet:

> The poet turned away, and gave himself up to a sort of vague reverie, which he called thought. Sometimes he watched the moon, pouring a silvery liquid on the clouds, through which it slowly melted till they became all bright; then he saw the same sweet radiance dancing on the leafy trees which rustled as if to shake it off, or sleeping on the high tops of hills, or hovering down in distant valleys, like the material of unshaped dreams; lastly, he looked into the spring, and there the light was mingling with the water. In its crystal bosom, too, beholding all heaven reflected there, he found an emblem of a pure and tranquil breast. He listened to that most ethereal of all sounds, the song of crickets, coming in full choir upon the wind, and fancied that, if moonlight could be heard, it would sound just like that.

The poet is finally moved to compose a "Farewell to his Harp," which, we are told, "with two or three other little pieces, subsequently written," he later will have published in the New Hampshire *Patriot*.

For Josiah and Miriam, the poet's account of his rejection hardly serves as a cautionary tale. Having no ambitions like the poet's, Josiah says, "we need not fear thy disappointments." The next speaker is the ruined merchant, proud of the vast extent of his failure, chagrined that Josiah has never heard of it, and still confident of his genius. He expects that the Shakers will have "a due respect" for his experience, and that they will allow him to manage their finances so as to double their capital in four or five years. Josiah shrewdly says that he sees "a sort of likeness" between the poet and the merchant, although he cannot justly say where it lies.[9] But since the ambitions of Josiah and Miriam are no more like those that led to the merchant's ruin than they are like those the poet is abandoning, the young lovers are as little affected by the merchant's story as they had been by the poet's.

9. Hawthorne gives a group of entrepreneurs a prominent place in "The Hall of Fantasy" (*Mosses*, pp. 200–1).

And now there is a shift in the tale, not of narrative point of view but of tone. The poet and the merchant are handled satirically; the farmer and his wife sympathetically. The shift is successful because it is morally consistent: folly and misfortune should be apprehended differently, and here in this neutral territory that the maker controls they are. Yet the shift is accompanied by a reversal of expectation, of the expectation of Josiah and Miriam, and of the reader's along with theirs. In a prettier parable than this one, a fulfillment and not a reversal would have been contrived.

The farmer tells how he had married a girl much like Miriam, how he had asked only "an ordinary blessing" on the sweat of his brow, so that his family might live decently. "I thought it a matter of course," he says, "that the Lord would help me, because I was willing to help myself." Josiah demands, "And didn't He help thee, friend?" and the farmer replies, "No, for then you would not have seen me here." The young lovers are taken aback: "here was one whose simple wishes had resembled their own, and who, after efforts which almost gave him a right to claim success from fate, had failed in accomplishing them." They had thought that the rewards of good intentions and honest efforts must be even-handed. Nor does it occur to either of them that the woman who accompanies the farmer could have been the pretty young girl like Miriam of whom he had spoken, now grown sad and fretful. She identifies herself, and she has her warning to give Miriam:

> If you and your sweetheart marry, you'll be kind and pleasant
> to each other for a year or two, and while that's the case, you
> will never repent; but, by and by, he'll grow gloomy, rough, and
> hard to please, and you'll be peevish, and full of little angry fits,
> and apt to be complaining by the fireside, when he comes to rest
> himself from his troubles out of doors; so your love will wear
> away by little and little, and leave you miserable at last. It has
> been so with us; and yet my husband and I were true lovers once,
> if ever two young folks were.

As the farmer's wife ends speaking, her children, wakened by the sound of their mother's voice, add "their wailing accents to the testimony borne by all the Canterbury pilgrims against the world from which they fled."

The testimony Josiah and Miriam have heard is true testimony within the purview of the witnesses. The young lovers do not disbelieve it; they do not disregard it so far as it has application to their hopes and desires; they can only affirm that their love supports them. "We will not go back," they say. "The world never can be dark to us, for we will always love one another."

In "The Maypole of Merry Mount," Endicott remarks that "the troubles of life have come hastily" for the Lord and Lady of the May. In this tale the narrator remarks that the young lovers have hardly stepped into the world when its cares and sorrows array themselves before them. Both pairs of young lovers leave what were for them, untouched in their youth and innocence, Edens of irresponsibility. Each Eden is for any who stay in it a false Eden—the Shaker Eden of asceticism is quite as false as the Merry Mount Eden of sensuality. Both pairs of lovers go out in the world of "mortal hopes and fears." The last sentence of "The Canterbury Pilgrims" is this: "The lovers drank at the Shaker spring, and then, with chastened hopes, but more confiding affections, went on to mingle in an untried life." Hawthorne surely trusted that it would recall to some of his readers the last sentence of "The Maypole of Merry Mount," and turn their minds again to the way in which, within greatly different sets of circumstance, human experience repeats itself.

The Canterbury pilgrims—for it is only the poet, the merchant, and the farmer and his family that the title comprehends—take their way to the haven of the Shakers. They are a set of pilgrims ironically different from Chaucer's. But Josiah and Mariam are not Canterbury pilgrims at all, and their pilgrimage we can in part foresee. It may be sometimes through Sloughs of Despond; it will often be up Hills of Difficulty. But Miriam and Josiah may view or even ascend the Delectable Mountains too.

"MY KINSMAN, MAJOR MOLINEUX"

"My Kinsman, Major Molineux," like "Young Goodman Brown," has been much discussed. And with "My Kinsman" we have a kind of paradox. First printed in 1831 in *The Token* for 1832 (and apparently originally intended for "Provincial Tales"), it was neglected by Hawthorne until he reprinted it to fill out his last collection.[10]

10. That Hawthorne gave "My Kinsman" the final position in the volume

Everything he had said in disparagement of his uncollected pieces includes it as surely as, say, "The Man of Adamant." And until the 1950s "My Kinsman" was virtually ignored by Hawthorne's critics. But now we are faced with an amazing number of readings of the tale.[11]

The number of these readings, and the extravagance of some of them, force us to consider whether it is just because Hawthorne did not have full control of the tale that such diversity of interpretation is invited. For the diversity of interpretation may arise, not really from the tale's profundity, nor even from a calculated ambiguity on Hawthorne's part—although there surely is some—but from his failure to fulfill his intention. Of "Ethan Brand," so much later than "My Kinsman," Hawthorne wrote to an editor: "At last, by main strength, I have wrenched and torn an idea out of my miserable brain; or rather, the fragment of an idea, like a tooth ill-drawn, and leaving the roots to torture me."[12] If, despite the authorial interpretation included in "Ethan Brand," Hawthorne thought the essential idea was not worked out, he may well have had his doubts about "My Kinsman, Major Molineux"—this tale so many writers have felt impelled to work out for him.

Some of the difficulties of the tale may arise from the discomfort Hawthorne felt in working in the period of the Revolution. In the "Legends of the Province House," we have realized, he felt it necessary to cast "the spell of hoar antiquity" over events so recent. In "My Kinsman" he apparently means to accomplish a comparable removal, partly by the dream-like atmosphere of the tale, and partly by obscuring the relationship of the tale to particular historical events. In the introductory paragraph, the time of the action is indicated as "a summer night, not far from a hundred years ago," at a time of "temporary inflammation of the popular mind." But in the tale the detail of the mob action is unmistakably of a sort that belongs to a time about 1765, perhaps particularly to that year. The first paragraph, indeed, has a calculated vagueness throughout. Indicating that he is

---

may indicate a regard for it on his part. The first four pieces in the volume are the ones he had written most recently.

11. It is dismaying to find that Robert Lowell has made a play, not so much of the tale as of one strain in the interpretation of the tale. His "My Kinsman, Major Molineux" was printed in the *Partisan Review*, Fall 1964.

12. Conway, p. 122.

drawing on Thomas Hutchinson's history, but drawing upon it in a confusing fashion, Hawthorne writes of "six governors in the space of about forty years from the surrender of the old charter" and of their difficulties with the people of the province of Massachusetts Bay.[13] The successors of the six, he says, "till the Revolution, were favored with few and brief intervals of peaceful sway." Only a single sentence suggests what is to be the subject matter of the tale: "The inferior members of the court party, in times of high political excitement, led scarcely a more desirable life."

Major Molineux[14] in the tale is an inferior member of the court party, most probably concerned in the effort to enforce the Stamp Act, whose offense is loyalty to his king and to his commitments. The Sons of Liberty forced all the stamp agents in the colonies, often by violence, to resign before November 1, 1765, the effective date of the Stamp Act. Tar-and-feathering is just the sort of activity the Sons of Liberty were carrying on in the summer of 1765.[15]

13. Hawthorne's sentence with its allusions identified is this:

The annals of Massachusetts Bay will inform us, that of six governors in the space of about forty years from the surrender of the old charter [1684], under James II., two were imprisoned by a popular insurrection [Sir Edmund Andros, governor 1686–1689, and Joseph Dudley, governor 1702–1715, but imprisoned with Andros in 1689]; a third, as Hutchinson inclines to believe, was driven from the province by the whizzing of a musket-ball [Samuel Shute, 1716–1728; see Hutchinson, 2: 217]; a fourth, in the opinion of the same historian, was hastened to his grave by continual bickerings with the House of Representatives [William Burnet, 1728–1729; see Hutchinson, 2: 275]; and the remaining two [Sir William Phips, 1692–1694, and the Earl of Bellamont, 1699–1700], as well as their successors, till the Revolution, were favored with few and brief intervals of peaceful sway.

14. There was a historical personage named William Molineux (1717–1774), remembered as an agitator against the authority of the crown and a participant in the Boston Tea Party—by no means a Tory. Hawthorne seems to have used only his name; Hawthorne would have found two references to him as "Mr. Molineux" in Hutchinson (see 3: 121, 278). Longfellow in the "Prelude" to his Tales of a Wayside Inn speaks of "jovial rhymes" inscribed on the inn window "By the great Major Molineaux," / Whom Hawthorne has immortal made." Longfellow may possibly have identified the title character of the tale with William Molineux.

15. In his Annals of Salem, Felt says, writing of tar-and-feathering, "It was a mobbish custom with a small portion of the people here and elsewhere, before and at the first of the Revolution, to punish individuals, charged as traitors, with a coat of such materials" (2nd ed., 2: 562).

Since Hawthorne mentions Hutchinson's history in the first paragraph of the tale, it is likely that he used it for some of the detail. And he does seem to draw upon Hutchinson's account of a mob attack on his own house, a story Hawthorne retold for children in *Grandfather's Chair.*[16] Hutchinson writes that, shortly before the attack on his house, there had been attacks on royal officers, considerable tension, and then a sermon preached by Jonathan Mayhew which, intentionally or not, incited the people of Boston to further excesses. On the night of August 26, 1765, the mob destroyed as much of Hutchinson's house as it could manage, and all of his public papers and private historical documents.

Some of the detail in Hutchinson's account is parallel to matter in "My Kinsman." The mob that attacked Hutchinson's house was directed by two men in disguise, with staves of office in their hands. (In the tale, the man with the red and black face is such a disguised leader, and hardly needs a Freudian explanation.) The plans for the riot were generally known, even to persons unsympathetic to them: "they would give no aid in discountenancing it," Hutchinson says, "lest they should become obnoxious themselves." (The urbane gentleman who counsels Robin at the end of the tale may be such a person.) "The town was, the whole night," Hutchinson continues, "under the awe of this mob; many of the magistrates, with the field officers of the militia, standing by as spectators; and no body daring to oppose, or contradict." The day after Hutchinson's house was attacked, citizens assembled at a public meeting in Faneuil Hall and by a unanimous vote condemned the mob action, but, Hutchinson says, "It could not be doubted, that many of those who were immediate actors in, as well as those who had been abettors of, those violent proceedings, were present at this unanimous vote."[17]

Now in "My Kinsman," what is bewildering to Robin is that, without any knowledge of recent events in the city, he has arrived in Boston on the night of a planned riot, a riot in which his kinsman is to

16. *Grandfather's Chair*, pp. 574–82.

17. Hutchinson, 3: 89–91. Hutchinson also records two previous disorders: the hanging in effigy of his son-in-law, Andrew Oliver, the newly appointed distributor of stamps for Massachusetts, and the subsequent destruction of a building he had intended for a stamp office (pp. 86–88).

be the victim, a riot virtually everyone he comes upon is informed about and is looking forward to, for the most part with pleasure. He encounters the leader of the mob; he sees people disguised "in outlandish attire," who address him by the password of the Sons of Liberty, and who, when he does not understand, curse him in plain English. Whenever he inquires for his kinsman, he speaks a name that is in everyone's mind. The "ambiguity" of his night's experience has in part a historical explanation.

But Hawthorne intends an allegory which, even while it is using history, will have a certain imaginative removal from history. The importance of the pervasive moonlight to the tale is generally recognized, and some connection with A *Midsummer Night's Dream* is apparent. The connection does not depend alone on the single direct reference to Shakespeare's play,[18] but primarily upon repeated mentions of the moon and moonlight that must be intended to recall the play and its similar iteration. The tale is a sinister Midsummer Night's dream; Robin is ill met by moonlight. But, although the associations with A *Midsummer Night's Dream* are clearly intended, exactly what they are intended to accomplish may not be so clear.[19] Shakespeare's play seems to have no specific connection with the ancient customs of Midsummer's Eve, and probably Hawthorne's allusions to the play are primarily intended to suggest that a seemingly

18. The one direct reference to the play comes in the description of the watchman: "A heavy yawn preceded the appearance of a man, who, like the Moonshine of Pyramus and Thisbe, carried a lantern, needlessly aiding his sister luminary in the heavens."

19. Robin is of course Robin Molineux, but it is late in the tale that we learn that the Major and his father were "brothers' children." If, early in the tale, the expression "The youth, one of whose names was Robin . . ." reminds us of the lines

> Either I mistake your shape and making quite,
> Or else you are that shrewd and knavish sprite
> Call'd Robin Goodfellow . . .
>
> [2.1.32–34]

the association may suggest that Robin is an ordinarily good young man, as Goodman Brown's name suggests that he is. (The fact that "Goodfellow" must have been in its origin a propitiatory name probably would not intrude.) The quoted lines may be connected also with the iteration of "shrewd" in the tale. And the curious time scheme of the play may have influenced somehow the condensing of so much experience for Robin into a single night.

enchanted world presents itself to Robin. Robin might well ask, as Amphitryon in Dryden's play asks, "What's this? midsummer-moon! Is all the world gone a-madding?" (4.1).

As Hawthorne is likely to do, he comments directly in the course of the tale on his use of "the moonlight of romance": "the moon, creating, like the imaginative power, a beautiful strangeness in familiar objects, gave something of romance to a scene that might not have possessed it in the light of day." The phrasing is Coleridgean, but the reference of the passage is not to the tale in general, but to the scene in which Robin seats himself at the church door in his weariness and dreams of home, whether asleep or awake. Everywhere else in the tale, the moon lights up a world that presents itself as hostile, irrational, and finally cruel. The moonlit scene of the tale for the most part does not seem to be this time that "neutral territory" of romance, where the Actual and the Imaginary may meet, but a territory of lunacy, where nothing seems actual, and the imaginary a nightmare. There is even a likelihood that the moonlit atmosphere of the tale, which so much affects its tone and mood, will for some readers inhibit a clear realization of the events.

It will be well, then, briefly to trace the story line before any attempt at interpretation. Since "My Kinsman" does offer special difficulties, we need to be sure that interpretation is interpretation of the whole action.

As the tale begins, Robin, who has walked more than thirty miles carrying his cudgel and wallet, crosses a river on a ferry and arrives in a city, the ferryman surveying him narrowly at parting. He sets out to find the house of his kinsman, Major Molineux, whom he expects to provide him great opportunities in the city. He assumes that of course the Major is a prominent and highly respected citizen. In searching for his kinsman's house and inquiring the way to it, he has a series of encounters. Briefly set down, they are these: Robin encounters an old man who carries a long polished cane (a constable with his staff of office) who says he has "authority," who threatens to put Robin in the stocks, and who has a peculiar mannerism of sepulchral "hems." Then he encounters an innkeeper, who pretends to think him an escaping bound boy. Next he encounters a prostitute, who pretends that her dwelling is the Major's house; and immediately afterward a watchman, who also threatens him with the stocks. Finally Robin encounters a man in disguise, his face painted red and black, whom

Robin recognizes as a man of striking features he has seen earlier undisguised. This figure tells Robin to watch where he is an hour and the Major will pass by. Robin has been everywhere unaccountably rebuffed—except by the prostitute—and laughed at.

Weary and bewildered, Robin sits down to rest on some church steps, and thinks or dreams of home. But when he perceives a passerby, he calls out to him confusedly, "Hallo, friend! must I wait here all night for my kinsman, Major Molineux?" The passerby is personable, in middle life, and the first man to have spoken kindly to Robin all the long evening. Robin tells him why he has come to the city and of the difficulties he has been having in trying to find his kinsman. This urbane gentleman tells Robin that the word of his informant with the black and red face may be trusted, that the Major will pass by. Almost at once come the sounds of an uproar afar off.

A mob in procession comes into view. Within the procession is a cart carrying Major Molineux, who has been tarred and feathered. Robin is excited by the mob, by his recognition within it of all who had rejected him, and particularly by their laughter. Suddenly he finds himself in spirit part of the mob: his laugh is the loudest there. When the procession has passed—there is a line of suspension points to indicate a short time lapse—the urbane gentleman recalls Robin from a trance-like state. Robin inquires the way to the ferry, but his companion suggests that he remain a few days—or permanently, and rise in the world without the help of his kinsman.

Now, unless the first paragraph has entirely misled the reader about the time of the action of the tale, an important effect of the narrative is surely a sustained sort of dramatic irony. Robin is so much in ignorance of the world of Revolutionary politics that he cannot interpret the responses to his requests for guidance, or see any pattern in his rebuffs. The reader who knows something of the history of the period before the Revolution and of the activities of the Sons of Liberty will be ahead of Robin at every moment, and watch him act in ignorance of conditions that are historically clear enough. Thus the insistence on Robin's shrewdness, on his feeling that his troubles might be solved with his cudgel, and on his vanity in being related to the great Major Molineux are all felt in high contrast to the reader's knowledge. The narrative point of view, however, constantly includes Robin's perceptions, in order that the reader's realization of the irony will not preclude his sympathy with Robin in his bafflement. Yet the dramatic irony may be so strong an interest—or, if it be not fully recognized, so confusing an effect—that it obscures instead of reinforces the allegory.

The recognition of the dramatic irony depends upon an awareness of history, and the allegory itself has a basis in history, but, like the allegory in "The Maypole of Merry Mount," the allegory in "My Kinsman, Major Molineux" transcends history. Although the tale has been confidently interpreted as an allegory of historical change,[20] there are some real objections to considering it so primarily. The first objection, although perhaps not insuperable, has a good deal of force. Hawthorne ordinarily makes his intention in historical allegory clear. Although there is some ironic reservation, we are in no doubt whatever about the direction of the historical allegory of "The Gray Champion," or "Endicott and the Red Cross," or "Edward Randolph's Portrait" (a tale which, like "My Kinsman," has its action in the time of Lieutenant-governor Hutchinson's administration). Each of these three tales, moreover, glorifies the Revolutionary idea, which "My Kinsman" hardly does. A second objection seems to have even more force. If the tale were intended to be an allegory of historical change, the episode with the prostitute, so vivid and disturbing in itself, would have no allegorical purpose, would be, rather, a confusing digression in the allegory. Finally there is this: If the tale were intended to represent the beginning of a new epoch in national experience, Robin would have some realization of the new order, some awareness of the change. His experience can hardly stand for historical change if he has no realization of historical change. But from first to last in the tale, he is given no political awareness whatever. There is not even any indication that he knows why his kinsman is being tarred and feathered, and we are left to determine for ourselves why he thinks of returning home. There is no evidence in the tale that Robin's urbane companion, when he counsels Robin to stay, is thinking in a political context. Judging by all we know of Hawthorne's practice, had he intended us to read back into the tale later attitudes toward the Revolution, he would have moved our minds toward that interpretation.

20. See Q. D. Leavis, "Hawthorne as Poet," *The Sewanee Review* 59 (1951): 198–205; Roy Harvey Pearce, "Hawthorne and the Sense of the Past," *Journal of English Literary History* 21 (1954): 327–49.

"My Kinsman, Major Molineux" also has been persuasively interpreted as an allegory that represents an initiation ceremony in which Robin, through his night's experience, suddenly achieves a moral maturity. Although interpretations of this sort may be made to depend too much upon anthropological or psychological ideas Hawthorne could hardly have known about, "My Kinsman" does seem to represent a common kind of experience in the lives of young men. Seymour L. Gross, in his influential article on the tale, speaks of "a thousand moral years" passing for Robin within his night's experience.[21] It will be here urged that Robin's "evening of ambiguity and weariness" represents in allegorical condensation not only a great moral change but a development that in ordinary experience would go on over months or years.[22]

{"The youth, one of whose names was Robin," stands for many youths who go by many names: he comes into the world with confident preconceptions and he finds them all mistaken.[23]}Under a condition of the allegory, Robin, by his decision to leave home, cannot return—just as going out into the world is decisive for most boys. And this condition is established clearly enough in the tale. When Robin is in reverie or dreaming on the church steps, his life at home is as vividly present to him as his new experience has been; but when Robin, picturing his family entering their house, would enter with them, he sees the latch fall and himself excluded.

The moral ideas that arise in the allegory are traditionally Christian moral ideas. Their traditional nature may be obscured, however, by a

21. "Hawthorne's 'My Kinsman, Major Molineux': History as Moral Adventure," *Nineteenth-Century Fiction* 12 (1957): 97–109.

22. This allegorical method is roughly comparable to that in some scenes in Goethe's *Faust*—in the Auerback's Cellar scene in Pt. 1, for example, or in the Baronial Hall scene in Pt. 2.

23. Robin's predicament is strikingly like the predicaments of the young heroes of a number of the novels of Sir Walter Scott, from *Waverley* on, who become involved in political events they do not understand. See Ian Jack, *English Literature 1815–1832* (Oxford, 1964), pp. 188–89. Robin might well have spoken the complaint of Roland Graeme, the young hero of *The Abbot*: "A land of enchantment have I been led into, and spells have been cast around me—every one has met me in disguise—every one has spoken to me in parables—I have been like one who walks in a weary and bewildering dream" (chap. 28). In Scott's novels, of course, the heroes do come to some understanding of the events they are caught up in, but there is surely a connection between Scott's bewildered young men and the bewildered Robin.

degree of failure on Hawthorne's part in managing the delicate balance between the interest of his persons and his action, on the one hand, and the interest of his allegory on the other. The moral ideas need to be distinguished from the complexity of their embodiment. For in Robin's appalling evening he is subjected to the three great temptations that the Litany calls "the deceits of the world, the flesh, and the devil." They come to every young man; what gives this tale its nightmare quality is that they and their attendant spiritual confusions come together, almost at once.

From the deceits of the devil, the temptation to the sin of pride, Robin is in no very great danger. He is by no means a Young Goodman Brown; he has perhaps a degree of pride—it is not worse than a boyish vanity—pointed up by the iteration of "shrewd" on his part and the narrator's part. Even when he is giving an account of himself to the urbane gentleman who seems to befriend him, Robin takes care to say that he has "the name of being a shrewd youth." But his vanity has been shaken by the rebuffs and laughter that have met his inquiries for the Major, and he begins to develop a self-distrust that, at least in young persons, is quite compatible with vanity, and indeed often its concomitant.

In his encounter with the prostitute, Robin escapes the temptation of the flesh—but very narrowly, and as much through fortune as by virtue. At the moment when the woman in the scarlet petticoat has drawn Robin nearly into her dwelling, the watchman frightens her away. When the watchman proceeds on his rounds, she reappears at an open window. But Robin is now free of her touch, and able to follow the dictates of his conscience. The narrator comments: "Robin, being of the household of a New England clergyman, was a good youth, as well as a shrewd one; so he resisted temptation, and fled away."

To the temptations of the world, Robin, like most of us, is susceptible; and to them he yields, at least for the time being. The scene in which he does so is presided over by the mysterious figure of the urbane gentleman who may stand for them—the narrator is careful not to identify him. He has been taken to be a helper figure or Robin's sympathetic friend. But the narrator never vouches for him; the narrator tells us how prepossessing this gentleman is, how kindly and pleasant his manner—but nothing more. The narrator does not say, for instance, that the urbane gentleman is kind, but that he speaks to

Robin "in a tone of real kindness." In a tale peopled with apparently sinister figures, he may be the most really sinister of them all.

Whatever the nature of Robin's companion, Robin is under his tutelage as Major Molineux appears in his "tar-and-feathery dignity" and as Robin recognizes, somehow individually present to him within the mob, the several persons whose apparent rejection of him had so shaken his confidence in himself. Robin is appalled by his kinsman's plight, "the foul disgrace of a head grown gray in honor," and stares at him "with a mixture of pity and terror." Yet he betrays, not his kinsman, but his own love and respect for him, and thereby for the time being loses his feeling of rejection. The narrator's account everywhere emphasizes the contagion of group attitudes, and the excitement and a kind of pleasure for Robin in his symbolic unity with the mob:

> A bewildering excitement began to seize upon his mind; the preceding adventures of the night, the unexpected appearance of the crowd, the torches, the confused din and the hush that followed, the spectre of his kinsman reviled by that great multitude,—all this, and, more than all, a perception of tremendous ridicule in the whole scene, affected him with a sort of mental inebriety. . . . The contagion was spreading among the multitude, when all at once, it seized upon Robin, and he sent forth a shout of laughter that echoed through the street,—every man shook his sides, every man emptied his lungs, but Robin's shout was the loudest there.

This passage, surely the crux of the tale, seems to represent what in our ordinary lives is the slow, insidious process in which a man, without full consciousness of depravity, makes his compromises and abandons his loyalties, avoids rejection, and comes to feel himself at one with his society.

When the mob has passed, Robin is bitterly aware of his betrayal of himself. He thinks of returning home—but intellectually and spiritually he can never be the boy he was, he can never go home again.

He may even have some insight into the nature of his companion; he does equate him with the other persons he has encountered, and, "rather dryly," he says, "Thanks to you, and to my other friends, I have at last met my kinsman." But we cannot be sure of Robin's future relationship with his companion.)Every reader will have his questions as he finishes reading the tale; he may answer them as he likes. A critic, it seems to me, should stay within the limits of the tale.

When the young Hawthorne wrote "My Kinsman, Major Molineux," he was in full possession of his powers. It would be hard to find an example of another fiction writer whose abilities developed so early. But in that plenitude he tried in "My Kinsman, Major Molineux" to use too many of his abilities at once. The tale has too many interests and makes too many suggestions for any reader to be sure of them all. Hawthorne's reluctance to collect the tale suggests that he thought it a kind of failure. But by an irony of literary history, it is just that fascinating kind of failure that has attracted critics of our time to it.

13. SYMPATHY AND CRAFTSMANSHIP

Since the work Hawthorne did at the Old Manse took new directions, and since he considered his early tales a resource in writing *The Scarlet Letter* and *The House of Seven Gables,* a discussion of the tales written 1825–1838 may have a kind of completeness. Certainly Hawthorne has achievement in the period that he does not parallel in his later work.

The tales of the period are of course of most unequal value. It is no service to literature or to the study of Hawthorne to exalt his weak work with its occasional puerilities. But there is an opposite disservice. What Lionel Trilling calls "the characteristic highly developed literary sensibility of our time,"[1] proceeds into some fascinating criticism, but it is likely to cherish Hawthorne's tales only as they furnish a very few pieces of material especially useful for its exercise. Hawthorne's excellence is neither so wide as the number of his tales portentously discussed might seem to indicate, nor so narrow as the multiplication of discussions of a few might suggest. The tales in which

1. In "Our Hawthorne," *Hawthorne Centenary Essays,* ed. Roy Harvey Pearce (Columbus, Ohio, 1964), p. 448.

Hawthorne's special kind of insight and his craftsmanship fortunately come together deserve our admiration.

Although Hawthorne could write delightful self-mockery,[2] he took himself and his role as fiction writer seriously; and he was able to feel, at least part of the time, that he had escaped triviality and justified his storytelling. In a letter of February 27, 1842 to his fiancée he writes of himself and of his work in a tone in which he of course would not have written in anything intended for publication:

> A cloudy veil stretches over the abyss of my nature. I have, however, no love of secrecy and darkness. I am glad to think that God sees through my heart, and, if any angel has power to penetrate into it, he is welcome to know everything that is there. Yes, and so may any mortal who is capable of full sympathy, and therefore worthy to come into my depths. But he must find his own way there. I can neither guide nor enlighten him. It is this involuntary reserve, I suppose, that has given the objectivity to my writings; and when people think that I am pouring myself out in a tale or an essay, I am merely telling what is common to human nature, not what is peculiar to myself. I sympathize with them, not they with me.[3]

The passage is especially pertinent to our concern, for in it Hawthorne is reflecting on the work of his first period. But the essence of its last two sentences is repeated in prefatory pieces, by implication in the 1851 preface to *Twice-Told Tales*; explicitly in "The Old Manse," where he says that he has "appealed to no sentiment or sensibilities save such as are diffused among us all"; and emphatically in the prefatory letter for *The Snow-Image*. He "has been burrowing," he says there, "to his utmost ability, into the depths of our common nature," proceeding "as well by the tact of sympathy as by the light of observation."[4]

2. See a passage in a letter to his fiancée beginning "Here I am, in my old chamber, where I produced those stupendous works of fiction which have since impressed the universe with wonderment and awe!" (*Passages*, pp. 334–35) This letter of January 20, 1842 is printed entire in *Love Letters*, 2: 73–76. And see the playful preface to "Rappaccini's Daughter," *Mosses*, pp. 107–9.

3. *Passages*, pp. 335–36. This letter of February 27, 1842 is printed entire in *Love Letters*, 2: 77–81.

4. Earlier Hawthorne had assigned a tact of sympathy to the "I" of "The Seven Vagabonds" (1832): "If there be a faculty which I possess more perfectly

In the prefatory letter for *The Snow-Image*, Hawthorne's mind turned back to his early work, not only because he used a good deal of it in that collection, but because he addressed Horatio Bridge, who had made the first edition of *Twice-Told Tales* possible. In the course of the letter he remarks, "In youth, men are apt to write more wisely than they really know or feel. . . . The truth that was only in the fancy then may have since become a substance in the mind and heart." Whether or not the remark is sound as a generalization, it describes a condition of Hawthorne's work, for neither his insight nor his skill seems to have developed greatly after his late twenties and early thirties. If as a young writer he complains of his lack of experience and knowledge of the world, he hardly seems to feel as he writes in 1851 that it was so great a disadvantage after all.

The ability Hawthorne claims for himself may be known only by its effects; Henry James in "The Art of Fiction" best describes the gifts required. James has been praising an achievement of insight on the part of a woman novelist, and concludes: "The power to guess the unseen from the seen, to trace the implication of things, to judge the whole piece by the pattern, the condition of feeling life in general so completely that you are well on your way to knowing any particular corner of it—this cluster of gifts may also be said to constitute experience, and they occur in country and in town, and in the most differing stages of education." It is only the recognition of such a cluster of gifts that will account for the work Hawthorne did in his young manhood, and we may call the cluster "the tact of sympathy," by Hawthorne's own term.

The term is a complex metaphor for which there may be no satisfactory literal equivalent. "The tact of sympathy" is paired with "the light of observation" and distinguished from it. The light of observation is external and shared by any writer with all other men; Hawthorne had fewer opportunities for the exercise of observation than great fiction writers usually have. In "the tact of sympathy," *tact* seems to combine something of its ordinary English sense, a fitness of response, with the sense of Latin *tactus* from which it comes. The tact of sympathy is the touch of sympathy, intentional, more active than just

---

than most men, it is that of throwing myself mentally into situations foreign to my own."

response. In Hawthorne's best tales, our common nature is represented
by persons who, since they are flawed like ourselves, elicit our concern.
And at its best, his tact of sympathy seems the imaginative operation
of Christian charity, asking of us not only concern but compassion too.

Ultimately, an estimate of Hawthorne's quality as a writer must
depend upon whether or not there is realized in his best work a tact of
sympathy enabling him to deal with human experience more by that
tact—that touch—than by observation. On his own testimony, he is
important for his imaginative realization, not certainly of himself, not
especially of particular persons, but finally of our common nature.

Not that Hawthorne's tact of sympathy is always embodied in a
successful tale. In comparison with Dr. Heidegger's four friends, or
with the ruined merchant and the poet in "The Canterbury Pilgrims,"
the types in "The Great Carbuncle" are inept and labored. Sometimes the very means Hawthorne uses to achieve a narrative balance of
interest in an allegorical tale seem not perfectly under his control.
The portrait painter in "The Prophetic Pictures," for example, is too
much a Gothic figure ever to stand for a part of our common nature,
or to bring a moral problem home to us. With such a tale, Henry
James's contention that Hawthorne's preoccupation with the sense of
sin has an *"imported* character," that it seems to exist "merely for
an artistic or literary purpose," perhaps could be sustained. But what
is said in "Drowne's Wooden Image" of the woodcarver—that he was
most consistent with himself in his best achievement—is true also of
any writer and particularly true of so uneven a writer as Hawthorne.
When we find him most consistent with himself, we experience the
kind of recognition that Aristotle so long ago found a fundamental
value in literature; we say, "That's right," or "Yes, it must be that way."

But in Hawthorne's early career he would have known of few persons who had experienced that recognition, few who had found their
way into his depths. Even in 1851, a year in which he could feel
himself a successful writer—then more than ever before and probably
after—he remarked in a letter to Bridge: "The only sensible ends of
literature are, first, the pleasurable toil of writing; second, the gratifica-
tion of one's family and friends; and, lastly, the solid cash."[5] In the
long years before the publication of the *Twice-Told Tales*, there had

5. Bridge, p. 125.

been very little solid cash, and few friends to gratify;[6] Hawthorne had to find his reward in the pleasurable toil of writing.

The reward was the pleasurable toil, not, apparently, the glow of success, the feeling that this time a tale was right, or even as excellent as Hawthorne could hope to make it. For he was troubled by his persistent awareness of the discrepancy between intention and fulfillment. Now we cannot, as it seems to me, dismiss this feeling in him as just a conventional Romantic attitude. It was too important to him, too often connected with a real sense of failure for that. Nor can we dismiss it as a pose Hawthorne liked to take in his prefatory pieces. The feeling does appear in them in graceful disparagement, but it also appears in what he said privately, and it is projected in his work.[7]

Perhaps Hawthorne's own ideal of his work was never fulfilled: in the prefatory letter to *Our Old Home* he wrote of "a certain ideal shelf, where are reposited many . . . shadowy volumes of mine, more in number, and very much superior in quality, to those which I have succeeded in rendering actual." If we do not quite know what his own conception of a successful tale was, we know it to have been exacting. We find him expressing a feeling of failure not only about tales that seem to us failures, but also about tales the world has taken as successes. When he said of "The Man of Adamant" that he had failed to give shape and substance to what had seemed a fine conception, we think we know what he meant, for we recognize in the tale an

6. Probably Hawthorne's small circle of friends in the 1830s were not much aware of what he was writing. Even the concerned Bridge, as we have seen, had not read "The Gentle Boy" until it was collected; and it is clear that Jonathan Cilley, another friend from college days, knew nothing of Hawthorne's work in 1836. See Cilley's letter, *Hawthorne and His Wife*, 1: 144–45.

7. In "The Prophetic Pictures," the painter's portraits of Walter and Elinor are successful "so as barely to fall short of that standard which no genius ever reached, his own severe conception." Georgiana, in "The Birthmark," recognizes that Aylmer's "most splendid successes were almost invariably failures, if compared with the ideal at which he aimed." Aylmer's journal, which records great achievements, also records continual failure to realize his own aims, and the narrator remarks, "Perhaps every man of genius in whatever sphere might recognize the image of his own experience in Aylmer's journal." This attitude is not, of course, limited to Hawthorne or to nineteenth-century writers. Compare a statement by Wallace Stevens: "It is not what I have written but what I should like to have written that constitues my true poems, the uncollected poems which I have not had the strength to realize." Quoted in Roy Harvey Pearce, *Historicism Once More* (Princeton, 1969), p. 261.

important conviction and an inadequate embodiment. When in 1850 he reread "Peter Goldthwaite's Treasure" and "The Shaker Bridal," he found them "painfully cold and dull."[8] "Peter Goldthwaite's Treasure," a satire of the financial speculator (written during the depression of 1837), has at least an interesting allegorical scheme, but we had not supposed it intended to have any warmth; the compassionate "Shaker Bridal" seems so different a tale as not at all to deserve the same adjectives. When he wrote a preface for "The Gentle Boy," he remarked that he had some sense of "imperfect and ill-wrought conception" in the tale—but we hardly know the intent of the stricture. In a letter to Longfellow, he disparaged the pieces in *Twice-Told Tales* his readers have most liked, and preferred those they have cared for least. The most earnest tales in *Mosses from an Old Manse* do not, he said, express "satisfactorily the thoughts which they profess to image." "Roger Malvin's Burial" and "Young Goodman Brown" are earnest tales, and Hawthorne tried again in *The Scarlet Letter* to image some of the thoughts in them.

Yet we hardly know what Hawthorne himself thought even relatively successful. We cannot say, on his own testimony, that any tale nearly achieves his own conception. We cannot say what tales seemed to him less imperfect and ill-wrought than "The Gentle Boy." What he says of the two great romances merely complicates the problem of understanding his judgment of himself. He complained in a letter to Bridge that *The Scarlet Letter* lacked "sunshine," and that it seemed to him an inadequate representation of his own nature as a writer; *The House of the Seven Gables*, he told Bridge, was a work more characteristic of his mind, "more proper and natural" for him to write.[9] Now since *The Scarlet Letter* takes up into itself so much of his work in his early tales, the implication of the judgment is that they, too, were not quite characteristic of his mind as he would have it be. In trying to understand Hawthorne's own estimate of his work, we must proceed largely by inference, and, as we have seen, inference

8. *American Notebooks,* ed. Stewart, p. 247.

9. Bridge, pp. 112 and 126. Hawthorne often let "sunshine" stand for a quality or qualities he felt his work lacked. In "The Custom House" he says of *The Scarlet Letter,* "it wears, to my eye, a stern and sombre aspect; too much ungladdened by genial sunshine." Close to the end of his life he writes to James T. Fields: "I wish God had given me the faculty of writing a sunshiny book" (Fields, p. 109).

from the clearest evidence we have—his own choices in collecting his tales—indicates that his judgment was often at variance with that of his readers, and especially with that of his readers today.

But it is clear that when Hawthorne was dissatisfied with one or another tale, it was because he felt a discrepancy between conception and execution: the tales that disappointed him were "ill-wrought." We may see the tales somewhat differently from the way in which he did; but our judgment of any particular tale, like his, is a judgment largely of his management of his complex technical means. When he so manages them that we recognize a quality of experience we hardly know in any other fiction writer's work, his success is so far technical, a success of craftsmanship. Yet in Hawthorne, perhaps more than in most fiction writers, one technical matter so depends upon another that a consideration of structure leads into a consideration of style, and the discussion of style may involve an attempt to define the narrative assumptions of a tale. What can be said about Hawthorne's technique in the tales must be inference from the tales themselves. And since we do not know much certainly about the order of composition of the tales, we cannot trace stages of Hawthorne's early development—if, indeed, there were any such stages.

There is, however, a clear place to start. It is with the four tales in *The Token* for 1832—"The Gentle Boy," "My Kinsman, Major Molineux," "Roger Malvin's Burial," and "The Wives of the Dead"—for we know that the first two and probably all four were complete by December of 1829. Now in these four tales we have examples of the three narrative structures Hawthorne uses best. "The Gentle Boy" and "Roger Malvin's Burial" have a sort of time span common in the short fiction of the day, a sort we find, for instance, in the work of Miss Sedgwick. "My Kinsman, Major Molineux" has a time span of but a single night, yet draws into it a wealth of experience and implication, and in allegorical condensation represents a development in its central figure. "The Wives of the Dead" is an early example of the highly concentrated tale that Hawthorne so often writes successfully.

When Hawthorne uses a time span that extends over months or years, he apparently chooses carefully what he will represent directly and in detail and what he will handle in summary narrative, always with the intent to give a sense of the whole elapsing time. He succeeds in that intent with the more-than-two-year time span of "The Gentle

Boy." The eighteen-year time span of "Roger Malvin's Burial" offers more difficulty; at least the reader is quite aware of a contrast between represented action and rapid summary narration. Likewise, in the later "Prophetic Pictures" the reader is aware, even as he reads the tale, that the account of the painter's travels in the wilderness is a calculated device to fill the interval between the painting of the portraits and the denouement—although it is also used for analysis of the painter.

But in these tales the handling of the time pattern is not greatly different from that of competent storytellers before and after Hawthorne. His triumph in handling a long time span, as we have seen, is in the skillful use of the narrator in "The Minister's Black Veil"—a narrator whose transitions from one sort of narrative to another are so well handled that in reading the tale we are not aware of their careful calculation. Hawthorne succeeds in a way of his own, too, with the shorter time span of "Old Esther Dudley," in which the narrative depends, not on direct representation, but on an account of what is generally known and imagined of old Esther's life alone in the Province House.

The way of storytelling in "My Kinsman, Major Molineux" and later in "Young Goodman Brown" seems to be Hawthorne's invention;[10] surely no fiction writer before him had condensed so much experience into such short spans of represented time, and written tales so enthralling on their surface and so arresting in their implications. "My Kinsman" must have been written at about the same time as "The Gentle Boy"; both are skillful, although as we have noticed, "My Kinsman" may be too complex an attempt and not completely in Hawthorne's control. Nevertheless, its technique has interested students of Hawthorne more than the technique of "The Gentle Boy," for in "My Kinsman" Hawthorne is beginning what distinguishes the best of his tales—the seizing on a representative short period which implies the previous experience of the major figure or figures, and predicts the future or, as in "My Kinsman," teases us into speculation about it. In such tales Hawthorne escapes the limitations of plot, and makes the tale a way of representing not just an episode but the very quality of a life or a relationship.

10. The scheme of "Ethan Brand" has some likeness to that of these tales, for it begins just after sunset and ends at dawn. But its structure as "A Chapter from an Abortive Romance" separates it from them.

"The Wives of the Dead," which has a time span from dusk to, apparently, some time in the small hours, sets the pattern for more concentrated and less complex tales than "My Kinsman" and "Young Goodman Brown," but tales that, like them, look before and after. For this structure, an initial influence on Hawthorne was certainly the single, highly wrought incident of Scott's novels, and the connection is apparent in some of the early historical tales. But the structure that represents only a moment in the lives of the figures in the tale is used variously. In "Dr. Heidegger's Experiment" the action of an afternoon conveys the whole quality of four wasted lives and the inevitable bleakness of their remaining years. Within the time it takes the little company that meet at the Shaker spring in "The Canterbury Pilgrims" to tell their stories, we know the essence of four lives, and move forward into a somber hope for the young lovers. Very short periods are represented in "The Ambitious Guest" and in "The Shaker Bridal"; but in each we comprehend lifetimes.

Just how Hawthorne worked out this distinctive structure we cannot say. The influence of Scott partially accounts for it; a letter of Hawthorne's to Goodrich suggests that Goodrich had asked for short pieces.[11] Yet the technique is surely inherent in Hawthorne. It is not just the result of what F. L. Pattee calls Hawthorne's "keen eye for situation"; it is a manifestation of his bent toward allegory, his interest in the situation meaningful beyond itself, and for what it holds of past and future. But Hawthorne's achievement in these sharply focused tales may be underestimated just because it is gained so briefly.

Henry James, who here as often manages at once to praise and to patronize Hawthorne, writes: " 'The Grey Champion' is a sketch of less than eight pages, but the little figures stand up in the tale as stoutly, at the least, as if they were propped up on half-a-dozen chapters by a dryer annalist, and the whole thing has the merit of those cabinet pictures in which the artist has been able to make his persons look the size of life." The sentence seems to recognize the economy as an achievement, but to accord it only a kind of success in miniature. Yet the figure of the Gray Champion looms in our imaginations; and,

11. In a postcript to his letter of December 20, 1829, Hawthorne says that if he writes any such short pieces as Goodrich has inquired about, he will send them to Goodrich. The letter is printed in Adkins, "Early Projected Works of Hawthorne," pp. 127–28.

indeed, in our final estimate of Hawthorne there may be a question of where *his* success is greatest—whether it is in those tales in which he works within narrow, self-imposed limitations, or in the romances where he resorts to half-a-dozen chapters of analysis.

What we need to see—and what James may not have seen—is that the economy of a tale like "The Gray Champion" depends upon its focus on a single event, and that within the limits of the tale, the treatment is a full one. Hawthorne's style in the tales of the period of our concern is a leisurely style, adapted to their structures. Since he is using a restricted subject matter and time span or, as in "The Gentle Boy," representing only a small part of the time span of the action, he can gain his effects deliberately, lingering on the nuances of experience, taking the time to write a prose far better finished than any we can find in the American writers of his day except Irving's at its very best.

Now there are objections to Hawthorne's style, but almost all of them arise when a passage conflicts with our own twentieth-century taste—and we might remember that Hawthorne wrote in a time when the praise for a writer of imaginative prose was commonly that he was "a true poet." Yet there is much that our taste can admire in Hawthorne's prose. Although his sentence pattern may not have the interest in and for itself that we find in, say, "Rip Van Winkle," there are single sentences of remarkable economy and accomplishment, sentences that convey at the same time accounts of actions and their moral or spiritual concomitants. Such a sentence comes as Goodman Brown makes his way into the dark wood: "He had taken a dreary road, darkened by all the gloomiest trees of the forest, which barely stood aside to let the narrow path creep through, and closed immediately behind." Or, to take but one more example, there is this sentence from "My Kinsman": "So saying, the fair and hospitable dame took our hero by the hand; and the touch was light, and the force was gentleness, and though Robin read in her eyes what he did not hear in her words, yet the slender-waisted woman in the scarlet petticoat proved stronger than the athletic country youth." But, although we can find many such separable sentences, it is not in them that Hawthorne's greatest skill is to be found.

For Hawthorne's special stylistic excellence is in the careful calculation of his whole pattern, the adaptation of style to the structure and to the narrative assumptions of particular tales. A cadenced sentence from "The Minister's Black Veil" may serve us: "In this manner Mr. Hooper spent a long life, irreproachable in outward act, yet shrouded in dismal suspicions; kind and loving, though unloved, and dimly feared; a man apart from men, shunned in their health and joy, but ever summoned to their aid in mortal anguish." The sentence is a major transition in the narrative, yet it enforces by its series of antitheses the parodox the tale discovers. But it can serve us only as an instance. Any illustration of the effect of Hawthorne's prose is necessarily inadequate, for one can quote only a part of the pattern; and for that matter Hawthorne's patterns are so much determined by the direction of the narrative that it would be misleading to say that one pattern or another is typical.

William Charvat remarks of Hawthorne's romances that their style is "essentially parenthetical and . . . this characteristic reflects the basically essayistic, generalizing, and speculative quality of his fiction."[12] The parenthetical habit grew on Hawthorne; the style of the tales of the period of our concern, although it is deliberate, is far less parenthetical than that of the romances, and immediately adapted to the differing structures and narrators of the individual tales. The style of "The Minister's Black Veil," for instance, is distinct from the style of "Dr. Heidegger's Experiment," both as the greatly different time spans of the actions require differences in the kind of narration and as the narrators differ in temper. Even in "The Gentle Boy," where there seems no narrator distinct from Hawthorne, we are sometimes stayed on a single, dramatic scene—Catharine ascending the pulpit and preparing to address the congregation, for instance—and sometimes carried along with rapid summary narration.

Hawthorne's flexible narrative assumptions, although we may easily be aware of their importance, offer certain difficulties in definition. We cannot say how he defined them to himself. He had read no discussion of "the disappearing author"; he could not have guessed what William Dean Howells and Henry James were to say on the authorial relationship to the story. He does not mind confessing that his story is a story; in "The Ambitious Guest," for instance, after an immediate account of the guest's reception at the inn, a paragraph begins "Let us now suppose . . . ." Yet narrative points of view in Hawthorne's tales

12. Quoted in the textural introduction to the Centenary Edition of *The House of the Seven Gables*, p. xlvii n.

may be intricate. Indeed they are intricate enough so that the terms commonly used to distinguish narrative points of view seem never quite suitable to our discussion.

Hawthorne's practice suggests that he did a good deal of thinking about the techniques of his narratives. In most of the tales written before 1839, he did not use an "I" narrator; he may have generally avoided one in order to keep the tales distinct from his essay-like sketches, which are often written in the first person. And it is likely that he wished to keep himself distinct from the tales, and that he understood that the use of an "I" narrator leads readers into confusion about the separation of a writer from his work. Such confusion is entirely apparent in naive readers, who may, for instance, identify the "I" in a Poe tale with Poe himself. But the same confusion may exist in more sophisticated readers without becoming so apparent; it sometimes makes trouble in discussions of *The Blithedale Romance*.

The authorial "we," when it occurs in historical tales, may indicate a narrative assumption special with them in which the action is related with immediacy and interpreted in historical perspective. Endicott, in "The Maypole of Merry Mount," is described even to his changing facial expression, yet he is interpreted as he is historically representative, "the Puritan of Puritans." But of course narrative point of view in these tales does not depend upon a pronoun. In "The Gray Champion," in which there is no authorial intrusion into the narrative itself,[13] there are yet the same assumptions about the storyteller's power to relate the action with immediacy and to interpret it historically; he knows both what an unidentified voice in the crowd calls out and what the scene symbolizes in New England history.

But narrative point of view, even in a historical tale, may not be only a matter of relationship of author to story. In the frame of "Howe's Masquerade" we are told that the tale is Hawthorne's redaction of Mr. Bella Tiffany's story. Yet in portions of the tale, the action is represented as it is perceived by some—not all—of the persons in the tale. For example, the last figure in the procession of figures representing the governors of Massachusetts the reader realizes through the apprehensions of "some of the spectators," and the pattern of the paragraph is the pattern of their growing perceptions.

13. There is a rather surprising "I" in the last, prophetic paragraph.

In some tales the realization of an identity for the narrator has considerable critical importance. The reader will have noticed that sometimes in the foregoing discussions of individual tales a narrator distinct from Hawthorne is referred to, and sometimes not—and the reader may not always have agreed with the distinction, for the matter is difficult. But we are surely aware of a narrator in "The Minister's Black Veil," aware even of something of his nature; the limitations on his knowledge are of the same kind that belong to our own knowledge of friends and acquaintances in ordinary life. And it would be difficult to account for the effect of "Young Goodman Brown," or of "My Kinsman, Major Molineux," without assuming a narrator, although in neither tale does the nature of the narrator fully emerge. In "My Kinsman," moreover, the narrator speaks sometimes in a historical perspective (he comments, for instance, on our ancestors' liking for the "Good Creature" rum). Yet the narrator in "My Kinsman" does not interpret figures or incidents that bewilder Robin; the narrator in "Young Goodman Brown," although he is cognizant of Goodman Brown's innermost life, will only speculate on the relationships of some of his perceptions to external reality. The ambiguity in these tales turns upon the limitations of the narrators' knowledge or of their candor, or perhaps of both; and it is these limitations that invite us as readers into speculation and a kind of collaboration.

Another difficulty in the definition of point of view is the frequent assumption in the tales of some "chimney corner" tradition or body of legendary material. The tales are not narrated as tradition, to be sure; tradition does not preserve dialogue nor the subtleties of human interactions. The purported recalling of a tradition—as in "The Great Carbuncle," for instance—often provides a preternatural suggestion that the narrator (or Hawthorne) does not make himself responsible for. Even in "The Maypole of Merry Mount," after an immediate account of Endicott cutting down the maypole, it is remarked that "as it sank, tradition says, the evening sky grew darker, and the woods threw forth a more sombre shadow." But this assumption is not essentially different from the narrative assumption for *The Scarlet Letter* as Hawthorne defines it in "The Custom House": there, it will be remembered, he purports to be working from Mr. Surveyor Pue's account and at the same time insists upon the full privileges of the omniscient convention. This likeness in narrative assumption is another evidence of the close connection between the tales and the romance.

But we cannot make rules about the way Hawthorne uses his devices. The account of Dr. Heidegger's study and of the marvelous occurrences therein is prefaced with "If all the stories were true." But in the same tale is ascribed to general report, not a preternatural explanation, but a suggestion that the happenings of the summer afternoon were illusions: "Yet, by a strange deception, owing to the duskiness of the chamber, and the antique dresses which they still wore, the tall mirror is said to have reflected the figures of three old, gray, withered grandsires, ridiculously contending for the skinny ugliness of a shrivelled grandam." The narrator has proceeded as if he had seen the doctor's four friends as young as they felt themselves to be. But he does know what the mirror is said to have reflected; and the mirror we took to be a magic mirror seems in this instance incapable of illusion. Hawthorne's device of unvouched-for suggestion clearly stems from Scott and William Austin, but his refinements on it are complex.

What emerges when we try to analyze the narrative devices with which Hawthorne works is a kind of legerdemain, adroit, yet for the most part not beyond detection, and perhaps not really so greatly involved as some writers on Hawthorne have lately been insisting. But the legerdemain is realized in analysis; it does not intrude itself in ordinary reading. In the best tales the illusion is maintained, and the only requirement we need make of any narrative device or assumption is imaginative success. We are hardly aware of even the repeatedly used devices except in the artificiality of critical analysis; and the reason must be that the even tone and the pattern of the style—its care and calculation—induce an acceptance.

But Hawthorne's narrative procedures only partly account for a peculiar quality of his work. Nor does this quality inhere solely in such passages as those commonly used as examples of his ambiguity, although they may serve to point it up. In the last chapter of *The Marble Faun* Hawthorne remarks, "The actual experience of even the most ordinary life is full of events that never explain themselves, either as regards their origin or their tendency." The sentence may have a special application to the romance, but it recognizes a quality which is in much of Hawthorne's fiction, and which (as it seems to me) is more impressively present in the early tales than in later work. That quality is the realization, not so much of the complexity, as of the opaqueness of experience, a quality we know in our own. There is likely, therefore, to be a residue of mystery in Hawthorne's best tales which good criticism will always leave intact.

Just as in particular tales we must accept a residue of mystery as part of Hawthorne's realization of experience, so we must accept the difficulties in understanding his intention and his estimate of his work. Of course Hawthorne is not the only writer whose estimate of some of his work is out of accord with that of even his devoted readers. Nor is he the only writer to feel the discrepancy between the work he envisaged and the work he produced. But his feeling that his work never quite represented his own nature as he realized it does seem to be special and part of his mystery. It is not only that he believed he had failed in one or another tale. He had some ideal, some measure of excellence for himself that his work in its entirety never fulfilled. The excellence he sought is not at all the excellence with which his critics invest him.

In "The Custom House" Hawthorne imagines a shadowy forefather who scorns him as a writer of "story-books." From his youth Hawthorne was determined to be a storyteller. But he was never willing to be merely a storyteller, never willing to merit that ancestral scorn.

To be a professional writer of fiction in America in the 1830s was to face great difficulties in finding and understanding a market, and greater in discovering a usable tradition. Regarded in itself, what served Hawthorne as a tradition seems makeshift, but clearly his work is strongest when it most depends upon the tradition he devised from what he had at hand. He found a way to be a storyteller in his time and place, and yet to move his fiction into territories no fiction writer had occupied before him.

Hawthorne's necessity to be more than just a storyteller may account for the puerility of some tales in which he seeks and does not find a moral purpose. But the same necessity accounts for those tales in which we recognize our common nature and the opaqueness of our own experience. The residue of mystery in his work is the sign of his humility as an artist; his complex technical means have purposes beyond themselves. He required his storytelling to do more than any fiction writer before him had required, sometimes, it may be, more than fiction can do.

BIBLIOGRAPHICAL NOTE

Most of my indebtedness is indicated in the text and notes, but my use of
certain tool works has not resulted in citation. I have used Nina Browne's
A Bibliography of Nathaniel Hawthorne (Boston, 1905) and the several
bibliographies that list scholarly and critical works on Hawthorne. I have found
still useful Elizabeth Lathrop Chandler's pioneer "Study of the Sources of the
Tales and Romances Written by Nathaniel Hawthorne before 1853," *Smith
College Studies in Modern Languages*, 7 no. 4 (1926). Harry Hayden
Clark's "Literary Criticism in the *North American Review*, 1815–1835," *Trans-
actions of the Wisconsin Academy of Sciences, Arts and Letters*, 32 (1940):
299–350 is most valuable and has been useful to me, as has William Charvat,
The Origins of American Critical Thought, 1810–1835 (Philadelphia, 1936).
Edward Wagenknecht, *Nathaniel Hawthorne: Man and Writer* (New York,
1961) is a balanced consideration of Hawthorne's character. I have long been
in debt to the introduction and notes in Austin Warren's anthology *Nathaniel
Hawthorne* (New York, 1934). If one is not too proud to use a book prepared
for high schools years ago, J. Hubert Scott's edition of *Twice-Told Tales*
(Boston, 1907) furnishes much information and some curious specimens of late
nineteenth-century criticism. Some works that are cited in my text or notes
have been more useful to me than the citation indicates, particularly Frank
Luther Mott, *A History of American Magazines, 1741–1850* (New York, 1930);
and Randall Stewart, *Nathaniel Hawthorne: A Biography* (New Haven,
1948).

INDEX

The names of figures in Hawthorne's fiction are not indexed; when names belong both to figures in the tales and to historical persons (e.g., John Endicott), only references to the historical persons are indexed.

Abbot, The. See Scott, Sir Walter
Adams, John Quincy, 8
Addison, Joseph, "The Vision of Mirzah," 67
"Address . . . to the Phi Beta Kappa Society." *See* Tudor, William
Adkins, Nelson F., 28, 94, 141
Aeschylus, *Agamemnon*, 142
Agrippa, Cornelius, 60
Alcott, Bronson, 52
Alison, Archibald, 16
Allegory, 44–45, 62–71; in "Dr. Heidegger's Experiment," 181–82; in "Fancy's Show Box," 155–59; in "The Gentle Boy," 165; in "The Great Carbuncle," 149–51; in "Lady Eleanore's Mantle," 129–30; in "The Man of Adamant," 220–22; in "The Maypole of Merry Mount," 99–101; in "The Minister's Black Veil," 172–76; in "My Kinsman, Major Molineux," 231–32, 234–38; in "Roger Malvin's Burial," 198–200; in "Young Goodman Brown," 203–4, 206–10
Ambiguity: in "The Gray Champion," 91; in "The Minister's Black Veil," 174–76; in "The Prophetic Pictures," 115
American Magazine of Useful and Entertaining Knowledge, 11
American Monthly Magazine (ed. N. P. Willis), 9
American Monthly Magazine, 73, 75, 78
American Quarterly Review, 15, 17, 35
American Stationers' Company, The, 73, 83
Andros, Sir Edmund, 85, 88
Anecdotes of his Own Times. See King, William
Annals of Salem. See Felt, Joseph B.
Arabian Nights, The, 34, 60
Arcturus, 8n., 81–82
Ariosto, Ludovico, 56
Aristotle, 168, 241
Arnold, Matthew, 176
Atlantic Souvenir, The, 8
Austen, Jane, *Northanger Abbey*, 47, 55, 61–62

Austin, William, 49; "Peter Rugg, the Missing Man," 19, 49–52, 151, 187, 189, 251
Axton, William F., 55

Bancroft, George, *History of the United States*, 90, 93, 162n.
Barker, James Nelson, *Superstition*, 86n.
Barlow, Joel, 18
Beaumont and Fletcher, *The Knight of the Burning Pestle*, 98
Belcher, Jonathan, 171
Benjamin, Park, 72; reviews of *The Token*, 75–78, 81–82
Bible, the, 34, 35; Old Testament (cited), 100, 198; New Testament (cited), 158, 168, 199, 203, 218, 219, 223
Blackstone, William, 97
Blackwood's Edinburgh Magazine, 24, 54
Blair, Walter, 45–46
Boswell, James, *Life of Samuel Johnson*, 33
Bourne, Henry, 98
Boylston, Dr. Zabdiel, 128
Bradford, William, *History of Plymouth Plantation*, 95, 96, 99
Bradstreet, Simon, 89
Bride of Lammermoor, The. See Scott, Sir Walter
Bridge, Horatio, 73, 84, 213, 240, 241, 243; letters to NH, 77n., 170
Brown, Charles Brockden, 35–36, 53, 54; *Arthur Mervyn*, 128; *Edgar Huntly* (preface), 13, 57
Brown, Thomas, *An Account of the People Called Shakers*, 138
Brownell, W. C., 21, 30–31
Brownson, Orestes, review of 1842 *Twice-Told Tales*, 84n.
Bryant, William Cullen, 5, 118; *Lectures on Poetry*, 18–20; review of *Redwood*, 16
Buckingham, Joseph T., 49, 71–72, 201
Bunyan, John, *Pilgrim's Progress*, 33, 66–67
Burnet, William, 109–10
Burrough, Edward, 168n.

Calef, Robert, *More Wonders of the Invisible World*, 204n.
Camus, Albert, *The Fall*, 171
Carey & Lea, 7, 8, 10n.
Carey, Lea, and Blanchard, 79
Carrier, Martha, 202
Castle of Otranto, The. See Walpole, Horace
Channing, Ellery, 184
Channing, William Ellery, 83
Charles II, 162
Charvat, William, 7, 248
Chaucer, Geoffrey, 227; "The Squire's Tale," 60
Cheney, John, 8
Choate, Rufus, "The Colonial Age of New England," 88; "The Importance of Illustrating New-England History . . .," 24–26, 29, 30, 160
Chorley, Henry F., review of *The Token* for 1836, 75
Christian Examiner, 73
Cilley, Jonathan, letter to NH, 35, 242n.
Clark, Lewis Gaylord, letter to NH, 181
Clark, Willis Gaylord, 8
Cloyse, Sarah, 202
Cole, Thomas, 8
Coleman, Ann, 160
Coleridge, Samuel Taylor, 114
Collections, Topographical, Historical, and Biographical. See Farmer, John
Cooper, James Fenimore, 7, 10, 15; *Notions of the Americans*, 6, 19–20; *The Spy*, 5, 22; *The Wept of Wish-ton-Wish*, 34, 86
Copley, John Singleton, 187
Corwin, John, 202
Cory, Martha, 202
Cox, William, 78
Cranch, Christopher Pearse, 64, 176
Crawford, Ethan Allen, 141–42, 147
Crawford, Mrs. Lucy, *The History of the White Mountains*, 147

Dante Alighieri, *Paradiso*, 113, 220
Davenport, Richard, 162
Davidson, Edward H., 212
Davis, Eleazer, 193
Democratic Review, 9, 80n., 82, 83, 117–20
Dixwell, John, 86
Dostoevski, Feodor, 170
Drowne, Deacon Shem, 187–88
Dryden, John, *Amphitryon*, 232

Ductor Dubitantium. See Taylor, Jeremy
Dunlap, William, 18; *History . . . of the Arts of Design . . .*, 109, 111–12
Durand, Asher B., 8
Duyckinck, Evert A., 40, 81–82, 84n., 119n., 213
Dyer, Mary, 79, 162, 165n.

Edgeworth, R. L., *Memoirs*, 35
Edinburgh Review, 5
Emerson, Ralph Waldo, 5, 64, 83, 155, 184; "The American Scholar," 14
Emlyn, Sollom, *A Complete Collection of State Trials*, 39
Endicott, John, 92–94, 95, 101–4, 162
Euripides, *Medea*, 140
Evans, Catherine, 163n.
Everett, A. H., 8
Everett, Edward, 8

Farmer, John, and Jacob B. Moore, *Collections . . .*, 193
Farwell, Lieutenant, 193
Faulkner, William, 54
Fay, Theodore S., 78
Feke, Robert, 109n.
Felt, Joseph B., *Annals of Salem*, 1st ed., 39, 86, 95, 102–3, 105–6, 108; 2nd ed., 93, 229n.
Fielding, Henry, *Amelia*, 35; *Tom Jones*, 35
Fields, James T., 10n., 33, 45, 63, 77, 134, 171n., 186n., 215, 243n.; *Yesterdays with Authors*, 39–40
Fisher, Mary, 163n.
Fowler, H. W., 222
Franklin, Benjamin, "Rules by Which . . .," 123–24
Frazer, Sir James, *The Golden Bough*, 115
Freneau, Philip, 18, 53
Frost, Robert, 13, 153, 176

Gardiner, William Howard, 30; reviews of Cooper's novels, 20, 58–59, 97, 137n.
Gentleman's Magazine, 37
Godey's Lady's Book, 186
Godwin, William, 54; *Caleb Williams*, 34–35; *Mandeville*, 34; *St. Leon*, 34, 71
Goethe, Johann Wolfgang von, *Faust*, 235n.
Goffe, William, 86, 88
Goldsmith, Oliver, "Asem, an Eastern Tale," 67; "The Looking-glass of Lao," 60, 67

Goodrich, Samuel Griswold, 6, 7, 8–11, 28, 71, 73, 215, 246; *Recollections of a Lifetime*, 6, 8, 10, 15, 16
Gothic, the, 35, 46, 47, 52–62; in "Dr. Heidegger's Experiment," 178–79, 180–81, 182; in *The House of the Seven Gables*, 134–37; in "Legends of the Province House," 121–23, 127–28, 130–31; in "The Prophetic Pictures," 109–11, 117; in "Young Goodman Brown," 57–58, 210
Graham's Magazine, 9, 133n.
Greek Anthology, The, 144
Greeley, Horace, 8
Gregory the Great, Saint, *Pastoral Care*, 155n., 157n.
Gross, Seymour L., 161, 235

Hale, Sarah Josepha, 79
Hancock, John, 132
Hart, Francis R., 16
Hathorne, Elizabeth (sister of William), 102
Hathorne, John (son of William), 86, 127, 201–2
Hathorne, Mrs. Nathaniel (mother), 141
Hathorne, William (first American ancestor), 32, 93, 102, 127, 159–60, 201
Hawthorne. See James, Henry
Hawthorne, Elizabeth (sister), 27, 33, 37
Hawthorne, Louisa (sister), 34–35, 139
Hawthorne, Nathaniel, LETTERS: letters (quoted or cited) from NH, to Horatio Bridge, 84, 241, 243; to Carey & Lea, 10n.; to Evert A. Duyckinck, 40; to James T. Fields, 10n., 45, 63, 134, 171n., 186n., 215, 243n.; to Samuel G. Goodrich, 28, 246; to Louisa Hawthorne, 34–35, 139; to his mother, 141; to Washington Irving, 36; to Longfellow, 12, 41, 138, 243; to Elizabeth Peabody, 10; to Sophia Peabody, 45, 83, 184, 239, 239n.; to Richard Henry Stoddard, 11, 33, 36, 138; letters (quoted or cited) to NH, from Lewis Gaylord Clark, 181; from Jonathan Cilley, 35, 242n.; from Horatio Bridge, 77n., 170; from John L. O'Sullivan, 117–18, 119n.
Hawthorne, Nathaniel, PROJECTED COLLECTIONS:
"Old-Time Legends: Together with Sketches, Experimental and Ideal," 213

Hawthorne, PROJECTED COL. (cont.)
"Provincial Tales," 6, 28, 94, 192, 215, 227
"Seven Tales of My Native Land," 6, 27–28
"The Story-Teller," 71–73, 84, 141, 170
See also Arcturus
Hawthorne, Nathaniel, WRITINGS:
"Alice Doane's Appeal," 27–28, 57–58, 109, 215
"The Ambitious Guest," 83, 141–45, 246, 248
The American Notebooks, 4, 53n., 61, 63, 107, 111, 133, 135, 139, 218, 220, 222, 243; the North Adams journal, 4, 53, 138, 222
The Ancestral Footstep, 133
"The Artist of the Beautiful," 65–66, 191
"A Bell's Biography," 29
"The Birthmark," 70, 116, 149, 171, 180–81, 186, 221, 242n.
The Blithedale Romance, 36, 181n., 249
"The Canal Boat," 138
"The Canterbury Pilgrims," 9, 65, 80, 138–39, 148, 215, 216, 222–27, 241, 246
"The Celestial Railroad," 67, 148, 185
"The Custom House," 31, 61, 63, 65, 120, 159, 201–2, 214n., 223, 243n., 251, 252
"David Swan," 9, 67, 69, 217
"The Devil in Manuscript," 6, 11, 27
"Dr. Bullivant," 29, 60, 94
Dr. Grimshawe's Secret, 52
"Dr. Heidegger's Experiment," 12, 57, 60, 61–62, 68, 70–71, 150, 159, 178–82, 241, 246, 248, 251
"Drowne's Wooden Image," 19, 52, 58, 127, 183, 186–92, 241
"Earth's Holocaust," 133, 148
"Edward Fane's Rosebud," 82
"Edward Randolph's Portrait," 22, 38, 47, 58, 59, 120–21, 123–28, 134, 145, 234
"Egotism; or, the Boston Serpent," 46, 155, 190
"Endicott and the Red Cross," 22, 83, 85, 92, 94, 101–8, 120, 212, 234
The English Notebooks, 66, 136–37n.
"Ethan Brand," 4, 70, 113, 116, 149, 180–81, 213, 221–22, 228, 245n.

Hawthorne, Nathaniel, WRITINGS (cont.)
"Fancy's Show Box," 67, 151, 155–59, 178
Fanshawe, 5–6, 42
"Feathertop," 26, 183
"Fragments from the Journal of a Solitary Man," 11, 82
"The Gentle Boy," 13, 24, 28, 79, 159–70, 243, 244–45, 247, 248
Grandfather's Chair, 30, 45, 104, 126, 128, 230
"The Gray Champion," 22–23, 31, 51, 85–95, 104, 107, 120, 126, 127, 201, 234, 246–47, 249
"The Great Carbuncle," 38, 44, 57, 65, 141, 145–51, 196, 223–24, 241, 251
"The Great Stone Face," 138, 141, 213
"The Hall of Fantasy," 225n.
"The Haunted Mind," 83
"The Haunted Quack," 10n.
"The Hollow of the Three Hills," 57–58
The House of the Seven Gables, 40, 45, 57, 58, 59–60, 133, 134–37, 238, 243
"Howe's Masquerade," 59, 120–21, 122–23, 188n., 249
The Italian Notebooks, 62
"Jonathan Cilley," 119n.
"Lady Eleanore's Mantle," 44–45, 61, 120–21, 128–30
"Legends of the Province House," 22, 29, 83, 117–37, 228
"The Lily's Quest," 67, 70, 217
"Little Annie's Ramble," 80
"Main Street," 29, 34, 39, 40, 79, 94, 105, 108, 160, 163, 201, 213
"The Man of Adamant," 34, 66, 67, 184, 190, 215, 218–22, 228, 242
The Marble Faun, 251; preface, 20
"The Maypole of Merry Mount," 22, 31, 68, 70, 75, 85, 91, 92–101, 107, 216, 227, 249, 251
"The Minister's Black Veil," 9, 52, 67n., 68, 75, 80, 150, 159, 170–78, 211–12, 245, 248, 250
"The Minotaur," 175
"Monsieur du Miroir," 183–85
Mosses from an Old Manse, 3, 7, 67, 80, 182–86, 213, 243; 1854 edition, 71, 141, 183, 214
"Mr. Higginbotham's Catastrophe," 71n., 80
"Mrs. Bullfrog," 183–85
"Mrs. Hutchinson," 23, 29, 30, 93, 214
"My Kinsman, Major Molineux," 9, 13,

Hawthorne, Nathaniel, WRITINGS (cont.)
22, 28, 31, 38, 41, 69, 80, 169, 214–15, 216, 227–38, 244–45, 247, 250
"The Notch in the White Mountains," 141, 148
"Old Esther Dudley," 61, 68, 120–21, 130–33, 134–35, 245
"The Old Manse," 34, 60–61, 65, 182–83, 239
"Old News," 29, 72
"Our Evening Party Among the Mountains," 21, 141, 145, 147, 148
Our Old Home, 33, 41, 242
"Passages from a Relinquished Work," 71, 183
"Peter Goldthwaite's Treasure," 243
Peter Parley's Universal History on the Basis of Geography, 11
"The Prophetic Pictures," 46–47, 49, 57, 58, 59, 61, 108, 109–17, 135, 142, 154, 180, 241, 242n., 245
"P's Correspondence," 66n.
"Rappaccini's Daughter," 62, 120, 186, 221, 239n.
Reviews of books by Longfellow, W. G. Simms, and Whittier, 26n.
"A Rill from the Town Pump," 72
"Roger Malvin's Burial," 13, 28, 80, 108, 125, 169, 183, 185–86, 192–200, 216, 243, 244–45
The Scarlet Letter, 3, 30, 38, 40, 45, 58, 90, 106, 107–8, 113, 153, 173, 176–77, 195, 199, 210–12, 238, 243, 251
Septimius Felton, 64
"The Seven Vagabonds," 71, 83, 84, 134n., 239–40n.
"The Shaker Bridal," 138–41, 222, 243, 246
"Sights from a Steeple," 9, 224n.
"Sir William Pepperell," 29
"Sir William Phips," 29–30
"The Sister Years," 84
"Sketches from Memory," 141, 183
"Snow-Flakes," 224n.
"The Snow-Image," 213
The Snow-Image and Other Twice-Told Tales, 3, 29, 80, 213–15; preface, 3, 213, 214, 239–40
"The Threefold Destiny," 67, 69–70, 84
"The Three Golden Apples," 187
"The Toll-Gatherer's Day," 83
Twice-Told Tales: 1837 edition, 3, 4, 5, 9, 29, 58, 71–81, 74–75 (contents), 86, 243; 1842 edition, 3, 7, 81–84; 1851 preface, 69, 81, 213, 239

Hawthorne, Nathaniel, WRITINGS (cont.)
"The Village Uncle," 9, 83
"A Virtuoso's Collection," 49–50, 60, 183
"Wakefield," 64–65, 151–54, 216
"The Wedding Knell," 44, 75, 80, 155, 180
"The White Old Maid," 82, 83
"The Wives of the Dead," 28, 215–18, 244, 246
"A Wonder-Book," 36, 45
"Young Goodman Brown," 12, 24, 31, 34, 48n., 58, 72, 80, 169, 183, 185–86, 200–12, 243, 245, 247, 250
Helwyse, Gervais, 129n.
Hibbens, Ann, 211n.
Higginson, Thomas Wentworth, "A Precursor of Hawthorne," 50
History of Boston, A. See Snow, Caleb
History of . . . the Christian People Called Quakers, The. See Sewel, William
History of the Colony and Province of Massachusetts-Bay, The. See Hutchinson, Thomas
History of the District of Maine, The. See Sullivan, James
History of the Rise and Progress of the Arts of Design in the United States, A. See Dunlap, William
History of the United States. See Bancroft, George
History of the White Mountains, The. See Crawford, Mrs. Lucy
History of the White Mountains. See Willey, Benjamin G.
Hoffman, Charles Fenno, 73
Hogg, James, Tales, 34
Holmes, Oliver Wendell, 8, 52
Homer, Iliad, 195; Odyssey, 142, 195
Hone, William, Every-day Book and Table Book, 37
Hooker, Thomas, 221
Hours in a Library. See Stephen, Sir Leslie
Howe, Sir William, 122
Howells, William Dean, 41n., 248
Hutchinson, Ann, 30, 221
Hutchinson, Thomas, 124, 230, 234; The History of . . . Massachusetts-Bay, 38, 87–88, 89, 123–26, 161, 162–63n., 192n., 206, 229–30

"Importance of Illustrating New-England History, The." See Choate, Rufus
Irony: in "The Ambitious Guest," 144; in "Edward Randolph's Portrait," 125,

Irony (cont.)
128; in "Endicott and the Red Cross," 106–7; in "The Gentle Boy," 166, 169; in "The Gray Champion," 92; in "Lady Eleanore's Mantle," 112; in "The Prophetic Pictures," 115; dramatic irony, in "The Ambitious Guest," 142–44; in "My Kinsman, Major Molineux," 233–34; in "The Prophetic Pictures," 117
Irving, Washington, 7, 10, 36, 54, 141, 247; Abbotsford, 15; "The Author's Account of Himself," 19–20; "The Bold Dragoon," 52; Bracebridge Hall, 27; "Dolph Heyliger," 197n.; "The Legend of Sleepy Hollow," 18, 51–52, 56, 57; "Rip Van Winkle," 18, 151, 247; The Sketch Book, 5, 27, 78; "The Stout Gentleman," 52, 56; "Strange Stories by a Nervous Gentleman," 56; "The Storm-Ship," 19, 187; Tales of a Traveller, 27, 56, 59, 73

J. B. H., "Indian Troubles at Dunstable," 193
James, Henry, 248; "The Art of Fiction," 240; Hawthorne, 20, 85, 121, 241, 246; "The Turn of the Screw," 210
James Munroe and Company, 83
Jewett, Sarah Orne, 217
Johnson, Edward, Wonder-Working Providence, 64, 93
Johnson, Dr. Samuel, 33; oriental tales, 67

Keats, John, 144
Kesselring, Marion L., 37
King, William, Anecdotes of his Own Times, 152
Knickerbocker Magazine, 9, 54, 75, 178

Lamb, Charles, 84n.; "Witches and Other Night Fears," 201
Lang, Andrew, 146
Lang, H. J., 217n.
Langtree, S. D., 118
Laud, William, 99
Leslie, Eliza, 78, 79
Levin, David, 206
Levin, Harry, 17, 100
Lewis, C. S., 203
Lewis, Matthew Gregory, 54; The Monk, 60; Romantic Tales, 35
Lockhart, John Gibson, Life of Scott, 15
London Athenaeum, 75

Longfellow, Henry Wadsworth, 8, 12, 41, 52, 73, 82, 84n., 118, 119–20n., 138, 192, 229n., 243; "Our Native Writers," 31–32; *Outre-Mer*, 78
Lowell, James Russell, 20n., 84, 118
Lovejoy, David C., 193
Lovewell, Captain John, 192

Macaulay, Thomas Babbington, 90
McHenry, James, *The Spectre of the Forest*, 86n.
Mark Twain, 13, 16
Marquis, Don, 176
Martin, Susanna, 207
Massachusetts Historical Society Collections, 38
Mather, Cotton, 89n., 97; "The Return of Several Ministers . . .," 207; *Wonders of the Invisible World*, 202, 204–5n., 206, 207, 208
Mather, Increase, *Illustrious Providences*, 64
Matthiessen, F. O., *American Renaissance*, 5
Maturin, Charles Robert, 54; *Melmoth the Wanderer*, 35, 59
Mayhew, Jonathan, 230
Melmoth the Wanderer. See Maturin, Charles Robert
Melville, Herman, 13
Metamorphoses. See Ovid
Milton, John, 33; *Paradise Lost*, 100
Mitchell, Isaac, 56; *The Asylum*, 54
Molineux, William, 229n.
Montaigne, Michel de, "Of Experience," 200
Moody, Joseph, 173
Moore, Thomas, *Lalla Rookh*, 73
Morison, Samuel Eliot, *Builders of the Bay Colony*, 94
Morton, Nathaniel, *New England's Memorial*, 94, 96
Morton, Thomas, 95, 96; *New English Canaan*, 95, 96, 99, 101
Mother Ann Lee, 138, 140
Mott, Frank Luther, 9
Mysteries of Udolpho, The. See Radcliffe, Ann

Narrative point of view, 248–51; in "The Canterbury Pilgrims," 222–24; in "Dr. Heidegger's Experiment," 179; in "The Great Carbuncle," 149–51; in "Legends of the Province House," 120; in "The

Narrative point of view (cont.)
Minister's Black Veil," 171–72; in "The Wives of the Dead," 216–17; in "Young Goodman Brown," 204–5
Neal, John, 24, 35
New-England Galaxy, 49
New-England Magazine, 9, 10, 11, 71–72, 75
New England Primer, 101
New England's Memorial. See Morton, Nathaniel
New English Canaan. See Morton, Thomas
Newgate Calendar, The, 33
New Yorker, 216
Norris, Edward, 163
North American Review, 5, 8, 16, 17, 20, 21, 23, 58, 73
Northanger Abbey. See Austen, Jane
Norton, John, 163
Notions of the Americans. See Cooper, James Fenimore

Orians, G. Harrison, 96, 161–63, 192–93
Osgood, Mary, 202, 206–7
O'Sullivan, John L., 117–20; introduction to *Democratic Review*, 118–19, 132–33; letters to NH, 117–18, 119n.
Overbury, Sir Thomas, 40
Ovid, *Metamorphoses X*, 187, 190, 191

Palfrey, John Gorham, 30; review of *Yamoyden*, 23–24, 94
Pattee, F. L., 246
Patton, James W., 118
Paulding, James Kirke, 17, 24n., 118
Peabody, Andrew Preston, 73
Peabody, Elizabeth (sister-in-law), 10, 75
Peabody, Sophia (Mrs. Nathaniel Hawthorne), 45, 83, 160, 184, 239
Pequawket Indians, 192
Perkins, Jacob, 8
Personal Recollections of Nathaniel Hawthorne. See Bridge, Horatio
"Peter Parley" books, 6
"Peter Rugg, the Missing Man." *See* Austin, William
Peveril of the Peak. See Scott, Sir Walter
Pioneer, 84
Pirate, The. See Scott, Sir Walter
Poe, Edgar Allan, 9, 54, 55–57, 62; "The Fall of the House of Usher," 55; "The Masque of the Red Death," 128; review of *Twice-Told Tales*, 54, 58, 78, 84n.,

Poe, Edgar Allan (cont.)
173–74, 181n.; "Tales of the Folio
Club," 8, 72n.
Ponce de León, 178
Pope, Alexander, 33
"Preamble to Nathaniel Hawthorne, A."
See Arcturus
Prescott, William H., 16
Preternatural suggestion, 58, 250–51; in
The Bridge of Lammermoor (Scott),
47–48; in "Drowne's Wooden Image,"
189; in "Edward Randolph's Portrait,"
127; in "Old Esther Dudley," 131; in
The House of the Seven Gables, 136–
37; in "The Minister's Black Veil," 174;
in "Peter Rugg, the Missing Man"
(Austin), 50–51; in "The Prophetic
Pictures," 110–11
Prince, Mary, 162
Prince, Thomas, *A Chronological History
of New England in the Form of Annals*,
96

Radcliffe, Ann, 54, 55; *The Mysteries of
Udolpho*, 34, 127
Randolph, Edward, 92, 126
Rawson, Edward, 164–65n.
Recollections of a Lifetime. See Goodrich,
Samuel G.
Reid, Alfred S., 39–40
Robinson, William, 162–63
Rousseau, Jean-Jacques, *Héloïse*, 35

Salem *Advertiser*, 182
Salem Athenaeum, charge books of, 37–40
Salem *Gazette*, 10, 73, 84
Saltonstall, Leverett, 93
Sands, Robert Charles, "The Man Who
Burnt John Rogers," 54–55
Scott, Sir Walter, 5, 14–18, 20, 22, 40–41,
42–49, 51–52, 54, 66, 217–18, 246, 251;
The Abbot, 34–35, 235n.; *The Antiquary*, 44; *The Bride of Lammermoor*,
43, 46–49, 112, 121; *Guy Mannering*,
165; *Letters on Demonology and Witchcraft*, 208n.; "My Aunt Margaret's Mirror," 60; *Old Mortality*, 165; *Peveril of
the Peak*, 24, 86–87; *The Pirate*, 146–
47; *Sir Tristrem* (introduction), 17, 85
Sedgwick, Catherine M., 8, 78, 79, 118;
Hope Leslie, 79; "Mary Dyre," 79; *Redwood*, 16, 79, 138; *Tales and Sketches*,
79, 79–80n.

Sewel, William, 79; *The History of . . .
the Christian People Called Quakers*,
159–60, 161–62, 162–65nn., 168n.
Shakespeare, William, 33, 170; *Hamlet*,
206; *Macbeth*, 143; *A Midsummer-
Night's Dream*, 99–100, 231–32
Shute, Samuel, 128
Sidney, Sir Philip, *Arcadia*, 32
Sigourney, Lydia H., 78–79
Sketch Book, The. See Irving, Washington
Smibert, John, 109n.
Smith, Captain John, 148
Smith, Sidney, 5
Smollett, Tobias, *The Adventures of Fer-
dinand, Count Fathom*, 34; *Roderick
Random*, 34
Snow, Caleb Hopkins, *A History of Boston*,
38, 97, 101, 106nn., 126, 128, 188n.
Sons of Liberty, The, 229
Southwick, Lawrence, 162
Sparks, Jared, 17
Spenser, Edmund, *The Faerie Queene*, 33,
56, 60, 66–67
*Sports and Pastimes of the People of Eng-
land, The. See* Strutt, Joseph
Standish, Miles, 95
Stephen, Sir Leslie, *Hours in a Library*, 48,
152, 177
Stevens, Wallace, 242n.
Stevenson, Marmaduke, 162–63
Stevenson, Robert Louis, "Thrawn Janet,"
210
Stiles, Ezra, 23; *A History of Three of the
Judges of King Charles I*, 87
Stoddard, Richard Henry, 11, 33, 36, 138
Stone, William Leete, 54–55n., 79
Story, Joseph, 93
Stoughton, William, 206
Structure and time span, 244–47; in
"Endicott and the Red Cross," 104–5;
in "The Gentle Boy," 164; in "The
Gray Champion," 90; in "The Minis-
ter's Black Veil," 171–72; in "Roger
Malvin's Burial," 194, 199; in "The
Shaker Bridal," 139–41; in "The Wives
of the Dead," 215–16
Strutt, Joseph, *The Sports and Pastimes of
the People of England*, 94, 97–99
Stuart, Gilbert, 112
Stubbs, John Caldwell, 65
Stubbs, Philip, *Anatomie of Abuses*, 97–98
Style, 247–48; self-parody in "The Canter-
bury Pilgrims," 224–25; in *The House
of the Seven Gables*, 136

Sullivan, James, *History of the District of Maine*, 38, 146

Swedenborg, Emanuel, 64

Swift, Jonathan, 37

Symmes, Thomas, *Historical Memoirs*, 193

Tales and Sketches. See Sedgwick, Catherine M.

Tales of a Traveller. See Irving, Washington

Taylor, Jeremy, *Discourses on Various Subjects*, 155; *Ductor Dubitantium*, 151, 155–57

Thomson, James, 33

Ticknor & Fields, 7

Tocqueville, Alexis, Comte de, 7

Token, The, 3, 6, 8–11, 27–28, 74, 75–77, 79; *The Token* for 1832, 28, 244

Tolstoy, Leo, *The Death of Ivan Ilych*, 171

Trilling, Lionel, 238

Trollope, Anthony, 63

True, Joseph, 188

Tudor, William, "An Address delivered to the Phi Beta Kappa Society," 21–23, 30

Turner, Arlin, 190

Turner, Frederick Jackson, 51

Tyler, Royall, 18; *The Contrast* (prologue), 13; *The Algerine Captive* (preface), 53

United States Magazine and Democratic Review. See Democratic Review

Upham, Thomas C., 193

Virgil, 170

Voltaire, François Marie, 37

Waggoner, Hyatt H., 169

Walpole, Horace, *The Castle of Otranto*, 36, 53, 54, 55, 59, 136–37n.

Walsh, Robert, 15, 21n.

Wendell, Barrett, 145

Wept of Wish-ton-Wish, The. See Cooper, James Fenimore

Whalley, Edward, 86

Whipple, Edwin P., *Character and Characteristic Men*, 185–86

Whitman, Walt, 118

Whittier, John Greenleaf, 21, 25n., 118, 145, 159

Wiley & Putnam, 7, 82n.

Willey, Benjamin C., *History of the White Mountains*, 142–43, 147

Willey, Samuel, 142–43

William of Orange, 89

Williams, Abigail, 202

Williams, Roger, 45n., 102–3, 221

Willis, Nathaniel Parker, 9, 184

Wilson, Deborah, 160

Wilson, John, 163

Winslow, John, 89

Winthrop, John, 94, 101; *Journals*, 38, 102–4

Wollaston, Captain, 95

Wonders of the Invisible World. See Mather, Cotton

Woodberry, George E., 42, 47

Yamoyden, review of. *See* Palfrey, John Gorham

Yesterdays with Authors. See Fields, James T.

York Town, review of, 15

Youth's Keepsake, 74